SPEAKING OUT

UNTOLD STORIES
FROM THE FALKLANDS WAR

SPEAKING OUT

UNTOLD STORIES FROM THE FALKLANDS WAR

Michael Bilton
&
Peter Kosminsky

ANDRE DEUTSCH

First published in 1989 by
André Deutsch Limited
105-106 Great Russell Street
London WC1B 3LJ

British Library Cataloguing in Publication Data

Bilton, Michael
Speaking Out: Untold stories from the Falklands War
1. Falkland Islands War
I. Title   II. Kosminsky, Peter
997'.11

ISBN 0 233 98404 6

Phototypeset by Falcon Graphic Art Ltd
Wallington, Surrey
Printed in Great Britain by
St Edmundsbury Press, Bury St Edmunds, Suffolk

Contents

List of Illustrations

Argentine soldiers carry away their dead (top: *Daily Express*; bottom: Times Newspapers)
General Mario Benjamin Menendez (Frank Spooner Pictures)
Brigadier Julian Thompson (UPI/Press Association)
The Community Centre at Goose Green (Times Newspapers)
Major Chris Keeble (UPI/Press Association)
Sergeant-Major Barry Norman (Yorkshire Television)
'J' Company 42 Commando:
　　On board *Canberra* (Ministry of Defence – Royal Navy)
　　At Government House in Port Stanley after the Argentine surrender
　　　(Ministry of Defence – Royal Navy)

Between pages 240 and 241

Argentine conscripts:
　　Carrying provisions (*Soldier* Magazine)
　　Waiting to leave (UPI/Press Association)
　　Preparing to return to Argentina after the surrender (*Soldier* Magazine)
Guardsman David Grimshaw, injured in the *Sir Galahad* bombing (UPI/Press Association)
A wounded sailor from HMS *Sheffield* (UPI/Press Association)
A casualty from the *Sir Galahad* (Times Newspapers)
Marine Chris White (Yorkshire Television)
Chris White and other survivors aboard the hospital ship SS *Uganda* (Chris White)
Nurse Marion Stock (Yorkshire Television)
Flight-Lieutenant Jeff Glover, the only British PoW in Argentine hands (Roberto Stvrtevcky)
Dee Glover, waiting for her husband's plane to land (Times Newspapers)
The Glovers' reunion (UPI/Press Association)
A young soldier of the Parachute Regiment is welcomed home by his relieved mother (UPI/Press Association)
Dead sailors from the *General Belgrano* are brought home to Argentina (Frank Spooner Pictures)
A rapturous reception for the British Task Force at Portsmouth (Times Newspapers)
Hulda Stewart, Falkland Islander (Yorkshire Television)
Dorothy Foulkes, widow of Frank Foulkes, killed on *Atlantic Conveyor* (Yorkshire Television)
Gillian White, wife of Marine Chris White (Yorkshire Television)
Anti-aircraft ammunition left over from the war (Times Newspapers)
A warning of minefields around Port Stanley (Times Newspapers)

List of Contributors

(Posts given are those held at the time of the Falklands War in 1982)

DIPLOMATS

Sir Anthony Williams, British Ambassador in Buenos Aires
Nicanor Costa Mendez, Argentina's Foreign Minister
David Gompert, US Deputy Under-Secretary of State for Political Affairs
Jeane Kirkpatrick, US Ambassador to the United Nations
Sir Anthony Parsons, British Ambassador to the United Nations

SAILORS

Captain Hector Bonzo, Captain of the *General Belgrano*
Captain Juan Antonio Lopez, Argentine navy doctor
Lieutenant-Commander Patrick Kettle, engineering officer, HMS *Sheffield*
Sub-Lieutenant Steve Iacovou, HMS *Sheffield*
Commander Alan West, HMS *Ardent*
Ken Enticknab, chief petty officer, HMS *Ardent*
Sam Bishop, petty officer, HMS *Antelope*
Surgeon Commander Rick Jolly OBE, commander of field hospital, Ajax Bay
Marion Stock, staff nurse, SS *Uganda*

PILOTS

Flight-Lieutenant Ian Mortimer, 801 Squadron, HMS *Invincible*
Flight-Lieutenant Jeff Glover, No.1 Squadron
Lieutenant-Commander Nigel 'Sharkey' Ward, leader of 801 Squadron
Major Carlos Antonio Tomba, Argentine Attack Group 3
Lieutenant Ricardo Lucero, Argentine Attack Group 4
Lieutenant Guillermo Owen Crippa, Argentine fleet air arm, 1st Attack
    Squadron
Captain Alberto Philippi, Argentine fleet air arm
Lieutenant José Cesar Arca, Argentine fleet air arm, 3rd Attack Squadron

Acknowledgements

We didn't set out to write a book, but to produce a film about a war. Our first task therefore is to thank all of those who were interviewed for the film *Falklands War: The Untold Story* whose stories appear in this book. In many ways being interviewed for a book or newspaper article is easier than appearing on film. The people who braved the camera to talk about their often very personal and emotionally harrowing experiences needed a special courage, to which this book is a tribute. We owe them a particular debt of gratitude. None of them are publicity-seekers but their individual contributions are an integral part of an important piece of oral history. Having conducted some eighty-seven interviews over the course of nearly a year we realised that we had unwittingly produced the makings of an interesting document. People often gave us a great deal of their time but the requirements of television meant that choices had to be made. In many cases only a few minutes of what people had to say appeared on the screen. In others the whole interview was dropped. Yet each contribution was fascinating. We hope they will feel that in the editing process we have kept the spirit of what they wanted to say.

Television is a team effort and we were blessed with the chance to work with some of the most talented people in the business, in both the technical and production areas. We would especially like to thank our Yorkshire Television colleagues who conducted many of the interviews: our bilingual Associate Producer Patrick Buckley, who was in his element in Argentina; and in Britain, three brilliant researchers – Ros Franey, Jill Turton and Clive Gordon. We made many friends in Argentina. Among those who provided us with invaluable help were: our consultant, Maria Laura Avignolo, one of the most gifted journalists in South America; Bernadita Giannuzzi; Juan Yofre; Joy Spalding of the British interests section at the Swiss Embassy; Roberto Roscoe and 'Jimmy' Tagan of the Argentine navy; Jorge Columbo; and George Nezvijinsky.

In Britain we were fortunate to have at our side as consultant, Major-General Julian Thompson, who commanded 3 Commando Brigade in the Falklands War. Julian put us on the right course even before he retired from the Royal Marines – his advice and expertise were invaluable, his companionship a delight. Lieutenant-Colonel Chris Keeble, of the Parachute Regiment, and Surgeon Commander Rick Jolly, RN, both served with distinction in the South

Atlantic campaign, and provided us with much early encouragement to go to Argentina and tell both sides of the story. Some people at the Ministry of Defence were unbelievably helpful; they know who they are.

In the Falkland Islands we must thank Denis Cornish of Laing Mowlem ARC; Patrick Watts of the Falkland Islands Broadcasting Service (FIBS); Gerald Cheek and the Falkland Islands Government Air Service (FIGAS) pilots; David Rose of British Forces Falkland Islands (BFFI) HQ; June McMullen of Goose Green and Hulda and Ian Stewart of Port Stanley for their wonderful hospitality.

In the United States, David Gompert allowed us to impose on him at unbelievably short notice; Ambassador Jeane Kirkpatrick kept a promise and an appointment, despite having just undergone a three-hour dental operation; and Tara Sonenshine and Tom Gunn opened doors which otherwise would have remained closed.

At Yorkshire Television, for standing four-square behind the place of the major documentary on British television, we have to thank Paul Fox, our former Managing Director, and John Fairley, Director of Programmes. We owe very special thanks to John Willis, our former Controller of Documentaries, who thumped the table once, signed the cheques and then trusted our judgement. Lastly we wish to thank Sara Menguç, our very patient editor at André Deutsch, and Steve Cox, our copy-editor, who expertly guided us to publication.

Chronology

1960 **14 December** UN Resolution 1514 calls for an end to colonialism; Britain lists the Falkland Islands as a colony and Argentina objects.

1965 **15 December** UN Resolution 2065 calls for Britain and Argentina to negotiate over the Islands.

1971 **1 July** Argentina and Britain agree on measures to improve communications between the Islands and the Argentine mainland.

1973 **April** Britain refuses to discuss sovereignty; negotiations stalled.

1974 **September** A commercial agreement gives Argentina's state-owned oil company the right to sell petroleum products in the Falklands at mainland prices.

1976 **January** Lord Shackleton visits the Falklands to investigate their economic future.

4 February A British survey ship heading for Port Stanley is fired on by the Argentine navy. Relations between the two countries at a low ebb.

July Lord Shackleton's report suggests that the major natural resources of the Islands – oil and fish – should be developed in co-operation with Argentina.

1980 **28 November** Minister of State Nicholas Ridley visits the Falklands to discuss political options including a 'leaseback' arrangement with Argentina.

2 December In Parliament Conservative, Labour and Liberal MPs attack Ridley's suggestions to the Islanders.

1981 **20 December** Argentine scrap dealer C.S. Davidoff visits South Georgia to inspect derelict whaling stations, without official permission.

1982 **3 February** British government protests at Davidoff's unauthorised visit.

19 March Davidoff's workers land on South Georgia, together with a contingent of Argentine Marines. Britain orders HMS *Endurance* to remove them.

24 March Argentine navy sends warships to South Georgia.

26 March Military junta in Buenos Aires sets date to invade the Falkland Islands.

2 April Argentine forces land at Port Stanley.

3 April UN passes Resolution 502 calling for an immediate end to hostilities and withdrawal of Argentine troops from the Islands. British Task Force prepares to leave for the South Atlantic to undertake 'Operation Corporate' – the recapture of the Falkland Islands.

8 April US Secretary of State Alexander Haig begins his peace shuttle to attempt mediation.

12 April Britain imposes a 200-mile Exclusion Zone around the Falkland Islands.

23 April Argentina warned any threat to the Task Force will meet with an armed response.

25 April British Marines and SAS recapture South Georgia. Argentine submarine *Santa Fe* attacked and disabled.

30 April Total Exclusion Zone introduced around the Islands.

1 May RAF bombs Argentine positions at Port Stanley, Goose Green and other strategic targets.

2 May Argentine cruiser *General Belgrano* is sunk by the British submarine, HMS *Conqueror*. The death toll is 368 men.

4 May HMS *Sheffield* destroyed by an Exocet missile.

14 May SAS troops raid Pebble Island and destroy 11 aircraft.

21 May 3 Commando Brigade lands on East Falkland and establishes bridgehead. HMS *Ardent* sunk. 15 Argentine planes shot down.

23 May HMS *Antelope* attacked (she sank on the 24th). 10 Argentine planes shot down.

25 May HMS *Coventry* lost and *Atlantic Conveyor* hit by Exocet missile (sank on the 28th).

28 May 2 Para recapture Goose Green. Lieutenant-Colonel 'H' Jones killed.

30 May 45 Commando secure Douglas settlement, 3 Para recapture Teal Inlet, 42 Commando advance on Mount Kent and Mount Challenger.

31 May 19 men from the Royal Marines Mountain and Arctic Warfare Cadre capture Top Malo House after a fire-fight.

1 June 5 Infantry Brigade land at San Carlos.

8 June RFA *Sir Galahad* bombed at Fitzroy – 48 men killed, including 38 Welsh Guardsmen. *Sir Tristram* also bombed, 2 crewmen killed.

11–12 June Mount Harriet, Two Sisters and Mount Longdon secured in a series of battles.

13–14 June Tumbledown Mountain, Wireless Ridge and Mount William secured. The Argentine military governor of the Falklands surrenders.

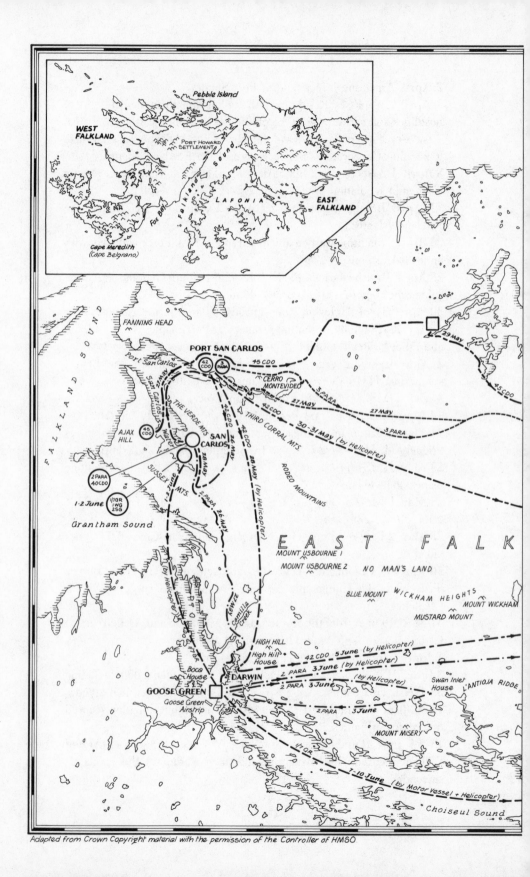

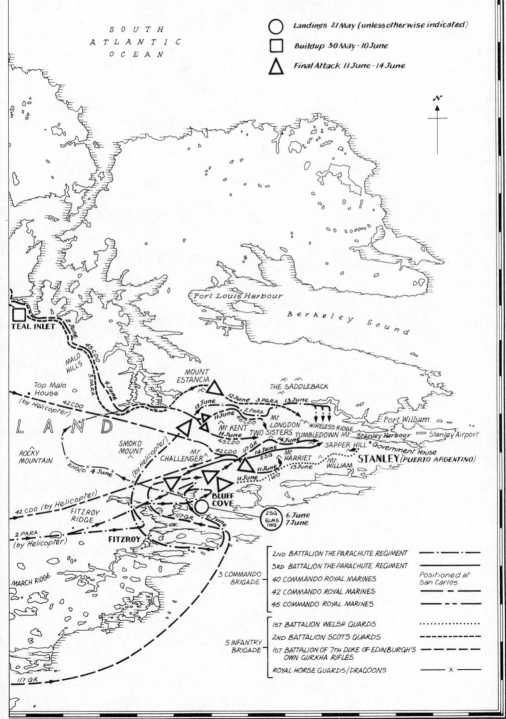

The Falklands Campaign, 21 May–14 June 1982
(Deployment of Principal British Land Forces)

SOUTH
ATLANTIC
OCEAN

○ Landings 21 May (unless otherwise indicated)

□ Buildup 30 May – 10 June

△ Final Attack 11 June – 14 June

N

Port Louis Harbour

B e r k e l e y   S o u n d

□ TEAL INLET

MALO HILLS

45 CDO

3 PARA

4 June

42 CDO

Top Malo House
(by Helicopter)

MOUNT ESTANCIA

THE SADDLEBACK

L A N D

17 June 12 June 3 PARA 13 June

3 SCDO

11 June 2 PARA

ROCKY MOUNTAIN

SMOKO MOUNT

(by Helicopter)

Mt. KENT
11 June
45 CDO

Mt. LONGDON WIRELESS RIDGE

Port William

Stanley Harbour Stanley Airport

TWO SISTERS TUMBLEDOWN Mt.

Government House

RHG/D 4 June

(by Helicopter)

Mr. CHALLENGER

42 CDO 1/7 GR

SAPPER HILL

STANLEY (PUERTO ARGENTINO)

14 June
2 SG

Mr. HARRIET

42 CDO (by Helicopter)

FITZROY RIDGE

11 June 1WG 13 June

Mt. WILLIAM

○ BLUFF COVE

2 PARA
(by Helicopter)

FITZROY

1/7 GR 5 June

2 SG
ELMS
1WG

6 June
7 June

MARCH RIDGE

1/7 GR

3 COMMANDO BRIGADE

2ND BATTALION THE PARACHUTE REGIMENT — — —

3RD BATTALION THE PARACHUTE REGIMENT

40 COMMANDO ROYAL MARINES   Positioned at San Carlos

42 COMMANDO ROYAL MARINES — — —

45 COMMANDO ROYAL MARINES —·—·—

5 INFANTRY BRIGADE

1ST BATTALION WELSH GUARDS ·········

2ND BATTALION SCOTS GUARDS – – – –

1ST BATTALION OF 7TH DUKE OF EDINBURGH'S OWN GURKHA RIFLES — — —

ROYAL HORSE GUARDS/DRAGOONS ——x——

Drawn by Sue Lawes

Introduction

The two and a half months' conflict between Britain and Argentina during the summer of 1982 was a full-scale war, the first experienced by a generation of young men. In a few short weeks a thousand of them were killed and two thousand injured. It was a campaign in which modern warships were sunk by sophisticated sea-skimming missiles and men fought against each other in trenches with bayonets. The media in both countries were victims of their respective governments' propaganda campaigns, some willingly, some unwittingly. So what have the people at home come to learn of the reality beyond the deeds of derring-do, the medal ceremonies and the victory parades? What do they know of the appalling horror and brutality of war as experienced by men serving in the Falklands campaign? The answer, sadly, is very little.

When those who were badly burned or had limbs amputated returned to Britain, the news media for the most part were kept at a distance. For there was another campaign being fought: the campaign of news management which deemed that the people at home might not support the war if they saw something of the cost in terms of broken lives. Those running the British propaganda war knew only too well that the sight of planeloads of wounded soldiers and tens of thousands of coffins returning to America in the Sixties and Seventies had helped lose popular support for the Vietnam War.

What the Falklands War confirmed yet again is the lesson that each generation seems to have to learn afresh. That warfare, whichever side you are on, is an horrific, frightening and bloody business. This is particularly so at the point of human contact, whether it be mortar or artillery rounds or anti-personnel bombs falling from the sky, or hand-to-hand fighting in the trenches cut out of peat at Goose Green or the expertly defended bunkers among the rocks and crags on Tumbledown Mountain. But it is equally true that endless waiting for an enemy which never arrives can carry its own terrors. The torpedoing of the *General Belgrano* brought home to the Royal Navy just how vulnerable they were.

1

The crew of HMS *Sheffield* never saw the aircraft which fired the missile which destroyed their ship. Fear played an enormous part in the way the war affected each individual. Morale was about overcoming that fear.

Perceptions differ, of course. It can depend on where you were, who you were with, whether you were winning or losing, whether you had good reason to be petrified because you were being shot at, or bombed. It might also depend on whether you had a safe job in friendly territory, especially if it was in Buenos Aires, Ascension Island or Whitehall. Clearly there was a different attitude on the part of British and Argentine servicemen who approached the situation from different standpoints, different cultures.

For both sides patriotism was important: the people at home were looking to them to win the war for their respective national pride. The Malvinas, as they call the Falkland Islands, are a national cause in Argentina. Argentine soldiers, the overwhelming majority of them teenage conscripts, had a very deep emotional attachment for the Islands even though they had never been there. They learned as children in primary school that the Islands belonged to Argentina but had been stolen by British pirates in the 1830s.

British servicemen, all of them volunteer professionals, were more detached. It's hard to imagine them caring about an event which happened 150 years ago. When one sailor proclaimed: 'Many of us thought the Falklands were at the top of Scotland' he spoke for a lot of people. The Islands were not a national cause for the British Task Force, but kicking 'Galtieri's gauchos' off them was. Many of them saw the Falklands War simply as part of their job, the serviceman's lot through the ages: to be ordered overseas to clean up the mess left by politicians. Even so, soldiers and sailors had a hard time coping with the reality of what they had actually been trained for – fighting in wartime. They did their duty, but many were not so keen on going to war as they thought they would be. Others were completely chastened by the experience. Like most men returning from war they could never forget what they had seen, and would rather not repeat the experience. Some, however, completely enjoyed the whole thrilling business.

Down on the ground in the battlezone the experience of the senior commanders on both sides was not dissimilar. The popular belief is that these high-ranking men enjoy a large degree of freedom to get on with their war as they think best. This notion is now completely nullified by modern sophisticated communications. The superior authorities back home in Buenos Aires and London looked at the 'big picture' and quickly relayed orders to the commanders in the field. General Menendez had to contend with regular interventions from the military command in Buenos Aires, and Brigadier Julian Thompson had his moments on the telephone by satellite to London, not all of them heartwarming. After one such frustrating call he angrily promised himself that he would win the war for the 'buggers' back in London and then retire.

Many of those involved never stopped asking themselves how they came to be fighting the war in the first place. We now know that the occupation of the Islands by the Argentines came as the result of a diplomatic fiasco. Each side either gave the wrong signals or misread what the other was saying, yet the mandarins who serve as our professional diplomats and intelligence analysts are there to prevent such things happening. If they can't get the little problems sorted out, what will happen if there is a major problem? The truth is that the Falklands *were* a major problem but were viewed as only minor until it was too late. How incredible it seems that this potential trouble-spot should have been simmering away for nearly twenty years, and that it then came as a total surprise when it ultimately boiled over into a full-scale war.

It was not only a shock to the people of Britain and Argentina. It also appeared as a thunderbolt on the world political scene, not least to the government of the United States, which enjoyed friendly relations with both sides in the conflict. We now know that a major concern for the Americans was that they should not be drawn into a superpower conflict with the Russians. Had the Soviet government intervened to exploit the rift between two Western nations, the United States would have been dragged in as well. As it turned out, America had to choose which side to back. It was anxious not to upset its cordial relations with the rest of Latin America, but the junta in Buenos Aires could not be relied upon. The Americans felt its initial aggression in attacking the Islands should not be rewarded. Nevertheless, Alexander Haig's abortive peace shuttle added to the general diplomatic failures associated with the Falklands War, failures which ultimately ended in the death and maiming of so many young men.

In Argentina there were few benefits for *Los Chicos de la Guerra*, 'the Boys from the War', not even the conscripts who returned home wounded. There was no South Atlantic Fund for them, and many found themselves outcasts in Argentine society for having been associated with a public national humiliation. It is a country with severe economic problems – not least a soaring inflation rate. Jobs are scarce and some conscripts were reduced to organising small co-operatives selling home-grown vegetables and fruit from market stalls in the poorer suburbs of Buenos Aires.

The British fared differently, of course. They returned to a grateful nation and a more sympathetic bureaucracy. All received payments for their injuries – some more than others according to rank. Some who lost limbs appeared before various army and navy employability boards and were allowed to stay in uniform. Others were so disabled they had to leave.

Rather than decreasing, the casualties from the Falklands War are actually increasing. Psychiatrists who travelled with the Task Force began treating soldiers and sailors even before the landings at San Carlos. Battle stress was a significant feature among the casualties in the South Atlantic: forty out of the 770 were judged to have psychiatric problems of one kind or another. As is shown in this book, the symptoms of stress due to acute battle reaction can vary from the sailor who, in his own words, put his wife and kids through hell for eighteen months after returning home, to the Royal Marine who twice tried to kill himself after surviving the bombing of *Sir Galahad* at Fitzroy in which forty-eight soldiers and crewmen were killed.

Now military and civilian psychiatrists are dealing with increasing numbers of men from the Falklands campaign suffering from the effects of delayed-stress syndrome. (Training and extensive service in Northern Ireland meant the army fared slightly better than the navy.) Their patients are both officers and other ranks. The Royal Naval Hospital in Portsmouth has so far treated 500 of these cases, and they expect to receive, on average, one a week for the next ten to fifteen years. Many of their patients have not been able to talk about their experiences, believing that their loved ones – families, parents and friends – just wouldn't understand what they had been through. The purpose of this book is to leave no one in any doubt.

Michael Bilton
York
1 January 1989

DIPLOMATS

SIR ANTHONY WILLIAMS

Sir Anthony Williams was Britain's Ambassador in Buenos Aires in 1980–82. He was closely involved in the diplomatic negotiations with Argentina before she invaded the Falkland Islands. When Britain broke off diplomatic relations, he was forced to leave the country. He returned to London and during the conflict was a close adviser to the then Foreign Secretary, Mr Francis Pym.

The negotiations between Britain and Argentina over the future of the Falkland Islands had been going on for seventeen years, which is an enormous length of time, particularly when you are dealing with a comparatively clear-cut territorial dispute. The basic question in that situation is always: 'Shall I have it? Shall you have it? Shall we share it?' There aren't any other choices. The difficulty for the British throughout has been that none of these solutions for the Falklands is at all politically satisfactory. Giving them to the Argentines would mean our surrendering the Islands. That clearly was not on politically. Our keeping them would mean moving into a Fortress Falklands situation, and government after government in Britain has felt that this would be desperately expensive. This was a dominating factor. Consequently, what was left was whether there was some possibility of working out a method of sharing: leaseback or condominium. But it was quite clear that the Islanders were not keen on this idea. Since we had committed ourselves to the proposition that the wishes of the Islanders should be paramount, our only negotiating ploy really was to wait until ideas evolved. To do that for over seventeen years requires a great deal of patience from those who see the issue simply, and a great deal of ingenuity from those who don't wish to come to any conclusion in the immediate future.

One of the ways in which it was possible to prolong this process was certainly to try to give the Argentines an opportunity to convince the Islanders that becoming Argentinian would be to their own advantage. In many ways this is what the negotiations leading up to the various agreements – the communications agreements of 1971 and 1974 [see Chronology] – were about. They were breaking down the isolation of the Islanders and giving them a chance to see that Argentines didn't have cloven hooves.

The delay was very frustrating for the Argentines. For them the situation was perfectly clear: they felt that a handful of Islanders – 1,700 or 1,800 – were really only colonial introducees. The Argentines wanted to get on and settle the issue. They were prepared to play along in an attempt to try and convince the Islanders. This is what the setting up of the airline link, the provision of oil supplies and the taking of children into their schools under the 1971 agreement was all for. It must be admitted that by 1980–81 even the Argentines could see that they weren't getting anywhere with this. The Islanders were not in any way becoming more reconciled to closer contact with the Argentine.

It wasn't easy for people on the spot, let alone in London, to realise that the situation was changing and that the amount of leeway, patience and negotiating space that one had was decreasing. It had decreased extensively after Nicholas Ridley's mauling in the House of Commons in 1981, which showed that leaseback was not going to be an immediate possibility. * In Argentina new, more nationalistic people such as Admiral Anaya and Costa Mendez were brought into the junta.

Although we were sending back warnings from the embassy that time was getting short and problems more acute, we were up against the difficulty that there were many other crises going on in the world. There was a tendency in London to feel that the dispute with Argentina had been going on for a long time and would go on for even longer, and so it could go lower down in the queue. Everybody could see that, in a sense, the sands of time were running out. The question was how quickly? The indications were that what the Argentines wanted was to

---

* Nicholas Ridley visited the Falkland Islands as a Foreign Office minister in November 1980, to outline his proposal for a 'leaseback' settlement with Argentina. When he gave Parliament details of the plan he was attacked by a large number of MPs on all sides and the proposal was scrapped.

put us publicly in the wrong so that if they took radical action, as we expected they might, they would get support in the UN, in the Western hemisphere and particularly in the United States. All this would be working up to the 150th anniversary of the original British landings in the Islands in January 1833.

I was sending warnings back that things were getting worse. I sent a very much more acute warning when I had a long talk with the Argentine Foreign Minister in September 1981. Then President Viola was displaced by Galtieri. The very hardline head of the Argentine navy, Admiral Anaya, was a person who believed in a forceful solution. We would draw the attention of London to this time and time again. I suspect the Foreign Office thought that this was a problem which it could let ride. So many times before it had come to a fairly high-decibel level and had cooled down again. They were by no means convinced that my information was necessarily better than what they were getting through other intelligence sources [i.e. Signals Intelligence, the interception of Argentina's diplomatic cypher traffic by Government Communications Headquarters (GCHQ)].

It was becoming increasingly clear that the atmosphere was getting worse and I mentioned this in all my reports. It was pretty frustrating. There wasn't a great deal of interest or a desire to focus on this in London. I started reporting not my own views but facts, very aggressive stuff, in the Press. I felt that if I gave them all the facts then perhaps they'd come to the conclusion that this really was blowing up.

It has to be realised that right up to the moment of the invasion there were no contingency plans in London for dealing with this situation. This is a subject which had been preoccupying me throughout the whole of 1981 – directly it became apparent that leaseback was not going to be viable. I was pressing very hard that we should have contingency plans drawn up. There was eventually a meeting at the Foreign Office which I was summoned back for. An attempt was made to look at the fact that the situation was obviously deteriorating, and with increasing speed.

The outcome of the meeting was that some attempt should be made to persuade the Islanders that something in the way of leaseback was the best way out for them. This suggestion was rejected by Lord Carrington in September 1981, at a meeting to which I was not invited. I only heard about it some time afterwards. It was rejected without any alternatives being taken up. I made the point as strongly as I could that if we were drifting and waiting for something to turn up, then we must have a contingency plan to deal with the situation if things went wrong.

Again this did not happen. The issue was about to be considered in the Cabinet's Defence Committee in the early part of 1982 when it was decided that before it was taken up, further questions should be put to the Argentines. And before it was put to the Argentines, it had to be cleared with the Falkland Islanders. This was the message which got overtaken by the South Georgia incident, and, consequently, it never really got delivered. When the landings on South Georgia took place it was a situation where a very highly charged atmosphere could easily lead to explosion. The feeling in London was: 'What the Argentines have done is wrong, we must send *Endurance* to go and arrest them.' *

HMS *Endurance* was virtually unarmed. The Argentine navy is quite strong. It was very important to bear in mind that in an explosive situation like this, either we were negotiating with the Argentines about these people [the scrapmen] or we were provoking them. And the provocation could produce an armed reaction. This was the warning which I put back to London straight away. I was doubtful whether sending a show of force from London would have done any good. It would have taken three weeks to arrive and it would have been too late. This dispute had been going on for so long that there had been various occasions when there had been a call to take expensive emergency preventive action, and in practice this proved to be unnecessary. Consequently, when the real thing happened it wasn't appreciated.

Because of the defence cuts there was no military presence in the area. In February 1982, the defence attaché in Buenos Aires and I had decided we must get some clear idea what the military situation was on the ground in the Falklands. But his remit didn't extend to the Islands, only to the Argentine Republic. There were only forty Royal Marines on the Islands and no plan as to what they should do in the event of an invasion. We suggested the defence attaché be sent down to do a recce. The Ministry of Defence didn't think this was worth while

---

* HMS *Endurance* was an ice patrol vessel, and the only British naval ship in South Atlantic waters. She was also gathering signals intelligence throughout South America. The British decision to withdraw the *Endurance* from the region was made in June 1981 on economic grounds. The Argentine government saw it as a signal that Britain was losing interest in its colony in the Falkland Islands.

and wouldn't authorise the journey. So we arranged that he should go down at his own expense. He made a report which was the basis really of the intelligence assessment which was used. We did an update on it again on our own initiative after the landing on South Georgia. It was another of the occasions when we were able to point out that the Argentine response very easily could be an invasion of the Islands themselves.

There was a serious miscalculation made in London during the time of the South Georgia crisis. But I would say that miscalculation goes back even earlier, to September the year before, when it was already clear that things were going wrong. By September 1981 plans ought to have been started and provisions made for meeting the possibility of armed conflict. And nothing was done.

The great tragedy of all this is that because the Falkland Islanders rejected attempts at a peaceful solution * their way of life has been undermined and destroyed in a way which is probably more disturbing and more tragic than if we had succeeded in negotiating a satisfactory leaseback agreement. The Argentines behaved in an extremely unwise and foolish way and I don't defend that for one moment.

To choose to live in the Falklands is to live away from the hurly-burly of the world. What has happened is that the hurly-burly of the world has been thrown at them. One can see that with the mines, the military presence and the history which has been made over these last years, it will never be the backwater it was again.

It can easily be forgotten that prior to 1982 it was regarded as grossly excessive to spend £2 million a year to keep *Endurance* in the area. The decision taken since the invasion was that after all we should be able to afford, and we must afford, the costs of Fortress Falklands. It's an expedient which has been forced on us.

*Over the previous years, the Islanders had received numerous delegations from the Foreign Office in London seeking to find an agreement with Argentina. In every case ministers had been told that the Islanders' wish was to stay under British control.

NICANOR COSTA MENDEZ

**Nicanor Costa Mendez was twice Argentina's Foreign Minister, in 1966
and again in 1982. He is a fervent nationalist whose lifetime ambition has
been to see his country regain sovereignty over the Malvinas. He advised
his government that America would remain neutral if Argentina invaded
the Islands, and that the British would not go to war to recover them.**

On 4 July 1966 I took over the Foreign Ministry for the first time
and called a meeting of all the under-secretaries. I asked them what
the most important issue was at that moment. They said it was the
meeting that we were due to have shortly to discuss our sovereignty
over the Malvinas.

In January 1982, nearly sixteen years later, I was again in charge of
the Foreign Ministry and again I called a meeting of my top officials and
diplomats. Again I asked what the most important matter was. They said:
a meeting with the British to discuss our sovereignty of the Malvinas. I
thought I must have been dreaming; at the very least that my mind was
fogged by old age. But that was the truth and that explains Argentina's
frustration. In sixteen years nothing whatsoever had happened . . . well,
a few things had happened. In 1968 I met with Michael Stewart [then
British Foreign Secretary] in New York and we very nearly reached
an agreement. We had agreed a draft document that did not establish
self-determination as a precondition for sovereignty. All the document
said was that Argentina should protect the interests of the Islanders.
Another important occasion was the agreement of 1971 – a very skilful
agreement from the British point of view. Under it Argentina would take
over – finance – the welfare state on the Islands without getting anything
in exchange. Finally, in March of 1982, there was a meeting in New York

and again we presented a proposal which we thought was quite balanced. All we asked for was monthly meetings following an agenda which would ensure results within a certain period of time; periodic meetings which would not be subject to the British recognition of Argentine sovereignty. But again that meeting was a fiasco and Argentine frustration kept growing.

Over these sixteen years there was a dialogue between diplomats, but there was a far more subtle dialogue through different signals which Britain sent to us, deliberately or not, and signals that we received, rightly or wrongly. The first one was Michael Stewart's attitude, which seemed to show a real British will and determination to reach an agreement. It was also important to remember that before that Britain had only abstained when the UN ordered both sides to negotiate the issue of sovereignty and stated that the interests of the Islanders should be protected but that their wishes would not be paramount. Britain did not vote against this, she abstained.

Another signal was the 1971 agreement in which Britain said let's negotiate this so that you will be able to persuade the Islanders.* This showed the British had nothing against handing the Islands over but wanted Argentina to establish their own dialogue with the Islanders. Later on Lord Shackleton went to the Islands and produced his very interesting report which concluded that there was no future for the Islands unless there was an agreement with Argentina.†

Later Britain decided to limit its defence role to fulfilling its role in NATO, especially its nuclear support. From then on it started reducing its surface fleet. What was the meaning of this? Obviously that the South Atlantic was of no interest to Great Britain because it was eliminating the possibility of having a surface fleet in that zone. Moreover the British government decided to get rid of *Endurance*, the only warship that Britain had in the area. How should we read this? We also heard that the British Antarctic Survey would close down its operations in the Georgias after 30 June 1982. So what we are talking about is a series of British steps

---

* In 1971 Britain and Argentina concluded an agreement which dramatically improved communications between the Falklands and the South American mainland. Regular flights to Comodoro Rivadavia were laid on, plus improved cargo and passenger travel by sea. The agreement also offered Islanders access to Argentina's superior educational and medical facilities.

† Lord Shackleton's report on the future of the Islands concluded that natural resources like oil and fish should be developed in co-operation with Argentina.

– concrete signals that they had no real interest in the Falklands.

We had not heard anything about any previous task forces sent by Britain. Had they sent a task force ahead of our occupation of the Malvinas, Argentina would have had to take another diplomatic course of action. It would have been obvious that Britain was prepared to act militarily since it was giving solid proof that it was prepared to defend the Islands. This doesn't mean we would have ceased our attempt to recover the Islands, but we would have had to adopt a completely different diplomatic and military strategy. This undoubtedly means that the invasion would not have occurred as it did.

President Galtieri asked me to prepare the diplomatic strategy for the Malvinas. I drew up an eight-point plan to be implemented immediately, starting with a protest against Britain. The plan was to climax in a very strong diplomatic offensive at the UN General Assembly, so as to reach the end of the year with maximum momentum. The British Secret Intelligence Service managed to get hold of this plan. I don't know exactly how, but the Franks Report* is proof of this. Unfortunately the British government took no notice and ignored or misread the plan and failed to understand our urgency. They made another mistake on the issue of South Georgia. Forty-two Argentine workers landed there with what we thought were the adequate documents – a white card. They did hoist an Argentine flag during a party but it was strictly a private thing. It wasn't formal because they were not representing the Argentine government and they certainly were not taking over. Neither the British government nor British public opinion could interpret it as such.

The British made a double error: sending HMS *Endurance* to expel the occupants was wholly disproportionate, you don't send a warship to expel forty-two workers without previously going through all the diplomatic motions. The second mistake was for the Foreign Office to say that Argentina had occupied South Georgia – that caused headlines the next day. At a debate in the House of Commons the MPs were shocked by the headlines, gave vent to their criticisms and forced the government to state that sovereignty would not be transferred. This of course had a negative impact in Argentina. We were not prepared to

---

* The Franks Report (*Falkland Islands Review*, Cmnd. 8787, 1983) was the British government's own enquiry into how the Falkland Islands were invaded by Argentina.

14

occupy at that stage because it was not in our interest to bring the occupation plan forward. It was better to wait for *Endurance* to leave and to wait for further reductions in the British fleet. We were also waiting for the warships which we had purchased from overseas, and we were about to receive more Super-Etendards and even more Exocet missiles. Also owing to the climate it was in our interests to wait longer.

The night of 1 April 1982 I could not sleep, and when the first news arrived I cannot deny that it was a tremendous thrill. We were enormously moved to see the people of Buenos Aires cheering the government, regardless of their political differences. Even the trade unions which had been on strike only a few days before were now supporting the Argentine action, and later all the political parties without exception supported General Menendez when he took over as governor of the Islands. As an Argentine it is hard to describe my emotions at that moment. As a diplomat I was aware of the difficulties ahead. I cannot deny, however, that that was one of the most moving and important moments of my life. On 26 March I was told by the military junta that the occupation was to go ahead. I was told of the conditions under which this action would take place. It was to be an occupation followed by an immediate withdrawal so that the United States or the United Nations would intervene.

The occupation therefore had the purpose on the one hand of limiting the Georgias' incident so that it would not escalate and on the other hand, from the diplomatic point of view, to provoke the intervention of a mediator. We analysed the position of the United States government and concluded that it was in their interests to prevent a conflict, an armed confrontation between two friendly Western nations which would have nothing to do with the East-West conflict. We were convinced that the US would mediate. It is important to note that the day that the Security Council debated Resolution 502* the US were not represented by Ambassador Jeane Kirkpatrick, they were represented by the third in command. We thought this was another indication that the US government wished to remain neutral. Obviously the US government needed Britain as its ally in NATO, but it also needed Argentina as an

---

* UN Security Council Resolution 502 of 3 April 1982 called for an immediate cessation of hostilities and the withdrawal of Argentine troops from the Islands. Proposed by Britain, it also called on both governments to solve their differences by diplomatic means and to respect fully the purposes and principles of the UN Charter.

ally in the Central American conflict. So we thought that the US would mediate and we were not wrong. We also thought that Britain would be hard put to organise a task force. On top of that we were thinking of a quick diplomatic solution that would avoid an armed confrontation.

The massive over-reaction by the British and the overwhelming support of the Argentine people for what we had done stopped us from carrying out this plan. The US government had to prevent this conflict and it did a lot to try and do so. General Haig in my opinion believed too much in the advantages of a general dealing with other generals, forgetting the differences between a North American general and an Argentine general. The psychological differences between North and South are far greater than the similarities in the military character. General Haig was wrong in terms of Britain's willingness to negotiate. He soon realised that the future of his shuttle diplomacy was quite bleak when he understood how intransigent Mrs Thatcher was. She insisted on restoring British authority over the Islands, the postponement of any debate on sovereignty and the Islanders' rights to self-determination. Haig's greatest mistake was thinking that he could persuade Mrs Thatcher, ignoring her intransigence, which is shown by her attitude in the negotiations before, during and after the war.

On 2 May the President of Peru made a very good and positive proposal that went beyond Haig's proposals in the sense that it didn't establish the need to restore British authority on the Islands and did not establish as a precondition the wishes of the Islanders. We accepted this proposal. I accepted it on General Galtieri's behalf but he asked for some time to obtain the agreement of the junta. It appeared, according to President Belaunde, that Britain was prepared to accept this proposal as well – then they sank the *General Belgrano*. This caused great anger in Argentina and the negotiations were called off. That was the moment when the negotiations were closest to success.

The British proposal of 21 May had a grave defect: by mentioning Article 73 of the UN charter it reintroduced the Islanders' wishes as a precondition for an agreement. Argentina could not accept this.

I don't think Argentina modified its position throughout the conflict – at no time did it accept any Soviet military support. We did not go to Cuba and ask for Castro's help; we went to a non-aligned conference which took place in Cuba. Naturally I greeted Castro because he was the head of state of that country. In Europe you shake hands, in Latin

America you hug each other. That embrace did not imply any ideological support for Castro, it was simply a way of greeting our host. Argentina has been in the non-aligned movement since 1973. Throughout the war Argentina made absolutely no statement that could be deemed contrary to Western, non-communist principles. What we did was to seek every possible support throughout the war, and you will remember what kind of allies Winston Churchill sought in World War Two.

I suppose that every defeat has its guilty party, and because I was in charge of Argentine diplomacy it is quite natural that those who are looking for scapegoats should point their fingers at me. I have made mistakes just like any other human being, but I don't think I was wrong in the fundamental advice I gave. When I supported the occupation I did it under the condition that it would provoke the intervention of the UN or of a mediator. I am not sorry that I rejected the British and American proposals during the negotiations but I did support the Peruvian proposals. I may have made diplomatic mistakes but I was never disloyal to my superiors and I always defended Argentine interests.

I thought the US made a serious mistake in its policy towards the Americas; it was not in their interest to support one of the sides in the conflict. Winning a battle does not mean winning the war and the British reoccupation of the Islands does not put an end to the conflict. The US decision to support Britain was severely criticised throughout the Americas and made Latin Americans very wary, and I do not think the US has completely recovered from the violent about-face in policy when they lent their support to Britain. The battle for the Malvinas in 1982 was not a decisive battle – the conflict continues. It has not helped towards a solution of the problem. I think Argentines understand that we were not defeated by Great Britain. We were defeated because they had US support. It was certainly not a fiasco. I am deeply sorry that it all culminated in a war which cost the lives of many Argentines and left many others wounded. I am very deeply moved by that, but Argentina was defending its rights.

DAVID GOMPERT

David Gompert was Deputy Under-Secretary of State for Political Affairs in the United States government. He accompanied Alexander Haig on his peace shuttle mission between London and Buenos Aires. He is now a vice-president of AT&T in Washington DC.

The Falklands crisis took the United States government and especially the State Department by complete surprise. We were ill-equipped to deal with it because there were only a few experts within the Latin American bureau who understood the merits of the issue. The rest of us at the policy level, supporting Alexander Haig as Secretary of State, were operating more on the basis of instinct and intuition, even impulse, than we were on a refined knowledge of the problem itself.

There was a tendency on our part to see the issue in the larger policy context. This determined our view of the problem and what we were going to do about it. At that particular moment in history the United States was dealing with two very major foreign policy challenges. On the one hand it was attempting to exert leadership within NATO, to bring about the deployment of new nuclear systems, to re-energise the NATO alliance around American leadership. On a different front, the US was attempting to reverse the tide of communism in Central America and for that reason was trying to build strong relationships with sympathetic regimes throughout Latin America, including Argentina. These two external challenges conditioned our approach and our understanding of the Falklands crisis.

It was clear that if we provided material and open political support to Great Britain, we would do very serious damage to our relationships

18

throughout Latin America, not just with Argentina. We may have over-estimated the damage that would have been done, but at the time it seemed as if we could put back our Latin America policy for years by coming out in direct support of Britain.

On the other hand, an even more absolute consideration was the imperative to avoid another Suez crisis. In 1956 the United States withheld support for France and Britain and our allies suffered a humiliation as a result. To us at the time, even before we understood the merits of the issue, the worst possible outcome would be for Britain to try and to fail to recover the Falklands, and to fail because the United States had withheld or withdrawn support. We were caught between two very difficult policy objectives and for this reason more than any other we felt an active American role to head off a conflict was essential.

The mood on the shuttle throughout the course of the negotiations changed dramatically. It began with a sense of excitement. No one had been killed and the forces were still thousands of miles apart. We were stimulated by a sense of challenge because we knew it was not going to be easy to find some basis for negotiation, but the sense of excitement turned to discouragement after the first visits to London and Buenos Aires. In London we did not find a very positive disposition toward negotiation. The view there was quite simple: 'Foreign troops have occupied land over which Her Majesty's Government is responsible. The issue at hand is the removal of the troops, not the negotiation of the conditions after those troops are gone.' That was about all we received by way of encouragement in London.

We delivered the message in Argentina that the British would fight and that we would not attempt to persuade the British not to fight. The Argentines did not take that well. It was clear they hoped the British wouldn't fight and that we would use our influence to persuade them not to. So we entered a period of discouragement during which we wondered whether we had launched ourselves into a dead end. Then, after another visit to London and back to Buenos Aires, we discovered that both parties were displaying pragmatism – they were willing to look for some basis to avoid further conflict. We had never been particularly optimistic that we would be able to find that common ground, but then we entered a phase where we saw some hope. That optimism turned to frustration rather dramatically when we discovered in Buenos Aires that the government we were dealing with was much less decisive, much less capable of making and sticking with decisions than the government in London. The democracy in London was extremely decisive, with a single figure able to exert powerful command over policy as well as over military strategy. In Buenos Aires we were dealing with a junta which didn't have sufficient authority to be able to make and stick with decisions.

While we found some difficulty in trying to get concessions in London, the frustration in Buenos Aires was that we *would* get concessions – sometimes rather significant concessions that could have averted the conflict – only to find the next day that those concessions had evaporated. The Foreign Minister and other members of their negotiating team had to check with more and more of the various constituents of power in Buenos Aires. They were bound to encounter some elements that did not want to support a particular concession. So it would all unravel – even more quickly than we were able to put such concessions together. We were discouraged and frustrated. After no more than a couple of visits to each capital we were beginning to feel that we were losing the race against the British fleet arriving in the South Atlantic. Once conflict began the whole climate would change, obviously; even the terms of discussion would change and we would lose the opportunity to bring about a peaceful solution.

The atmosphere in Buenos Aires was unreal, that is the only way to put it. We were advising the Argentine government the British would fight, and by implication they would win. We said we would support the British and we were painting a very gloomy picture for the Argentine leadership. At the same time they had whipped up the public and the crowds to the point where there was almost exuberance and joy about what had taken place. There were very high, indeed unmanageable, expectations. The mood in Argentina varied from the sombreness of the inner councils, where we were advising the junta and the negotiators of just how bad things were going to get, to the streets and the speeches to the crowds about how victorious Argentina already was, and how everything was going to work out fine. It was the leadership in Argentina which really created this contradiction by looking to the public for support. By fuelling public emotions they put themselves in a position where they had to show something. The only outcome of the negotiations that would have resulted in survival for the Argentine leadership was one in which they would be able to show they really had accomplished something significant – at the very least the Argentine flag flying over the Malvinas. Those sorts of fruits from the negotiations were impossible.

This was certainly the most gruelling of all the diplomatic missions in which I have been involved. The negotiations were exhausting. If we had only been able to retire to the aeroplane and sleep for the eighteen hours it took to get from London to Buenos Aires and vice versa, I think we would have been able to handle the situation. We weren't able to do that for two reasons. Firstly the sense of excitement and challenge. We really had to put the time to good use, so we spent most of those shuttle flights debating, drafting, arguing and collecting new information in an attempt to refine and redefine the negotiating parameters. The other reason we couldn't rest properly was the conditions we were in. The shuttle aircraft was a work space – it wasn't possible to disappear and catch a few hours' sleep. Secretary Haig is a man of enormous stamina and energy and he was constantly holding meetings, debating, looking at positions, looking for new ways to try and get one or other side to see things in a different light. We had this intense work environment and a not particularly comfortable setting. On top of it all was a requirement that we spend those eighteen hours in the air going over material to understand what had happened on the previous visit and plan for what we had to get across in the next visit.

The whole team was tired and grubby. I was certainly no exception. On the one hand, all of us could have used a break and were hoping that perhaps we would have an opportunity to go home and if nothing else get some fresh laundry. At the same time we all understood that we were racing against the clock. Every day was important and we simply had to stick with it as long as there was somebody at either end to talk to us. We were prepared to go on for as long as it took, even at the pace we were keeping. I was tired but also stimulated by the situation, excited by it. As the shuttle progressed we were all becoming more and more conscious of the gravity of the crisis. As we approached the point where we knew the British were going to arrive in the theatre of war, we appreciated how serious, how grave, how mortal the situation was becoming. There was a sense of personal responsibility to do what we could, to go the last mile, even at an individual level, to contribute that last idea or stay up just a few hours more to find a way to prevent men from killing each other. That was by far the most important emotion we all felt.

The most memorable recollection about London was Mrs Thatcher herself and the way she presided over the War Cabinet and spoke for Britain in the negotiations. She did so forcefully and eloquently, with a powerful command and a powerful set of convictions. I don't believe she wanted to see a conflict at any price. I think she was utterly prepared to use force to remove those troops. And she was unprepared to compromise, in any significant way, important principles or important interests in order to avoid the use of force. I never sensed she was really determined to see force used if another way could be found.

The War Cabinet met with us as a group. She presided and would allow others to speak, to address particular aspects of it, based on their expertise. But in all cases she would have the final word, and in some cases she would explicitly overrule a senior member of her Cabinet in order to be absolutely sure that there was no lack of clarity in our minds about the British position. We had told Mrs Thatcher how perplexing and confusing it was to deal with the Argentines. She made it very easy for us to understand where Great Britain was, what Britain would do, what the British position was. At the same time Mrs Thatcher did show pragmatism. Out of concern, I think, to avoid bloodshed she was willing to look at certain compromises that did not fundamentally deviate from the principles at stake, and did not undermine British interests in any fundamental way. She was prepared to give us concessions that we could use to help get the junta off the hook that they had put themselves on. She understood their problem. She is a politician and she understood the problems that politicians in Argentina can get themselves into by whipping up public expectations. She tried to help in that game but she never showed any inclination to make compromises that would create the appearance in her body politic, or the world at large, that Britain had surrendered the Falklands, that Britain had knuckled under to American pressure, or that Britain had abandoned the interests and the welfare of the Islanders.

She wanted to be absolutely sure – and we supported her in this view – that it was clear to the world, however this conflict turned out, that the Argentines were not to be rewarded for attempting to resolve the dispute by use of force. That was more important than the other principles involved, such as self-determination. She felt that if the Argentines could display the fruits of their actions it would give encouragement to other regimes to resolve disputes by force. On that principle we supported her completely and I think she understood that.

Mrs Thatcher was a bit impatient with us at the outset. She was not convinced that the negotiations could go anywhere, or were even wise, because she felt they would be futile and put pressure on Great Britain. She understood why we felt there ought to be negotiations once we got into them. In the final analysis, when they broke down and conflict began we provided her with political and material support. She was convinced the United States had acted properly and could be relied upon.

Looking back, as awful as it was, the crisis could have been a lot worse – it could have involved military action on the mainland of Argentina itself. We were motivated by a fear that it would get worse and the chances were that it *could*. We were concerned with an escalation of the war, direct bombing attacks on the Argentine and a possible spill-over into Chile. There was always concern about what the Soviets were up to, the danger that they would be able to benefit out of this, as a result of expansion and escalation of the conflict. We feared Argentina and other Latin American countries becoming increasingly dependent on Soviet arms. We had a rather terrifying scenario of the Soviets being able to gain geopolitical advantage as a result of this crisis and we shared those concerns with Britain because we wanted our closest allies to understand those fears. We feared what would happen if the junta fell and a less stable and perhaps leftist regime came into Argentina. We feared a loss of American influence throughout Latin America because of a backlash against us.

The shuttle ultimately failed because politics within Buenos Aires made it impossible for the junta to negotiate in good faith. The prospects for any military regime being ousted were not pleasant. These military officers were quite fearful of the consequences of being thrown out of office as a result of having to surrender. The junta felt they had to have something significant to show for the action they had taken, otherwise they would be ridiculed and ostracised. It was impossible to get those sorts of concessions from the British, and we didn't even try to get concessions from Britain that would have been significant enough to allow the junta to show that it had really given something to Argentina as a result of the invasion.

We felt acute disappointment that our diplomacy failed because of the knowledge that if we had been dealing with objective, rational and decisive governments at both ends, instead of at one end, then we would have been able to produce an agreement. We had no doubt about that. We had a fair solution and we had agreement in principle on both sides; it just didn't hold in Argentina. Then the sorrow set in as we saw the immediate consequences of our failure coming to pass. Obviously we weren't accountable or responsible for the fact that men were beginning to kill each other. We knew we had an agreement so close, almost within reach, and it was our failure to grasp that agreement, our failure to make it stick in Buenos Aires, that removed the last hurdle and permitted the forces to engage and the killing to begin.

JEANE KIRKPATRICK

Professor Jeane Kirkpatrick was US Ambassador to the United Nations from 1981 to 1985. She was also a member of President Reagan's Cabinet and the National Security Council (NSC). She is a senior fellow at the American Enterprise Institute in Washington DC and a leading figure in the Republican Party.

I had no idea that Argentina was going to invade the Falklands. It came as a total surprise to me, and the whole US government was taken by surprise. We had thought that Argentina might conceivably be preparing military action against Chile over the Beagle Channel dispute.* After the Reagan administration came to office I visited six Latin American countries, one of which was Argentina. I was very carefully briefed on raising the Beagle Channel issue, which I did at some length with Galtieri and the then Foreign Minister, Emilio Camilion. When the Argentines were in the United States, and again at the United Nations, I told them that we would regard any effort to settle the Beagle Channel dispute by force as really unforgivable. We made that very clear. Roger Fontaine, who at that time looked after Latin America for the NSC, and I made a very special point of talking to the Argentine Ambassador and a visiting Cabinet member about how important our government regarded it that the dispute should not be settled by force.

* Both countries claimed sovereignty of the Beagle Channel, a strip of water running between Argentine and Chilean territory at the foot of South America.

It is a fact that no one ever said to the Argentine government: 'The United States would not understand an effort to settle the Falklands dispute by force' because it never occurred to anyone that this was even a possibility. It is literally true that no one in the United States government, at any level of specialisation or authority, ever even conceived that possibility. So when it happened we had to try and make sense out of it. What I thought then was that Argentine had engaged in this absolutely unreasonable and reprehensible act of invading and occupying the Falklands in a spasm of nationalism. We were aware that they were at a height of nationalist feeling. As in the case of the Beagle Channel, they have always regarded the Falkland Islands as theirs. In an act of self-assertion presumably, they simply went in to claim what they considered to be theirs and to claim it by force. They did that with no expectation that Britain would resist, much less that the United States might assist Britain in resisting.

The whole conflict seemed to me to be very strange – right from the beginning. From an objective point of view it seemed to be much less important than it obviously seemed to both sides, because the Falkland Islands by themselves did not seem objectively to be that important to anyone. Yet suddenly they had become the focus of this enormously intense conflict. From the United States point of view it was very difficult. If you ask Americans in a poll, 'Who do you feel closest to, who do you care most about, who would you go to war to defend if they were invaded?', Britain is the country that most Americans feel closest to. I personally also feel close to Britain and always have because we share that Anglo-Saxon heritage.

On the one side there is that commitment. I would not say that there was a commitment of alliance that would have involved us in the Falklands on Britain's side, because the NATO alliance is, as Lord Carrington pointed out recently, limited to the area of defence of the NATO countries and limited in its relevance. Beyond the NATO alliance Britain and the United States have from the American point of view a special interest, a special relationship. So if Britain is going to war, it is obviously something the United States needs to care about.

Latin America is very near to us and we are also Americans. All the countries of the hemisphere are 'The Americas'. We share a heritage with 'The Americas', the whole experience of discovery and exploration and colonisation. Being part of the New World is an important experience. It is also a strategically relevant experience for us because the Caribbean and the northern tier of Latin America, particularly Central America and the Panama Canal, as well as the South Atlantic and the South Pacific, have strategic relevance which some other parts of the world do not. It is real. It is concrete.

Our ties with the countries of Latin America are significant. They always reproach the United States for not really caring about them, that is their principal reproach against us. There is an anti-Yankee current in the Latin countries generally, in all of them. The biggest reproach is: 'America doesn't care about us, you care about Europe.'

I knew from my experience at the UN particularly that the countries of Latin America backed Argentina's claim to the Falkland Islands, as they do now. That does not mean they all approved of Argentina's move in invading and occupying the Falklands. It does mean that when the chips were down they all supported Argentina, with the possible exception of Chile. Most of them did it with considerable intensity. At the United Nations I had a very strong opportunity to be reminded of the intensity with which Latin governments viewed this situation.

It seemed to me that while Britain and Argentina had an interest in the Falklands, the United States had a very special, intense interest in avoiding war, and in peaceful settlement of this conflict and in not being drawn into it. I thought we had more to lose than either of the potential combatants.

The night the Argentines invaded the Islands, a number of senior members of the United States government attended a dinner at the Argentine Embassy in Washington DC. The Argentine government had proposed to have a dinner in my honour during the period that I was president of the Security Council at the UN. That is a common diplomatic practice and I had accepted and chosen a date. They had invited all of the top-level officers of the US government concerned with Latin America. The Deputy Secretary of State, the Deputy Secretary of Defence, the chiefs of staff of the various services, the Assistant Secretary for Latin America – nine top officials of the United States government were invited. Once the Argentines began their invasion of the Falklands the question of whether we should attend or not became a major decision for our government. We knew the invasion was coming the day before, and the decision that we should attend the dinner was made by the President, Ronald Reagan. It was not my personal decision, it was a policy decision made by President Reagan. Why did he make it? Because he knew that he wanted to undertake every effort possible to stop the development of a conflict, and he had already decided on a mediation effort. He thought that to cancel the dinner would be an act of special hostility towards the Argentine government that would diminish his possibilities of successful mediation.

Frankly, at the time, I felt unhappy about it. I think most of us did. I was somewhat embarrassed as I saw the juxtaposition of events. I felt personally rather exploited.

The Argentines believed that they had given me a number of signals about their intentions towards the Falklands. I didn't realise they had given them until after they invaded the Islands. I then understood that they had in fact tried to communicate to me that they were going to do it and I had completely missed it. I suppose it seemed too far-fetched.

The Argentine Ambassador, Esteban Takacs, called one day and proposed we have lunch. During the course of that meeting he said that the British had arrested a group of Argentine scavengers [scrap men] on the adjoining islands, South Georgia. He said: 'You know we feel very strongly about it. All Argentina feels strongly about it. You know we feel even more strongly about this than we do about the Beagle Channel dispute.'

I think I must have waved it past because he came back to it and said: 'You know we really have to find a way to settle this issue because we all feel so strongly.'

I thought: Why don't we get on to talking about something important, and I paid no more attention. I never thought about the conversation again until after the invasion of the Falklands. Then I realised he had been trying to tell me that they intended to do this. I told him after it had happened, when it was all over, that I understood that he had been trying to give me a signal. I said I felt very badly that I had completely missed it, never reported it to my government, and never thought about it. He said I should not feel too badly because he had given Tom Enders [the US Assistant Secretary of State for Latin American Affairs] a good deal more clear signal than he gave me, and Enders had totally missed it too.

I was very surprised by Britain's final negotiating offer to Argentina . . . By that time I had been active, along with the UN Secretary-General, in trying to persuade the Argentines to become more serious about mediation and a peaceable settlement. I had been trying very hard to persuade them there was really going to be a war. It was clear now that it was going to be war and that they were going to be defeated if there was a war. They kept saying the British were absolutely unreasonable and that Mrs Thatcher refused compromise. On the very eve of the war there was an occasion when Nicanor Costa Mendez, the Argentine Foreign Minister, Enrique Ros, his assistant, and their Ambassador at the UN, Eduardo Roca, came to the US residence for the purpose precisely of discussing one last effort at mediating the conflict. We specifically discussed the Secretary-General's efforts and the Belaunde plan. * I was trying to persuade them to accept those proposals, telling them they were going to suffer a terrible defeat.

I was given at that time by the British Ambassador to the UN, Sir Anthony Parsons, a full description of the offer made by Mrs Thatcher as Britain's last position. I was very surprised, frankly, at how generous that offer was. I said again and again to the Argentines present that night, if they accepted that offer they could do it with honour, they would have even gained something from this unfortunate adventure. I believed Tony Parsons when he said that Mrs Thatcher would suffer political problems at home in Britain from such a generous offer. For the first time I understood how really serious Mrs Thatcher was, and her own desire to avoid that war. And for the first time I also understood fully just how impossible it was for those representatives of the Argentine government to make a decision not to continue. There was about their attitude a kind of frivolousness first of all, as though they were not really serious, as though they did not have a sense of what war would be like. They had no sense of the tragedy of war and the loss of life. They had no sense that they were going to be defeated. They had no experience of war. They would be fighting one of the world's great powers, which Britain is, and they couldn't even treat the matter fully seriously. They couldn't decide among themselves, and it was clear by then that they had decided, in fact, to go ahead, if for no other reason than that they were incapable of uniting in a decision not to go ahead to war.

* The peace plan proposed by the President of Peru.

SPEAKING OUT

I realised then that there was going to be a war and that young men would die. That was particularly meaningful to me because I had three young sons at just war age. Young Englishmen, young Argentines, would die in a war fought for stakes that seemed to me quite frankly, then and now, not really to be worth their lives.

SIR ANTHONY PARSONS

Sir Anthony Parsons, now retired, was a diplomat for forty years. When the Falklands crisis broke he was Britain's Ambassador to the United Nations in New York. Within a few days in April 1982 he steered Resolution 502 through the UN. It provided the legal basis under International Law for Britain to reclaim the Islands, by force if necessary.

When the crisis emerged the UN was preoccupied with a number of problems – the Middle East, the Lebanon, Arab/Israel, Nicaragua. The Falklands had hardly been near the UN, and never before the Security Council. The issue of sovereignty had been before the General Assembly but not for many years. So it took the whole organisation by surprise. The day before the Argentine invasion I was instructed by the Foreign Office to call an emergency meeting of the Security Council to try and take some pre-emptive action. I called my colleagues – other members of the Security Council. They simply couldn't believe it. It is perfectly true it was April the 1st. One or two of them literally thought that I was playing an 'April Fool' joke on them and that I wasn't serious. I had a lot of difficulty getting the Security Council round the table.

The issue had the unique quality in the modern United Nations of being absolutely fresh. In most UN debates the ground had been worked over for many years: Arab/Israel; South-East Asia; Southern Africa. But for the very first time, from the day before the invasion, everybody except myself and my Argentine colleague was coming completely new to the problem. As the debate rolled on in the first two or three days before we got Resolution 502, you could see delegates changing their minds in accordance with the way the debate was developing. It was the first real live debate in the genuine sense that I'd ever participated in at the UN. There was an astonishing atmosphere. Because of that and our appreciation that this was new territory to everybody we were absolutely determined to get the resolution as quickly as possible, not so much to take people off balance but to get them to make up their minds while it was still fresh. We felt that if a long-drawn-out negotiation period started different considerations would come into it. People would start horse-trading their agreement to this resolution against our agreement on some future occasion on something that was important to them. We felt we had to isolate it and get the whole thing through within a maximum of forty-eight hours – the minimum time possible for getting a resolution.

Luck was on our side. Firstly with the composition of the Security Council; the non-permanent members change every two years and the composition of the council varies a great deal. The Arab delegation was Jordan. It could have been Libya, which wouldn't have made things easy. On the Argentine side the previous ambassador to the UN had left shortly before. He was a very experienced man and was eventually the Argentine negotiator at a later stage of the crisis. His successor only arrived four or five days before the crisis broke. He had never served at the UN before and the poor chap was really completely at sea. So that was a great help. I had been there some time, my team were all experienced and we knew exactly what we wanted to do and how we wanted to do it.

When the debate actually started, we waited for twelve hours to let the Argentine Foreign Minister, Costa Mendez, come and participate. The Argentines felt that, being a Third World non-aligned country pitted against a former colonial power at the UN, they were bound to have the advantage, particularly since most of the UN accepted their view on the sovereignty issue. So when Costa Mendez came up, and the seven non-aligned members of the Security Council asked to see him before the debate started, instead of taking a lot of trouble to persuade them of the rightness of what the Argentines had done in invading the Falkland Islands, listening to their questions, answering them carefully and so on, he rather brushed them aside in a few minutes. I remember when we were all sitting around the great horseshoe table in the Council chamber, waiting for him to come out from his preliminary meeting with the non-aligned delegation. They came into the room much more quickly than we'd expected. We thought they would be another half-hour

– they came out after a few minutes. It was clear to me, looking at their faces, that the meeting hadn't gone very well. I think he just said to them: 'Look I'll deal with this, you just support me. No problem.' He didn't appreciate, of course, that what was on their minds was the use of force to settle a political problem, and not an issue of sovereignty.

He made one or two major mistakes during the debate itself which helped me a great deal, one in particular. When I had spoken three or four times about how the UN Charter laid down peaceful settlement of disputes he took the floor. He said that perhaps I didn't understand. This doctrine in the Charter only applied to disputes which had arisen since 1945, when the UN came into existence. Since most of the delegations round the table were involved in bloody disputes and hostilities which went right back to the nineteenth century and which were all very much up front at the UN, that was a major lead-balloon on his part. I could see votes changing in my direction pretty well as he said that. So we did have a lot of luck.

The position of the Soviets was very interesting. They were taken totally by surprise. Like everyone else they had scarcely been aware of the Falklands dispute over the years. In our delegation we were in a good position to observe them because alphabetically we sit next door to each other. Throughout the day or day and a half of the debate, they were constantly running backwards and forwards to the telephone outside the Council chamber to tell Moscow what was happening and get fresh instructions. It was pretty clear to us that they were in a mess. They didn't know what to do because they saw, as the debate wore on, that the non-aligned members of the council, with whom they always want to be on the same side for good propaganda reasons, were moving towards our side. They were faced with a very ugly choice, either of supporting, or rather not blocking, not vetoing, a British resolution, or offending a number of non-aligned states who were obviously going to vote for us. This is what explains the fact that they abstained on the resolution and didn't veto it. They simply couldn't bring themselves to vote in favour of a British resolution, but at the same time they couldn't bring themselves to sail across the bows of the non-aligned majority.

It's very difficult to look at the history of the negotiations between Britain and Argentina over the Falklands without taking advantage of hindsight, difficult to project oneself back into the atmosphere of the time. With full hindsight it seems to me now that we were too confident about the basic excellence of Anglo-Argentine relations. It's true to say that, over the past century or so, Britain and Argentina have probably been closer, except over the Falklands, than Britain and just about any other Latin American country with the possible exception of Chile. Before they invaded, we were always confident subconsciously that however the negotiations went, even if they broke up, the basic positive nature of Anglo-Argentine relations would prevail. You have to put this in the context of our other dispute in that area – Guatemala and Belize – where our relations with Guatemala had never been particularly good. Diplomatic relations were broken in the early Sixties. We had a series of negotiations with Guatemala on behalf of the Belizeans. I don't believe we would have ever risked a breakdown, a major breakdown, in negotiations with Guatemala if we had not had an adequate deterrent force present in Belize all the time to guard against any impetuous action following a breakdown in negotiations. *

We never did that with the Argentinians and the Falklands. We negotiated and the negotiations went on in a kind of desultory way for about seventeen years. But we never faced up to the question: 'If these negotiations finally fail and there is no way forward apparent to Argentina, is Argentina likely to do something?' We never raised the money for an adequate deterrent force in the Falklands in case the negotiations failed. So when the final crunch came, when the final negotiating process really broke down in 1980, we were – with hindsight – really left high and dry. There was no more juice to be got out of the negotiations. We had not provided an adequate defensive force. So the Islands were very vulnerable.

I think there was a major failure of diplomacy on both sides. Again with hindsight, on our side we failed to appreciate the depth of Argentine national feeling about the Islands and the fact that national feeling could explode if it got the right kind of government, as it were, at the right time in Argentina. Over the seventeen years before 1982 this hadn't happened. We had one or two scares and we had got into a bit of a 'cry wolf' attitude.

On the Argentine side equally they failed to appreciate the latent depth of feeling in this country about the Islanders: not the Islands,

* British troops and RAF fighter planes are stationed in Belize – formerly the colony of British Honduras.

but the Islanders themselves, the community in the Falklands. The Argentines felt that Britain, which had decolonised a quarter of the world's population since 1950, had always withdrawn when pushed rather hard by people seeking independence. The Islanders may have made a fuss but surely they were not going to react one hundred per cent to what Argentina believed was an ultimate piece of decolonisation.

There were the so-called missed signals. We took a number of steps in the months before the invasion which failed to appreciate their point of view; for example, the decision to withdraw HMS *Endurance*. There was another decision – not to give the Islanders full British citizenship – plus a number of others [including not providing the money to extend Stanley Airport, at a cost of £12 million]. As far as we were concerned all those were separate actions taken on their merits. But we can now see that to Argentina they were an accumulation of actions which suggested we were actually losing interest in that part of the world and specifically in the Islands. It helped lead them to the conclusion that if they did something violent like seizing the Islands we would be unlikely to do anything much more than jump up and down at the UN and accept the status quo.

The invasion would have been avoidable if from the very onset we had put an adequate force on the Islands to defend them. But we didn't. We decided that we could afford to negotiate even if the negotiations failed, and there was no danger, given the basic state of Anglo-Argentine relations. In the early months of 1982, when the negotiations at the UN in New York closed, and Argentina did not publish the agreed communiqué of their own, we clearly realised that we were in a more dangerous situation. Then when we had the business of the scrap dealers on South Georgia, we also realised the temperature was rising.

With the genius of hindsight, if we had anticipated at that stage, say a few weeks before, that an invasion was imminent, we could have called the Security Council at the UN into being, announced that we feared a surprise attack in the South Atlantic and focused the world's searchlight on that area. If we had done that it would have been much more difficult for Argentina to invade. The fact was that in February 1982, although we had nothing to offer in the negotiating round in New York, the atmosphere was extremely friendly. I remember commenting on this at the time.

But in the light of the history of the previous seventeen years of negotiations, in the light of the history of the century and a half in Anglo-Argentine relations, it would have been an incredibly dramatic decision to have made. Without hindsight, it would have needed a positive genius to have come to that conclusion and taken such a dramatic step. We must not forget that since our view on sovereignty of the Islands is shared by scarcely any of the members of the United Nations, we were never particularly enthusiastic about airing the subject in the UN, because we were on the sticky end of the poker.

I suppose we had become complacent. On the previous occasions when we had sent secret task forces [1952, 1966 and 1977] nothing had happened. On at least two occasions Argentina had not known that we sent anybody down there, so the overtly deterrent objective was not relevant.

My view as a professional diplomat is that there is no doubt that neither side comes out of this well. Both sides made miscalculations, both sides made false assessments, and we ended up at war with each other. This isn't an exceptional thing: since 1945 there have been between 100 and 150 inter-state wars, and pretty well every one of those has started through a miscalculation by one side of a certain set of events. It is arguable that it would have been avoidable. I cannot help feeling that if we were living through it all again, and we only had the information available to us of the present day and not of the future, then the same course of events might well have unfolded.

After hostilities broke out – with the sinking of the *Belgrano*, the attack on HMS *Sheffield* and the sending of the Task Force – the delegations at the UN found it difficult to believe that Argentina and Britain were at war with each other, and that real fighting was going to take place. Through April there was a certain amount of skirmishing here and there. Gradually the Security Council delegations began to realise that serious business was afoot. I was anxious to dismiss this atmosphere that it was all somehow a game. I kept impressing on them in the informal behind-the-scenes consultations we had two or three times a day with the whole Council present that we were pursuing two tracks. There was a diplomatic track to get the Argentines peacefully off the Islands, and a military track, if we couldn't bring about a peaceful withdrawal.

In the UN by the end of April there was a growing realisation that there was a war on. Although in Britain the sinking of the *Belgrano* caused shock waves of emotion, in New York it had surprisingly little effect. To start with most of the delegates were men of my age whose countries had been involved in wars over the years, and they were getting used to the fact that there was the possibility of a very serious war afoot in the South Atlantic. Coincidentally, the Secretary-General had just picked up the negotiating baton himself following the failure of the Haig shuttle mission. The minds at the UN were beginning to focus more on his negotiations than on various incidents in the war. There is no doubt the sinking of the *Belgrano* and the major casualties it caused came as a shock. Instead of being the victim of aggression, it looked as though we were going to start looking more like bullies. This was offset in a couple of days by the sinking of HMS *Sheffield*. Somehow psychologically this balanced the two in the minds of the UN as a whole. But this explosion of hostilities at the beginning of May didn't really materially affect the negotiating process in New York.

By the time I went back to London on 15 May we were at the end of a fortnight of the most intensive negotiations that I have ever been involved in, in all my life. I had been seeing the Secretary-General two or three times a day and so had my Argentine opposite number. We had worked out a whole series of draft texts of what would have been a treaty, an agreement of about fifteen to twenty articles. We had been exchanging telegrams with London, various texts, changes and amendments throughout this period. All this negotiating had been conducted against a background of greater public interest, media interest, in New York over this crisis than anything the oldest hands at the UN could remember over any crisis since the UN had been formed. Whenever I went near the UN building I was besieged by television cameras, radio, journalists. I couldn't walk up the street without having a great procession of people following me asking questions. It was the same with my Argentine opposite number. There was an atmosphere of tempestuous negotiation.

I clearly had to go home. The piles of telegrams and amendments and new drafts had built up to a point where it could only be sorted out face to face. I went back to Britain and had a long day with the full War Cabinet at Chequers. We went through these documents, line by line, word by word, comma by comma, stop by stop. Again and again and again. This was a very well-organised and orderly meeting, very methodically carried out. And by the end of the day we had reached a clean text of a draft agreement, which our government could live with. Essentially what it amounted to was an arrangement by which the United Nations would administer the Islands, with equal Argentine and British representation alongside it, for a period of six months which could be extendable, during which negotiations would go on under the Secretary-General's auspices to reach a definite solution of the problem. Before any of this could happen there had, of course, to be Argentine withdrawal from the Islands.

We had been going through the text in a line-by-line way. At the end of the meeting I was slightly anxious that the broad implication of what we had eventually agreed might have become a bit blurred because of our concentration on detail. I remember talking alone to the Prime Minister when it was all over, going through the thing in a more strategic way, to make absolutely sure that all the implications of it were completely clear to her.

At some stage the question came up as to whether or not Argentina would accept what we were proposing. I was asked for my view. I said I thought they would be absolute lunatics if they did not accept it, but that the evidence of the Haig negotiations suggested that they were in such a terrible mess down in Buenos Aires that they might find it very difficult to get their act together. I thought the possibility of it being accepted was below fifty per cent.

I was convinced then, and I am convinced now, that this was an absolutely serious offer. What the British government wanted was to get the Argentine withdrawal, and if we could get it peacefully, so much the better. If we couldn't get it peacefully then we would have to do it another way. I was convinced the Prime Minister and the whole Cabinet wanted Argentine withdrawal and they were perfectly genuinely pursuing two tracks. If the peaceful track worked that would obviously be the best thing. But if it did not work there was clearly a determination to recover the Islands, to redress the aggression whatever the cost. The suggestion that this was all a charade and that we put together a document which we knew was going to fail in order to have a scrap at all costs is complete nonsense. The document made an eminently reasonable offer which any sensible government would undoubtedly have accepted. The very fact that it was published to the House of Commons even when it didn't work demonstrated to me beyond a shadow of doubt that the government was serious. I certainly thought Mrs Thatcher would have trouble within the Conservative Party if it had been accepted by the Argentines. I reckoned there would be elements in the country and in her party, and not entirely confined to her party, who would feel that we were giving too much, that we were paying too high a price for Argentine withdrawal from the Islands.

At the end of the session – it was a Sunday – I had the document in my hand. I didn't even telegraph it to my people in New York. It was agreed that I would fly back on the first Concorde the following morning at the crack of dawn and present it to the Secretary-General himself by eleven o'clock New York time. With Concorde you arrive more or less before you leave.

I stopped at my office at the UN to have a couple of copies made and gave one to Perez de Cuellar. We went through it together. I think he was genuinely shocked by the flexibility we had shown. He said to me: 'Do you really mean this? I mean, do you . . . is this really your offer?'

I said: 'Yes it is. There is no question about this. But it is our final offer. We feel that the negotiations have gone on long enough, we cannot just let them drift indefinitely. This is our last offer and also we must have an answer from Argentina within forty-eight hours. We are not putting a pistol to their heads in the negotiating sense but we feel that they have had as much time as we have had to negotiate and that forty-eight hours is plenty of time to reach a final conclusion.'

Perez de Cuellar agreed with this. He didn't feel it was at all unreasonable. We discussed whether or not Argentina would accept it. I expressed very much the same views as I had to my own government back in London. We both felt rather the same: they should accept it with both hands, but the chaotic state of government in Buenos Aires was such that we had our doubts.

We had a reply a couple of days later. It was rather a dramatic evening. The Security Council proceedings in the UN had finished for the day and I was back working in the office at about ten o'clock at night. Perez de Cuellar rang up and said he had the Argentine reply but that it was in Spanish. It would take some time to translate. He asked: 'Can you wait until morning?' I said: 'No I can't. With the time gap that means a whole day gone. I must have it tonight. Can you not translate it in summary or go through it with me and translate it as we go along, for me to be able to give my government a clear idea of what the answer is?'

I got down to his office at about midnight. He was looking very gloomy. I could see from the expression on his face that the news wasn't good. We started going through his rough translation of the Argentine telegram. As soon as he started reading it I realised straight away that it was a negative reply. It didn't even address the detailed points in our negotiating document. It amounted really to a flood of rhetoric not even properly directed at the points at issue. I saw that that was it, we had reached the end of that particular road. And so did Perez de Cuellar.

We had rather an emotional scene. I said to him: 'You know, as a result of this document there are a lot of young men who are alive today on both sides who in a few days' time are going to be dead . . . Don't in any sense reproach yourself for this. I don't think anybody could have negotiated harder, more devotedly, or more expertly than you have. I feel a sense of great tragedy that the negotiation hasn't succeeded.' We parted on that note for the evening.

I got in touch with Perez the next morning. He said he wanted to talk personally with the Prime Minister and to Galtieri. I arranged for the Prime Minister to telephone him later in the day. He rang Galtieri. I was down in the Security Council at the time and was walking past his private room just as he was talking on the telephone to Argentina. He had been on the telephone with Galtieri for twenty minutes. He came out with a bewildered look on his face. I said: 'Was there any positive result?' He said: 'You know I don't really even know what we were talking about.' It had been a totally chaotic conversation.

Then the Prime Minister spoke to him. They had a friendly and rational conversation. He suggested one or two small changes to the text which didn't seem to me to alter things very much in either direction. Then he made the same suggestions to Galtieri. We were prepared to take the changes on board but we wanted to see how Galtieri would react. They didn't respond. So that was that. I felt very disappointed. I thought we had come very close and that there could have been a peaceful outcome if it had not been for the total Argentine failure to get their act together.

The strange thing about the whole crisis was that I don't think I ever felt tired. I had been working I don't know how many hours a day, I was never going to bed before the early hours of the morning because I was going on late-night American TV shows. I was then in action again at the crack of dawn. It was unremitting but I don't think I ever really felt tired. Right from the beginning there was never a break. There was always a great deal to do, and more and more and more.

I suppose for me and my little team, it was rather like being on a surfboard. We were being carried along by an enormous wave and we had to give so much attention to remaining upright that one didn't have time to think about being tired. There was an atmosphere of great gloom in my mission and among friendly delegations too when we realised that negotiations had finished and that there was no alternative to a military recovery of the Islands.

I had been a soldier myself and I knew what fighting was like and I thought about our soldiers bobbing around on boats in the South Atlantic. The whole time at the UN we were dealing with issues of war and peace. We were all very conscious of the fact that it wasn't a game and that people were actually going to die. They were going to die in substantial numbers in what seemed to us to be a completely unnecessary quarrel between two countries with very close relations with each other. I had relations of Argentine nationality who had been down there since the 1880s and it seemed awful. But there was no way out. I never wavered in my conviction that we were doing the right thing. There had been aggression and it was clearly against everything that the UN Charter stood for. That aggression had to be redressed. If it could be redressed peacefully, then fine; but if not, it had to be redressed in some other way.

It was extremely frustrating. We felt right from the beginning that for the first time for many years we had the strength of the international community behind us in our response to an act of aggression. From the moment we first got Resolution 502 we never lost that support. Then we had the negotiations, which by their very momentum created a kind of optimism in our minds. They were so intensive we thought they must succeed. It was a great let-down after that. Even after the British landings, Perez still tried to revive negotiations to avoid the ultimate battle. A number of delegations were calling for stand-stills and ceasefires. I made it clear to him all along that there could be absolutely no question of Argentina drawing us into a morass of endless negotiating in order to stop the momentum of the fighting and somehow reverse the diplomatic situation to our discredit. I made it absolutely clear that although we would welcome any initiative there was one unalterable condition: immediate and unqualified Argentine agreement to withdraw from the Islands. Only in those circumstances would we contemplate a ceasefire or anything of the kind. We never got that, and so we had to carry on to the end.

If the agreement offered by Mrs Thatcher had been accepted by them, a six-month period of diplomatic negotiations would have started under the Secretary-General's aegis. Admittedly that period was extendable and it might not have ended in six months. We would have had the scenario of the UN/Argentine/British flags flying on the Islands and the pressure which those negotiations would have generated. Against all that background, I find it very difficult to believe that those negotiations would have ended in failure. I am not saying that they would have ended in Argentina simply taking over the Islands like that. This is pure speculation but I cannot help feeling that they would have ended up with some kind of recognition of Argentina's presence in the Falkland Islands, with a lot of safeguards built in.

One thing is certain. The Argentines, if they'd accepted them, would be a damn sight better off, vis-à-vis their claim to the Islands, than they are in the present circumstances. I just don't believe the world as a whole would have allowed those negotiations to collapse after everything that had happened.

SAILORS

HECTOR BONZO

Captain Hector Bonzo was a career officer in the Argentine navy. He was skipper of the cruiser *General Belgrano* when it was torpedoed just outside the Exclusion Zone around the Malvinas on 2 May. Now retired from active service, he is vice-president of a company building new submarines for the Argentine navy.

When the occupation of the Malvinas took place the *General Belgrano* was in dry dock having one of its engines overhauled. We said goodbye to the ships which were going with our forces to re-take the Islands. From the dock we waved to them and wished them luck. Two weeks later we sailed ourselves to consolidate their operation.

The day in which the Argentine flag flew again over the Islands was memorable and unforgettable for all of us. Many of the traditions of the Argentine navy are English traditions because we have had, and still have, English friends and had been at sea together and fraternised closely. When you are taking part in something like the occupation of the Malvinas your patriotic feelings go beyond any possible friendship.

I was given the command of the *General Belgrano* in November 1981. I had been an officer on that ship, so for me to become the captain gave me tremendous pride. When I took over at a special ceremony on 4 December it was an unforgettable moment, an indelible memory. That, of course, was in peacetime. We did manoeuvres and training exercises. At the start of the South Atlantic conflict we became a warship in which every member of the crew had the same goal. They were a wonderful crew and they would show their worth at war. Our mission was patrolling the southern zone of the Argentine sea, that is to say, south of the Malvinas. We were to go out on an east–west line and then return west. We always sailed outside the Exclusion Zone, never any closer than thirty-five or forty miles.

In the early morning of 2 May the ship was coming back from its patrol heading west at a fair speed, following a 280° course, straight back to the Argentine mainland. We were ninety-five miles south-east of Estados Island and there was a strong headwind. At 16.01 hrs we heard the first explosion. I thought immediately that it was a torpedo, some others thought that it could have been an air attack. That first explosion was the one which caused the greatest number of deaths, either through the initial blast or through heat and flooding. The second impact came four seconds later. The torpedo hit fifteen metres from the bow and those fifteen metres practically disappeared under water. The two explosions wrecked all the emergency services, especially the first torpedo, which hit under the engine-room and destroyed the pumps, the fire-fighting system and the emergency lights.

From that moment on it all happened very quickly, but it seemed to last an eternity. I was coming up to the bridge at the moment of the first explosion and when I reached the bridge I could already see the ship listing. Five minutes later it had a 15° list to port. I could see movement on deck where an officer was preparing the crew to abandon ship and the wounded sailors were being brought up from the lower decks. Medics were trying to give morphine or first-aid to those suffering burns. All the conscripts and NCOs were trying to help each other. It was all very well organised. There was no panic, although this may be hard to believe. There were people who went down five or six times to the lower decks to bring up the wounded.

At 16.15 hrs the ship had a 19° list, but I still withheld the order to abandon ship, hoping that we could save more people. When I saw that the situation was hopeless, that there was no possibility of saving the ship, and when everyone was at emergency stations – that's when I gave the order.

It is the most tragic order that a captain can give in his life. We have all studied it but we had never actually done it. Here a situation occurred which reveals the attitude of the crew. I thought there was no one left on board, by now the ship had a 40° to 45° list; the deck was covered in oil but the fires were being extinguished by the floods of sea-water. I was still aboard trying to release a few more liferafts, although we had more than we actually needed. Then I heard the voice of an NCO behind me. I had not seen him before and he said: 'Let's go, sir.' I turned round. He was a gunner who wanted to be with me up to the last moment. I ordered him to his liferaft but he refused and he would only jump when he had made sure that I was jumping behind him. We jumped into the water and reached four liferafts that were about fifteen metres away from the ship waiting for us, refusing to leave the side of the ship despite the danger of being dragged down when the ship sank.

The *General Belgrano* was as noble in its death as it had been throughout its life. It capsized very slowly and started sinking, showing the gaping wound on its hull but not dragging any of the liferafts with it. Forty or forty-five rafts surrounded the ship and in some of them they sang the Argentine national anthem and shouted: 'Three Cheers for the *General Belgrano*.'

At that moment all a captain can think about is his ship and the heroes who are going down with it. It is hard to explain what I felt – it was a part of my life sinking with the ship. I felt immediately much older. But there were other things to think of. I was on the liferaft and there were other people with me and a gale was blowing. There was not time any more to think of the ship. At that time I didn't even think of my family. I had no family, only a ship and over 1,100 men. Of these 770 had survived. All this in one of the most dangerous seas in the world, with winds of up to 120 kilometres per hour and freezing temperatures. This was no coincidence, it was due to our training and team spirit. When we reached Puerto Belgrano [the main Argentine naval base 500 miles south of Buenos Aires] we kept the crew together for the next thirty days. They wanted to stay together but at that time they were needed in other units.

On 2 June the time came for us to separate and there was a Mass. I talked to the crew for an hour and I would say that a very strong bond has remained between us. To this day we maintain our Belgrano Association. I still visit many of the relatives of those 368 heroes who remain at the bottom of the sea.

JUAN ANTONIO LOPEZ

Captain J. A. Lopez was a navy doctor aboard _Bahia Paraiso_, an Argentine hospital ship painted white and operating under the rules of the Geneva Convention as a non-combatant vessel. She was allowed to sail between the Malvinas Islands collecting wounded Argentine soldiers. There was a rescue-zone north of the Islands where the British medical teams handed over wounded enemy soldiers to their Argentine counterparts.

We were shocked to hear the _General Belgrano_ had been sunk because we all had a large number of friends in her crew. We sailed as quickly as possible to the rescue-zone. We were worried because it was a very cold sea. The liferafts from the _Belgrano_ were drifting with the current further south towards the Antarctic. They were not the best conditions for survival. The fact that seventy per cent of the _Belgrano_'s crew did survive is due to their good training and efficiency. Some of them were picked up at the point where they were almost frozen, virtually dying from exposure. We sent our helicopter ahead to find the liferafts. He would give us their position and we would try and reach the location as quickly as possible. When we came close to a liferaft two frogmen would dive in and attach a lifeline to it. Most of the survivors were so tired that we had to winch them aboard. We removed their clothes and gave them warm clothing, a hot bath and plenty of hot liquid like tea and chocolate. After that they were put to bed.

Many of them were found with bad burns and had to be treated immediately. The most painful side of the rescue was finding liferafts where the survivors had died from heart failure because of the cold, even though they had survival suits on and had rations with them. They had followed all the procedures. All we could do was identify

Left: *Petty Officer Sam Bishop of* HMS Antelope.
Below left and right: *Sub-Lieutenant Steve Iacovou and Lieutenant-Commander Patrick Kettle of* HMS Sheffield.

Right: *Captain Hector Bonzo, skipper of the ill-fated Argentine cruiser* General Belgrano.

David Gompert, a US State Department official on Alexander Haig's abortive peace shuttle between London and Buenos Aires.

Deputy Prime Minister William Whitelaw leaves a Downing Street Cabinet meeting during the crisis.

Top: *Esteban Takacs* (right), *Argentina's Ambassador to the UN, held a dinner in Washington DC for Jeane Kirkpatrick* (far right) *on the night his country invaded the Falkland Islands. Pictured alongside the Ambassador's wife is the Deputy Secretary of State, Walter Stoessel, one of the nine top US government officials who attended the dinner.*
Above: *On opposite sides at the United Nations in New York: Nicanor Costa Mendez, the Argentine Foreign Minister, and Sir Anthony Parsons, the British Ambassador to the UN.*

Top: *Sergeant Lou Armour* (front with arms raised), *one of the Royal Marine Commandos garrisoning the Falkland Islands on 2 April 1982, captured by Sergeant Manuel Batista, an Argentine Marine* (with gun).
Above left: *Lou Armour.* Above right: *Manuel Batista.*

Surgeon Commander Rick Jolly commanded the field hospital at Ajax Bay, which was nicknamed the 'Red and Green Life Machine'.

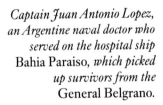

Captain Juan Antonio Lopez, an Argentine naval doctor who served on the hospital ship Bahia Paraiso, *which picked up survivors from the* General Belgrano.

Lieutenant-Commander Nigel 'Sharkey' Ward (Royal Navy fleet air arm).

Lieutenant Ricardo Lucero (Argentine air force).

Major Carlos Antonio Tomba (Argentine air force).

Pictured outside the Argentine fleet air arm base at Commandante Espora near Bahia Blanca are Lieutenant José Cesar Arca (left) and Captain Alberto Philippi.

Los Chicos de la Guerra – *Boys from the War. Then they were still in their teens, now they are in their mid-twenties.*
Top: *Patricio Perez.* Above: *Horacio Benitez.*

the bodies and prepare them to be shipped back home. I remember one case in which we saw a raft with three bodies in it. One of them was lying on the roof. It seemed that he was acting as lookout and fell asleep and froze to death. But when we first saw the raft he seemed to be peacefully asleep with his hands folded under his face. He had a survival suit on and was really wrapped up well. All you could see was his face peeping out of his survival kit. When we brought him on board we realised he was dead. This man was Lieutenant Gerardo Sevilla.

We had periodic encounters with the British hospital ship *Uganda* north of San Carlos, where we would take on board the wounded Argentine soldiers who had been treated by the British doctors. Within the drama of war we had the paradox of being allowed to meet with the English doctors, to transfer wounded prisoners, in a specially designated zone which was an area of peace in the middle of war. We visited the *Uganda* on one occasion to take away our wounded and establish contact with our British colleagues, who then returned our visit by coming on board our ship. They were struck by the fact that our ship was very similar to theirs and had the same facilities. These contacts in a war-free zone allowed British and Argentine doctors to save many lives. I remember that during our visit to the *Uganda* we gave the British doctors anti-biotics, tranquillisers, X-ray plates and other medical equipment which they needed.

It was very sad to see all these young men who were wounded. The navy doctors did everything they could to help them. In our meetings with the English doctors we talked about the Islands and they all said that for them the war made absolutely no sense. I asked them why they wanted to recover them and it was obvious that they were carrying out orders. We explained our position and our geographic and historical rights over the Malvinas.

PATRICK KETTLE

Lieutenant-Commander Patrick Kettle, an engineering officer, served aboard HMS *Sheffield* during a five-month tour of duty in the Indian Ocean and the Mediterranean. She was on her way back – five days' sailing from Britain – when she was told to alter course for the South Atlantic. The ship never made it home. She was hit by an Exocet missile on 4 May some sixty miles south of the Falkland Islands.

Steaming towards Ascension Island I thought I was going to a shooting war, it had every probability of being that. I was aware there were problems with the Falklands in previous years, and because of the magnitude of the Force, and the impressions we gained from the radio and Press, there seemed to be no way out of it. I had a feeling of dread about the whole thing, a lot of people did, and we suddenly grew up very quickly, from the mere fact that we had to prepare the ship. We had to paint it from top to bottom, to make sure it was in a warlike condition. It was painted grey. We had to unload some stores and make sure we had enough food and ammunition. It brought it home to us.

I realised that going into a situation like this there was a possibility of losing my life. It was something I had to face. I had a wife and child at home and I was concerned that if I had to lose my life then they would not go without something from me. I thought about it for some time and decided to write my wife a letter to explain to her how much I loved her, my feelings for her, things she could remember me by . . . a piece of music, a place to go. I gave her some advice as to how to behave as a widow, as I remember. It was difficult for me to write. The more difficult one was to my son. I haven't re-read it but it was

50

certainly blotted with tears. Having written them, and it's the hardest thing I've ever done in my life, I posted them to my father and asked him to pass them on in the event of my death. I am glad now that I did so, and indeed my wife has read those letters since and it has made our marriage stronger.

In the few days before we were hit by the Exocet* we were positioned at the head of the Task Force, and only on the first day were we ever under attack directly from aircraft. These were flying over the Islands; we were picking them up at whatever range. We then found ourselves in action and we waited and listened to the messages as we shot down or splashed Argentine aircraft. We just sat there and waited. My job as an engineer was basically to keep the machinery running and to wait for action damage, so we had the terrifying long wait for something to happen. We realised it would only happen during daylight hours and we spent the few days beforehand living in dread through the daylight and getting some feeling of safety during the night.

The watches we had were long: we worked four hours on and four hours off and for someone in my position on the engineering side of life, that is a lot of time to fill. I filled it by speaking to the men in the damage-control parties and the machine-control room. I even did a little bit of reading. We had to find things to do to keep our minds occupied and not dwell on the bleaker side of life. For instance we might hear depth charges in the distance and one's mind could turn to wondering: Is there a submarine in the near vicinity? By and large they were normally sea animals that were depth-charged unfortunately. We lived through the long wait and the boredom in the three days that we were active in the waters of the Exclusion Zone.

The day we were hit I had gone on watch at midday. It was a very quiet watch, the ship felt as though it was on exercise on a Sunday, almost dead. I had spoken to the damage-control parties at the fore and aft ends of the ship. I'd even been into the operations room to speak to the principal warfare officer to find out what was going on so I could pass the message down the line to the damage-control head-quarters, HQ1. I decided to read a book for the next half-hour. After

---

* Exocet anti-ship missiles, manufactured by Aérospatiale of France, were launched from Super-Etendard jet fighters flown by Argentine navy pilots. Guided by radar and containing a high-explosive warhead, the missiles could skim over the surface of the sea searching for their target.

ten minutes there was a 'pipe' [a message over the ship's loudspeaker intercom system] on the ship's main broadcast, requesting the advance warfare officer to go to the ops room. I could tell by the edge of the voice speaking that something was happening, so I made a move to put my book aside, pull stumps and get ready for whatever was happening next.

I waited, it felt like ten, fifteen seconds. I looked around: nothing happening, no alarm, so I picked my book up again. I'd opened it and at that very instant there was a whoosh and a giant rushing wind passing through the machine-control room, out into the port passageway. People passed in front of my eyes, books, log sheets, and there was an awful lot of dust in the air. It was just like a rushing wind. I had been blown off my chair, which I discovered later had been broken into three or four pieces.

I picked myself up. My first reaction was: I'm still alive. My next reaction was to find my lifejacket and then to reach for the main broadcast alarm to make sure that we got the whole ship awake and moving to the right place to deal with the incident. I found that the main broadcast alarm was dead. I did have communication with the forward end of the ship and received a message that the ops room had been hit. We discovered later it wasn't the ops room but then we lost communications with the forward end. Almost immediately the compartment filled with smoke. To me it smelled like the normal chemical smoke we use during our exercises for damage control. It seemed unreal that in this action state I should feel we were in the middle of an exercise.

The smoke soon built up. I had the incident marked up on the incident board, but within minutes I couldn't even see my hand in front of my face. I realised that there was little more that I could do in my position, so I ordered the evacuation of both the machine-control room and HQ1. We made our way out, crawling on our hands and knees, with our noses as close to the deck as possible. There was air there and we could breathe and we made a relatively trouble-free exit from those compartments.

After I'd made my way to fresh air, I spoke to the marine engine officer who was dealing with a technical problem to make sure we could get rid of some of the smoke. I made it my business to go to the aft end of the ship to find out whether we were sinking or not and to look at the attitude of the ship in the water. We were floating upright at the time. I could see the whole forward end on the starboard side, and there was water pouring out through this hole which came from the ship's firemain, the water used for fire-fighting. Electric cables were broken loose and there was smoke pouring out of this hole. I could see that there was no immediate danger of the ship sinking and we set about trying to tackle the fire. We were not able to put water into the rest of the firemain of the ship, and therefore we had to fight that fire primarily with buckets on the end of a string. This was in 1982.

Fire-fighting went on for five hours – it seemed like half an hour. We had no means of communication; I had to rely upon myself walking around to make sure that it was all happening. I was thinking that this was an air-launched missile that hit us and I suspected that anyone who fires one of these missiles was likely to fire two, so I was concerned as to when the second one might strike. It was only a passing thought. I was talking to a petty officer later and learned the second Exocet had missed us and was seen going past the stern of the ship.

I didn't feel afraid, I was too busy to be afraid. I was initially, but those thoughts disappeared as I got on with the work of fire-fighting. I remember walking from one end of the ship and meeting a doctor I'd known on HMS *Fife*. I suddenly stopped to speak to him and said: 'Nice to see you, I haven't seen you in a long time, I'm too busy now, I must rush off.' For that moment or two I was somewhere else passing the time of day with this doctor who had been flown from *Hermes*. He'd got an MBE for his efforts at relief work we had done in Dominica when it had been struck by a hurricane.

It hit me that some of my friends on board were dead, and I knew I would have to detach myself from those thoughts and concentrate on those alive. Someone reported to me that a particular person was dead. I hadn't time to think about that, my thoughts were directed to the action in hand. I saw casualties who had been burned by the fire but I knew we had doctors; they and the petty officer medical assistant were handling it capably. It was their job and I left it to them.

We left the *Sheffield* and were taken to HMS *Arrow*. We were handed 200 cigarettes which I remember being thankful for. Things seemed to be quietening down. The light had gone, it was now coming on towards night-time and I felt relatively safe. Indeed, I had decided to have a shower to clean some of the smoke off. I took all my clothes off and had a nice hot shower in the ward-room showers. Unfortunately at that moment we heard the dreaded words 'Air Raid Warning Red' and here I was ready for action with no clothes on. I have never dressed so quickly in my life. I knew I was in the wrong clothes for the situation. For any kind of action the best chance you've got is to be fully dressed, so my instant reaction was to make sure I got each leg down the single hole of my pants at the time rather than putting two down one. I went and stood by the damage-control party of HMS *Arrow*. I didn't know that type of ship, the layout of it, so I couldn't really have been much help except in the immediate surroundings. I had just to wait for the all-clear. It was not a happy time.

I came home in a very sombre mood. I had been frightened out of my life. I had never been so frightened before. I had seen friends killed. I came home on an RAF VC10 and we landed at Brize Norton. I met my wife in the VIP lounge, which was very nice, then I had to suddenly face a barrage of the Press. I remember walking back to the car with my wife and my son in his pushchair, and we had all the American news channels with cameramen and sound recordists walking backwards along the pavements in front of us while we walked forwards. I couldn't understand this, I couldn't think why I was important.

We got in our car and drove to Portsmouth. I asked to go down to Southsea and drive along the sea-front before we finally returned home. As I drove along the front there were people having their summer holidays; they were eating icecreams, sitting in their deckchairs and passing the time of day, enjoying themselves. I felt as if I wanted to pick them up and shake them and say: 'Look, there is a war going on, people are getting killed.' I felt for them the war was something that happened at eight o'clock in the morning when they picked up their newspapers or switched on the radio, or at nine o'clock at night when the TV news came on. I think it took me a lot of time to re-adjust. Everywhere I went life was going on as normal, people were buying houses, going on holiday.

Throughout the Falklands conflict the Press were constantly being extremely jingoistic with banner headlines. There were large cheering crowds. To me it was just a reminder of August 1914. War is something that sometimes has to be done, but it doesn't have to be done in that state. I don't think until the *Sheffield* was hit people realised that we were really in a killing war.

I found it very difficult to speak to my wife about my experiences. The only way that I could ever let her know how I felt was actually to tell the story to other people but to make sure that she was within earshot, and I consciously did this on several occasions. This conflict has been working on inside me for some time, but I'm glad to say I've managed to get it out and tell her exactly how I felt, and I feel better for it.

I was left with the feeling of the absurdity of war. It's a message that has been said many times before. War is hell, believe me.

STEVE IACOVOU

Steve Iacovou was a Sub-Lieutenant in the Royal Navy serving aboard HMS *Sheffield* when it was sunk. He was one of the first people on the ship to spot the Exocet missile before it struck.

We had already taken up our station on patrol in the South Atlantic off the Falkland Islands. There are different levels of 'action stations' and we were at defence stations, which basically meant the whole ship was on alert. We weren't exactly expecting trouble at that time, but we were in a state of preparation in case it came.

I was on the bridge on watch. The quartermaster has a bosun's mate and you work hand in hand with him, taking stints on and off at the wheel. I stood behind him giving him some instruction. There were people milling around, a couple of officers-of-the-watch, the navigating officer and a radio operator. It was a beautiful day, the sea was flat calm and I don't think at the time we were terribly worried that something was going to happen.

At all times we kept a very good lookout for obvious reasons. I noticed something about the same time, I should think, as the officer-of-the-watch; we were both looking out to sea at the same spot. It looked like a torpedo was on its way because the sea was shimmering and shaking. So I said I thought there was a torpedo. The pilot also trained his glasses round to the same spot and said: 'No. It's an Exocet.' At that stage we didn't have very long before the missile found its way to us. It was on the horizon, so it was little more than a glimpse at first, just a heat shimmer, miles away. The visibility was as far as you could see; we'd picked it up pretty early.

They don't shoot Exocets at you in training. It is something that you see from the side view on training films. You don't actually see them coming head-on as we were experiencing at the time. I was transfixed by the missile coming at us. For a brief second nobody quite knew what was going on. The pilot seemed to make a quick exit. He'd left the bridge quite soon after spotting it and I found out that he went down aft to get the helicopter off. The rest of us made ready. We could do very little. We made a shout to 'Take Cover' over the main broadcast. That was all. We were not even sure if it came out – not many people remember hearing it. The officer-of-the-watch and the other members of the bridge crew started to take cover, but I remember myself and the second officer-of-the-watch becoming mesmerised by the missile. We watched it almost to the point of impact, when we quickly huddled together and dropped to the floor.

It was only a matter of seconds before the missile hit, not enough time to do anything else with the ship. I'd prepared myself for an explosion of some kind, which didn't happen. There was just a loud bang and a thud, rather than a ripping explosion. Everything shook, there was dust everywhere, things falling off bulkheads and the whole place seemed to be imploding. At the time everybody seemed to be running around: the officer-of-the-watch was trying to take charge, the second officer-of-the-watch was trying to man the intercom, the bosun's mate had made his way off the bridge, so I took the controls of the ship to see if we had any steerage. The smoke soon filled the bridge and we didn't see much from that point on. I soon realised when I was asking for instruction from the second officer-of-the-watch that nobody was answering me, so I made my way off the bridge as well. I found out that the officer-of-the-watch had actually ordered us off the bridge.

Fighting the fire was incredible. The heat is hard to describe, and it was getting closer. We had a case of someone running through a cross passage where there were no flames coming up but just heat. He had to run through this heat to get away from the point of impact and he had been scorched from top to bottom. He was, in fact, okay apart from a lot of scorch marks and very minor burns, but he was very lucky. The fire-fighting seemed to go on for a long while. We were trying to close the hatch at the top of the fire to cut off the oxygen and air to the flames. People were in boats down the side of the ship, trying to close the hole with water so that would also starve the fire. There were a lot of people trying to stop the fire which was raging, using anything they could to put the flames out. You are taught in training that gas masks only give you very short cover against smoke but I tried to use a gas mask and so did my friends who were also trying to fight the fire. We had minimal success, we managed to stem it rather than stop it. After a while we knew that we were not going to stop it, it was just a matter of whether we could hold it back for a while.

I was worried that we were going to have an explosion. It wasn't the fire that worried me, we were fighting that, it was the fact that the ammunition might go up, the shells and the missiles we were carrying. We seemed to have the fire under control, we weren't going to get hurt from that. In seconds our boots were sticking to the deck, it was that hot. It was a matter of peeling your feet off as you were trying to walk about.

We weren't cold to start with – we were spraying each other down to try and get as close to the fire as we could. When the captain ordered the fire-fighting to stop and for us to go to the foc's'le the bright afternoon had turned into early evening and it was very cold. The people down there had blankets and other warm clothing we could get into.

HMS *Arrow* made her way alongside us quite quickly and she was assisting with her hoses. Obviously they couldn't get very close to us because I suppose they were worried that the lot was going to go up. There was a curious incident shortly after the missile hit. An Oerlikon gun crew started to make ready to shoot down one of our own aircraft because it was coming close on the enemy arc. We were quite concerned that the Argentines might try and finish us off. I had mixed feelings when the order to abandon ship was given. Most of the ship's company were very sad to leave a ship that we'd been with for some months and in the case of most of them for two years. It's a strange liaison that you have with a hunk of metal, you become very much part of that ship. We were sad to be leaving but genuinely relieved that we were going to get off a ship that might explode.

The ship was abandoned with helicopters taking off the injured. People were jumping off the ship from down aft in once-only protective suits. I didn't quite fancy that because the water looked too cold, I must admit. I was always worried that you'd jump into the water and not be found. HMS *Arrow* had put down some scrambling nets and I'd decided that was the way I'd try and get across. I jumped the short distance between our ships. The scrambling net was put there just in case we didn't make it. I think two or three people came with me and we were pulled on board.

On the *Arrow* we were all put together on one mess deck and they tried to make us as comfortable as they could. People were very kind to us, giving us articles of clothing. Slowly but surely we started to look around, hearing the stories about the people that hadn't made it. You soon became aware of the people who had died because you couldn't see their faces; and you'd look round for friends, people you'd spent a lot of time with, to see if they had made it across. Everybody lost friends. We were a very friendly ship's company who had spent a lot of time together.

The crew of HMS *Arrow* were a little bit cautious about how they spoke to us, they didn't quite know how to approach us, how to talk about the incident. They showed a lot of anger for the Argentinians, but they didn't quite know how to broach the subject of us being hit, what it was like. They were probably very curious, as anybody would be, but couldn't quite bring themselves to ask the questions they wanted to. They left us pretty much to ourselves once we had assembled.

We were shocked about the loss of our ship – we hadn't expected it. I don't think anybody in a civilised world would really have expected us to have been sunk or to have been shot. We thought that we'd gone down there to do a job that wouldn't take any kind of hostilities. We thought there would be a purely diplomatic solution found for the whole conflict but we were wrong.

Seeing the missile from the bridge is something you don't forget. It was a sense of awesome power coming towards you. Rather than being able to recognise every fin on the missile it just seemed to be some sort of explosion on its way to you, quite incredible. For ages afterwards I closed my eyes and that's all I could see, that sort of imprint on my mind.

ALAN WEST

Commander (now Captain) Alan West commanded the frigate HMS *Ardent*, which was sunk as a result of Argentine aerial bombardment in Falkland Sound on 21 May. He was awarded the DSO and now commands a destroyer. He is president of the HMS *Ardent* Association. Each May former crew members gather at a naval church in Plymouth for a memorial service and reunion.

My ship sailed two weeks after the main Task Force left for the South Atlantic. About three or four days before we sailed I went up to Northwood, which is the command headquarters for the Royal Navy, where the whole operation was run. A vast amount of money was being released to fund equipment and to get things ready. It became very apparent because of the amount of organisation going on at Northwood, that unless the Argentinians pulled out of the Falklands voluntarily we would fight them. I felt that the Argentinians would not withdraw because that's not in the personality of the Argentine people. I don't think I had any doubts.

I went back home convinced there was going to be a fight, and indeed when I left my wife I said: 'You know we're going to fight.' I said this because a lot of people in Britain didn't think there would be a war. I said there would, and that if it came to a naval war we were not fighting against absolute beginners, so ships were going to be lost. It obviously worried her but I felt she ought to know the facts. Unfortunately I didn't realise my young son who was then aged six was listening outside. When I went to say goodbye to him I said: 'Goodbye William, I'm coming back soon and don't worry.'

He said: 'Ah, but you said ships are going to be lost Daddy.'

I said: 'Well, I promise you I'm going to come home.' When the *Ardent* was lost he jumped on his bicycle and pedalled around the patch, he wouldn't believe it. And then he went back and said: 'It's all right, Daddy said he'd come home.' That kept him going all the way through the conflict.

I didn't think about not coming home when I was on the ship or when we were under attack. When I was returning home I did, but things like that are quite difficult. They touch a chord and make one feel rather sad, because some of my boys didn't come back. It's an experience that changes people. I've learned a lot. I've made closer friends with a lot of people. My boys in the ship now are always 'my boys' and that's quite a thing. We have a reunion every year and we are a close-knit family. We try to look after the next-of-kin of the chaps who were killed. That is the marvellous thing.

May 21st was the day of the British landings at San Carlos. HMS *Ardent* went in first, down through the narrows into Falkland Sound. We took station in an inlet called Grantham Sound because our 4.5 inch Mark 8 gun had a long enough range to be able to hit Goose Green airfield. From early on our role throughout the morning of the invasion was to provide naval gunfire support to stop the airfield being used by enemy Pucara* aeroplanes, and also to give support for an SAS diversionary attack. We were firing shells over towards Goose Green at a range of about eleven miles and there was some very good shooting.

A couple of spotters had been landed some days before. We got in voice contact with one of them after arrival at our station. They clocked straight in and we opened fire. At the time one had to laugh at the dear old 'Brits', but I thought it was quite amazing. We had steamed eight thousand miles and arrived on time at four o'clock in the morning. These other chaps had come in other ships, landed, and were sitting in a little hole. They called up and 'Click' we talked to them and 'Bang' went the gun. I thought: It's quite something.

We kept firing but we were also under attack throughout the morning. It was a very beautiful day, which was unfortunate. The day before on the approach to the Falklands it was cloudy and misty, which was just what we wanted because we knew we were within reach of their aircraft.

* Pucaras were slow twin-propeller aircraft, highly manoeuvrable, used to mount low-level attacks on British ground troops and helicopters.

But on that morning it was absolutely crystal-clear. Sure enough, about an hour after sunrise the first raids, big heavy raids of jets, came in. We were bombarding the shoreline and then shooting at the aircraft as they came in and attacked us.

Later in the day, having finished our gunfire support, we moved in closer to the shore. We had been under some attacks, we had been straddled by bombs, but nothing very heavy. I signalled requesting further instructions, and we were put into a 'goalkeeper' position* to stop the air raids coming up from the south, because the raids were really heavy. Clearly the Commodore in charge of the amphibious force was worried because if they had started hitting amphibious ships or the shore where the troops were trying to land it would have been a very different day. We formed part of the gunline to stop those ships close in by the shore being damaged. The Royal Navy ships in the bay outside of San Carlos Water that day really took the brunt of the attack and stopped them getting at the other ships, which was crucial to the landing. I try and tell my boys that the great thing we achieved was that not a single soldier was killed in the landing. That was our job.

The first really heavy attack that hit us were Argentine navy A4s. The reason we knew they were navy was because they were white-coloured and you can see them much better. I was talking to the ship's company over the intercom. I saw these aircraft moving in towards us and told them another raid was coming in. They got closer and closer and they dropped their bombs. You could see them fall quite easily and I could tell they were going to hit down aft. I called: 'Take Cover,' so that the chaps down below would hit the deck. The bombs hit us and exploded, a bloody great explosion. The Seacat [missile] launcher was thrown about a hundred feet into the air. It came back down, landed on the flight deck, killed a number of people, and ripped a bloody great hole in it causing fires, flooding and things like that.

All the alarms went off on the bridge. Initially one was trying to work out what exactly had happened. We got it under control fairly quickly. The flooding was being tackled by damage teams and the fires were basically put out. I was able to establish what damage the ship had suffered from

---

* Royal Navy frigates were used as 'goalkeepers' in Falkland Sound on the day the Task Force landed. The term refers to the fact that the ships were positioned to draw attacks from enemy aircraft and stop them getting through to the ground troops disembarking at San Carlos.

the reports that came up to me. Sadly I lost my Seacat missile system. Also because of another fault the 4.5 gun was temporarily not working. *Argonaut* had just signalled the Commodore that she could float and fight but couldn't move because she had just been hit in her boiler. I sent a signal saying we can float and move but I cannot fight because I had no weapons at all.

The Commodore signalled to me to come back towards the other ships because I was clearly being singled out. I started to do just that when the next waves of attacking aircraft came in – Mirages and A4s [Skyhawks]. We were hit heavily again, mostly in the stern because I was steaming into the wind trying to cause them problems for their aiming. If you aim for the middle of a ship clearly steaming into wind, it causes a high crossing rate, so all the bombs tended to hit down aft all the time. That was bad because it killed a large number of my damage-control parties. Had they hit us amidships then an awful lot more people would have been killed. In that sense we were quite lucky.

There were very large explosions, lots of smoke and flames. Some injured people appeared on the bridge; my Seacat missile aimer was absolutely covered in blood. He had been blown out of the aiming stand over the ship's side, landed in one of our boats and crawled on board. I sent an officer quickly to give him some morphine. It became apparent from reports coming up that the ship was pretty badly damaged. I sent out another signal, this time saying that we were badly hit. Other ships had realised this and by then *Brilliant* and *Yarmouth* had come down to stand by because there were raids still going on. Then it was a question of working out exactly what the damage was.

From the reports that came up it became very clear that we were not going to be able to save the ship. It was a question of were we going to stay on board having a go at it, or would we use *Yarmouth* to get as many of my boys off as possible? I then had to make a decision whether to abandon ship. I thought about it because you fall in love with a ship, especially as its captain. Giving the order to abandon ship was probably one of the hardest decisions I have ever had to make. In the final analysis it's the people that you really like. You think it's the whole ship but it's the people. It was difficult. I had to weigh up the information I had got. I had to think of how long it might take, if there was any possibility of getting the fires and damage under control. From the reports I had that was not a possibility. If it had been peacetime we could have brought several other ships alongside us and used lots of other gear. We might possibly have been able to do something, although I still doubt it.

Finally I made the decision. It's something I had to do. I was the captain and no one else could do that. When I had made the decision the chaps disentangled themselves from fighting fires and in a very orderly manner made their way up on deck, got settled and then checked to make sure there was no one left alive. I sent them all off. I stood there on the bridge on my own; nearly all my men were off by then, and *Yarmouth* had put her stern on to our bow because we were sinking. I finally walked and stepped off on to her. It was very sad. As we moved away from her I know a lot of my chaps were in tears. I was in tears myself.

At that stage I didn't think about the pilots who were bombing me. As far as I was concerned they were aircraft that were trying to hit my ship and it was very much a military action to try and shoot those aeroplanes down. I didn't think of it in personal terms at all. That's one of the things about being in the navy, it's not quite as personalised as jumping into a trench with someone and trying to kill him. I thought the aeroplanes were hateful things I wanted to absolutely smash up, but I didn't think about the pilots. If you saw a plane splashing or blowing up everyone thought: Great, let's get some more.

In retrospect I think their pilots performed very much as I predicted. On the way down south when I talked to my sailors I said that their air force was the main threat to us, without doubt. You know in military terms you don't think about carrying out an amphibious landing until you've got air supremacy. In that sense I suppose it was a slight gamble, but I knew there would be major attacks. If you're a fast jet pilot you've got to be good or you're dead. I mean, it doesn't matter which country you come from because you've got to have bloody good reactions, you've got to be good. The Argentinians? If you imagine, what are they – racing drivers, polo players? What better sort of chap to have sitting in a fighter, flying at low level? He's got to have quick reactions. You know they were like 'The Few' but in Argentinian terms. I wasn't in the least surprised.

Their weaponeering capabilities, their ability at delivering ordnance accurately, was probably not that clever. They came in very low, a lot of it was free-fall type bombing, eyeballing it as they say. If it had been our fleet it would have been the weaponeering aspects that would look much better. They would have gone for the target they wanted. They wouldn't have been dragged off and seduced into attacking escorts. By doing that the Argentines lost the war. If they had sunk the amphibious ships or if they'd sunk a carrier they could have won the war. But they fell into our hands, and did what we wanted – which was attack the ships.

KEN ENTICKNAB

Ken Enticknab was in charge of one of the damage-control parties as a chief petty officer aboard HMS *Ardent*. He was badly injured and was rescued from drowning when he was pulled out of the sea by Surgeon Commander Rick Jolly, hanging on to a helicopter winch-wire. Later he was commissioned and received the Queen's Medal for Gallantry.

On board HMS *Ardent* I was a chief petty officer. I was the engineering chief looking after the refrigeration, air-conditioning and domestic machinery. At action stations I was in charge of the aft damage control which involved dealing with fires, floods and any other damage caused by attacks. When the ship is hit you have to send out two-thirds of your men to do a blanket search: to cover your section of the ship, find out exactly what the damage is and report back to you. They then take action to deal with the damage. My job was to get a picture of the damage which I could plot on a diagram of the ship. Then I talked to those co-ordinating damage control so that the command could be kept informed.

When the Argentine bombers came over we were in the dining-hall. We were lying on the deck taking cover. You have to cover your head with your hands and wait for any explosion. When it came I shouted: 'Go!' and my team went to do the blanket search. The ship actually bounced when the bombs hit. Water came through the deckhouse and there was a horrible smell of acrid smoke. When I got up I could see through the forward door that we had been hit in the next section. I was really petrified. We'd just been called out into the middle of Falkland Sound to draw the fire and we knew then we were going to be attacked and probably hit. Initially when it happened it was a relief because we now had something to do in our section. We had been lying on the deck all day, since the early hours of the morning.

The relief of being able to get up lasted a second or two. When I got my wits together I was able to see that the deckhead had caved in and water was pouring through the holes in the deckhead and the ceiling. My team were picking up equipment used to stop water coming in through the side of a ship. I shouted at them to leave that and organise a pump to get the water out. I went forward to appraise the damage in that section, smashed a couple of locks off doors to see the extent of the damage behind us, in the beer store and canteen. I realised that the water could only come from the pipes with fluid in them and isolated the systems quickly around the damaged area, so the water coming in steadily got less and less. I had a quick look at the other compartments and assessed the damage. I could hear a diesel engine running. When I went to the switchboard all the cables were dangling loose, severed in half. I remember tiptoeing out of there in case I got electrocuted.

The engineer officer, who is the co-ordinator of damage in HQ1, was standing at the door, shouting at me, wanting to know what was going on. I was able to give him a quick report and then went back down to the dining-hall to where my stateboard was. I wanted to make up the stateboard and receive the rest of the reports coming in. We were told to 'Take Cover'. The ship had keeled over somewhat by then and we were in six inches to a foot of water. On the starboard side it was waist-deep.

I remember waking up again after that. The dining-hall was pitch-black. I had a quick look round and I could see that my hand was injured. I had my anti-flash glove on and I could just see a mess, a mass of blood. There was no pain, no pain at all. I thought: Well, they can sew fingers back on these days, there's no problem. I had a quick feel over the rest of my body. I had a large piece of Formica sticking out of the top of my head. I pulled it away and then tried to get up. I was unable to. I could get up on all fours but I was unable to crawl out from whatever it was that was stopping me moving. It was a dreadful feeling. I just thought about getting out then. I felt a little cheated that I'd survived this far. You pray. I could hear somebody moving around in the debris and he came up to me and said: 'You alright mate? Alright?'

I said:'Okay. Get this thing off my back.'

He was able to move it out of the way and help me up. Having a quick look round I could see a fire and that's about all. We tried to stumble forward to get back into the ship. By this time we were gasping for breath and starting to choke. We both sat down. We couldn't see a thing. We thought that we weren't going to be able to make it. The rule is that in a lot of smoke you get closer to the deck because the smoke normally rises. We tried to get as low as we could but there was still no air.

I can remember what I was thinking. At that time my wife was five months' pregnant with our first child and I wanted to get home. Like a miracle the ship must have slewed round, because we got a breath of sweet-tasting air. The hole in the side must have caught some air. It wafted in and we took a large lungful. We started moving to the back end of ship but we couldn't climb out of the hole because that's where the fire was. We were unable to go through the fire. We went further up but we couldn't find a place to climb out because there was so much debris. However, there was a place to get out under the winch and we managed to struggle out under this little gap about two feet by nine inches. I must have been losing a fair amount of blood by then. I felt rather weak and fell into a hole.

Able Seaman Dillon [later awarded the George Medal] pulled me out. We stood on the side of the ship, put our lifejackets on, put some air in the bag and jumped into the water. He then grabbed me and pulled me away from the ship. My thoughts then moved to the propellers – I must keep away from those – and also the fact that the rest of the team were probably fighting the fires. They would have seen us jump in the water and would pick us up. We had heard that survival time in the water was under two minutes. We hadn't had time to put our once-only survival suits on, we just jumped in the water. Once we got away from the ship I looked back and could see the orange suits of all the ship's company on the upper deck, waiting to abandon ship. The horrible thought I had was that if the Argentines should come round again and attack the ship, many like us would have been lost.

I could see a ship coming to my right and I thought: Ah they're coming to pick us up, they've seen us. But they went right past, obviously going to take the survivors off the ship. Helicopters appeared from over the headland and I could see one stop and pick up Able Seaman Dillon. It then came over and picked me up. As the winchman was splashing in the water in front of me he hooked on to the blue nylon strap that comes in front of your lifejacket. Normally they used that only to pull you in to the boat. I thought: Oh no, he hasn't put the strop round me.* And as we were going up in the air I could see a surgeon commander who had come down to pick me up. We flopped on to the deck of the Wessex helicopter and I heard him shout: 'Get these to *Canberra* quick.' And then I woke up on *Canberra* feeling cold.

I was quite badly injured. I had severe lacerations of the skull and a large rip up my back from the thing which was trapping me. I eventually lost two fingers on my left hand, a small price to pay for my life. It's very difficult to think how I've changed from what I was beforehand. I think I'm more tolerant to other people. Things that mattered before don't matter so much now because I've been very close to death. I enjoy life.

* The 'strop' is a detachable loop at the end of a winch-wire by which the person being rescued is carried to safety.

SAM BISHOP

Sam Bishop, an Ulsterman, was a petty officer in the Royal Navy serving aboard the frigate HMS *Antelope*. The ship was bombed in Falkland Sound on 23 May 1982 and was evacuated when one bomb failed to detonate. Finally the ship exploded when the missiles for the Seacat guided weapons system blew up. A photograph of the explosion appeared in newspapers and on television throughout the world.

When it all happened we were at Portland on workout. We were sent straight back to Plymouth, our base port, to store up and top up with fuel and ammunition. I managed to phone my wife on the Friday night. Nobody knew when we were sailing, so I was taking a risk because I said: 'Can you try and get the children down tomorrow? Just get yourselves down. I'd like to see you before we go.'

The wife managed to get down on the Saturday with the two children. Although I was on duty I got her on board the ship. One of the other petty officers took her up to his house and put her up for the night. I was able to spend most of Sunday with them before they got the train back to Northampton. I felt very emotional but I tried to keep a brave face: 'We'll sail, the Royal Navy has never been beaten before, and when they hear us arriving they'll get out and I'll be home. Don't worry.'

Living in Northampton she wasn't near other navy people; she might get news a bit late so I tried to make sure that she felt a bit confident that I'd be coming home safe. But when her train pulled out, other thoughts started coming into my mind: Could it be real? What would happen if the worst comes to the worst, the extremes? Then you think: Well, that's what I've been drawing the wages for, although when

70

you join the navy you never imagine that you'll have to go to war or you'll have to fight.

I started thinking: Will I ever see the wife and kids again? I've always said if war breaks out I'm going back to Belfast where I was born. I didn't join for war. It's all a big joke.

I said to the wife when I took her to the station that I'd been in the navy for fifteen years and I couldn't just say: 'Look I don't want to go now.' You don't join a club and, when the going gets tough, say: 'Well, I'm not a member any more.' I said: 'I don't want to go, but I've got to go. The taxpayers have been paying my wages all these years and okay they've called my number, they've called all our numbers. It's our duty.'

I believed in what we were doing. The wife didn't believe in it, but women's attitudes are different to men's. I was a service man. I believed the Falklands were British, that we were doing the right thing to fight to get them back. I still believe that.

All of a sudden everybody had a great interest in the Falklands: where they were; what they were. We got paper cuttings, got the atlas out, got the books out and read about it. It was British. We couldn't let people walk in to what's British because if they did that then people would take other things that are British for granted and come in and take them. It's part of Britain even though it's . . . not part of Britain. It's part of Britain even though it's 8,000 miles away, and we just couldn't give it away.

There was good humour on board. We got all the reports through that the Royal Marines had taken back South Georgia. A big cheer went up and we got the scores on the doors going – one to us and one against them. We were sat in the mess and the rumours were going round that one of the ships had been hit but we weren't sure which. Then there was a broadcast from the first lieutenant that the captain was making a broadcast and everybody had to be in hearing distance of a tannoy. The captain said we all had to tune in to the BBC World Service. That's when we discovered that the *Sheffield* had been hit and sunk. We didn't know how many lives had been lost. It came as a great shock because up to then everybody thought: It's going to finish tomorrow – we'll never see no action.

It was all a bad dream. It came home with a sudden bang, to me anyway. It's happened. A Royal Navy ship has been sunk! We're in it this time. Why don't we go in and get it over with?

We didn't know what was happening. We weren't getting the news that we wanted to hear, we were getting filtered reports through. We thought: Why aren't they doing this and why aren't they doing that? We just do what we are told. But when the *Sheffield* got sunk the whole attitude on board the ship changed in as much that people were looking at things: Could we do this, or should we do that? I started putting all the fire-fighting gear from around the ship in various places so that we had different dumps . . .

We felt sick at losing mates who had been on the *Sheffield*, you feel as if it's part of you. You've seen Vietnam on television. You've seen World War One and World War Two. Then you see a ship getting hit and sunk, you see the survivors, people dying. All of a sudden you realise that it was one of our ships there. You feel as if it's part of you gone. Because it could have been you. Even if you don't know who is on board, you are bound to have some mates on every ship throughout the fleet when you've been in the navy a long time. You feel a great loss.

Until we heard that HMS *Ardent* had sunk we hadn't seen any action. That brought it closer because she was a Type-21 frigate, the same as the *Antelope*. We were all sitting around feeling a bit sorry for ourselves when the captain made a broadcast that we'd got the honour of replacing the *Ardent*. The following day we'd be going into the Falklands. That got the adrenalin going, especially after we realised the pounding *Ardent* had taken. That was when I learned the term 'goalkeeper'. I asked somebody what it meant and he said: 'We've got to catch anything and everything that they throw at us.'

That night was a bit tense. First thing next morning we were all closed up at 'Action Stations'. We knew all the 'pipes' to listen for, what action to take in the event of different 'pipes', and we went in.

I was closed up in the forrard engine-room with a stoker. We were sat around just checking the machinery, getting bored, thinking: Maybe it won't happen today, maybe they won't come today. Let's get in, get it over with, get out. It was going to be the first time in my life that I'd ever seen action. I didn't know how I was going to react under fire. That was more frightening, thinking about it, thinking about how I would react. Would I show myself up, would I crack up?

We went in and then we had a 'pipe' to go up for snacks, 'action snacks'. It still didn't seem real, yet we knew it was real. The whole ship's company were very tense. The young lads, the junior ratings, were amazing; they're all volunteers, but they were very professional. Everybody was scared but they weren't showing it.

A 'pipe' came: 'There's four planes coming in, we'll be under attack soon.'

I thought: Oh no.

The worst thing down below was that you couldn't see anything, you didn't know what was happening. You were hoping: Please let the gun work, please let everything on board work, which it did. One hundred per cent. You could hear the sound of the machine gun from the aircraft and our gun pounding away. And then we heard 'Zipper One', which meant there was a bomb attack coming in and you've got to hit the deck.

We were all over the place, moving about trying to avoid them. After the first attack we heard a bomb had come in forrard and a young steward, called Stevens, was killed. That came as a shock because he was in the petty officers' mess, which was the forrard first-aid post.

And you thought: That was lucky. The bomb didn't go off, thank God for that. Then we had another attack and lost the lighting in the forrard engine-room. I only heard the word 'Fire' from the aft engine-room because I was on a headset. Then I realised that there was a burn mark on the deck above my head. I thought: Well, that wasn't there before. A young stoker was with me. I said: 'How long has that been there?' He said: 'I think it was there this morning.'

There was water dripping down and I thought that water was coming in the wrong end of the Olympus*, so I piped to the ship's control centre. I said: 'There's a burn mark and there seems to be water there.' And they said: 'Oh we know all about that bomb!'

What I didn't know was that it had come in and broken open the air-conditioning machinery and that the gas got out. Then the gas alarm went off. That was the worst moment of my life, because I thought: It's not a proper bomb, it's a gas bomb. My brain just went. I lost control for a minute because I thought I could smell it and taste it. My imagination just went wild. I was trying to get my gas respirator out and the nerves in my legs started going. I thought: That's it, I'm

---

* HMS *Antelope*, like other RN frigates in the South Atlantic, was powered by two Rolls-Royce Olympus TM3B gas turbines, which gave the ship a top speed of 30 knots.

going to crack up, I can feel it, I'm a goner. I've come 8,000 miles, we've been bombed and I'm getting killed by gas.

It seemed like minutes, but was probably only seconds later that I realised what had actually set the alarm off. The first lieutenant got on and said we could take our respirators off. 'It's a false alarm.' He explained what happened. That was the greatest relief ever, to breathe fresh air again.

For a long time I was in the engine-room with an unexploded bomb. Thinking back it was silly. I thought: How much metal can I get between myself and that bomb above my head? It was about ten feet above my head and had wedges underneath which secured it, so that as we moved it didn't rattle. It was a bit reassuring to realise that the bomb was a little steadier. I tried to get outboard of the port Olympus engine thinking that would protect me, if it went off. Looking back at the effect the bomb had [when it finally exploded] it seems silly. It's self-preservation. I just kept looking at it and thinking: Well you haven't gone off yet. I thought: If that goes off, what damage will it do, how bad will it be? That was when I realised I had to do something to occupy my mind. So I told the stoker to check the air system while I checked the fuel system. We were keeping ourselves busy – it kept us going.

I prayed to God that day. I'm not a deeply religious man, but I think that's the guilty part of most human beings. We say we don't need religion, but when that bomb was there I was saying: 'Please God, I want to see the wife, Laura and Mark again. I want to see my family. I want to get home.'

(Sam Bishop along with the rest of the ship's crew had to move to a safer location on board while bomb disposal officers tried to defuse the bomb.)

Later I saw the bomb disposal blokes. I didn't manage to get a sight of the bomb, and I didn't really want to see it anyway. We reported to the control room and were told to go on the flight-deck. It seemed like a nice night, I cannot remember feeling cold. My nerves were calming down. I was feeling quite pleased – 'I went through it and I didn't crack up and make a fool of myself.'

They piped over that the first attempt to defuse the bomb had failed and they were going to try again. Now I noticed the cold and borrowed a submariner's pullover from one of the sailors. We went into the hangar where it was a bit warmer. We heard the second and third attempts at defusing the bomb were failures. The captain gave us a pipe that the bomb disposal bloke wasn't very happy about the bomb. It wasn't 'normal'. We didn't know what it was, we just knew it was a bomb and wanted rid of it. He was going to try for a fourth time. We were talking to each other in the hangar when there was an almighty bang. The ship seemed to disappear from beneath our feet. We were all over the place. Everybody calmed down, we went on to the flight-deck and when we looked up the starboard side it was in flames, from the water-line right to the top of the ship, where the bomb had gone off. We were still alive but I thought: God, look at it. It was terrible looking at the flames to think what could have happened if people had been below when that went off.

We took all the action we could, but there was nothing we could do. We attempted to get down from the flight-deck to see if we could fight the fire. Two men in special 'Fearnaught' suits [protective heat-resistant fire-fighters' clothing] went in. There was just no way we could get near the forrard engine-room where the fire was. It spread the whole way aft. We got a number of people out, including the second bomb disposal officer. The order was given to take to the boats. The injured were put into the boats first and we put our 'once-only' suits on, thinking: Thank goodness for that, because we knew that there was a lot of ammunition on board. We were very worried when the flames got near. We got into a boat from HMS *Intrepid*. The boat drivers were very brave. They came right along beside us. We didn't have to go near the water, we just stepped over and stood in the boat. They stayed there until we were topped up, and off we went. All those who had been aft didn't know whether the people forrard had got off.

Half a mile away from the ship you could see it burning brightly. That's when the big explosion happened. You could feel it. You could imagine the water hitting you, though it probably didn't. That was that really dramatic picture that appeared in the papers. That's when we all thanked our lucky stars. It only seemed like two or three minutes after we had left the ship. It was like a firework display, it just completely lit up the sky. You'd have thought somebody had arranged it, planted all the ammunition in the middle of the ship to give a fantastic display. It was just sickening. One bloke said: 'Two and a half years' wasted work.' But it was more than that. Having the family in Northampton I had lived on board when we were in port, it had been my home. You just feel a great sense of loss and shame. 'Why our ship? Why was it sunk?'

On the night we came off and walked up the ramp at the rear end of the HMS *Intrepid*, they didn't know what to say to us. We didn't know where to look. You felt like a prisoner-of-war even though you were coming on to one of your own ships. You thought: Well, do I smile and say 'Hello lads'? They'll think: He must be mad. Or do I look sad and dejected? We didn't know what to do and they didn't know how to speak to us, the way we'd react, whether we would be in shock or full of the joys of spring. It was a very strange experience.

The day after, we woke up and realised: Here we are, we're still alive. Then it started again. The ship went to action stations but we couldn't do anything because it wasn't our ship and it was out of our control. That was really nerve-racking. *Intrepid* was anchored in San Carlos Water. We were told just to stay in the mess because we didn't know the layout of the ship. We had no jobs on board, we'd only be in the way. When the attacks came in we could hear the Seacat going off, people firing rifles at planes. You thought: Why can't I do something? You just sat in the mess listening to it all and praying. You were helpless.

When I got back to Portsmouth, back on duty after leave, I saw all the other ships coming back: *Invincible*, *Hermes*, the *Bristol*; all of them. They were heroes because they came back, they brought their ships back. You felt as if you had lost out. I wouldn't want to go through a battle every day but you thought: Why didn't we bring back our ship? You felt guilty. You see other blokes and everybody says: 'You were on the *Antelope*. That was sunk, wasn't it?' as if it's something special. I mean, we weren't heroes. We went in for one day. The one day we actually saw real action we got sunk. You thank God you're alive but you also think: How ironic . . . so much work gone into that ship, costing so much, one day's action and it's all lost.

When you look back at the explosion you think that a lot of people knock God, but He's got to be there, no matter what form or what religion He takes, there's somebody there looking after us. You don't think: Well, He died and He probably thought exactly the same. You think: No; He answered me. It's a great relief that you're alive. You start thinking whether you have been good enough to the kids and wife. I could have been dead, have missed out on life. Had I been doing the right things in my life? I think my whole attitude to life changed that day.

I know when I got home I put the wife and kids through hell for eighteen months – just arguments, telling them off, I didn't realise it. At work I was normal. I was easy, happy-go-lucky, did my job. I never noticed. I didn't know I was doing it until one day the wife told me. If it hadn't been for her sticking by me, I don't know what might have happened.

RICK JOLLY

Surgeon Commander Rick Jolly, OBE, was one of a team of doctors looking after the Task Force during Operation Corporate. He commanded the field hospital at Ajax Bay on East Falkland where most battle casualties were treated. Currently he is conducting a major research project on the effects of stress upon senior commanders on active service.

Before we landed at San Carlos we had been at sea for six weeks, so there had been a lot of planning done. But there were certain things we couldn't plan for, like the weather. The Argentine navy had already demonstrated with HMS *Sheffield* that they had a certain competence. Hence there were a lot of variables when we went into the sheltered areas of San Carlos: were there mines around there, were we being suckered in? There was great relief the day before the invasion when the weather was awful, the cloud-base was low and the Argentine air force couldn't find us. When the sun went down on 20 May it seemed that we were going to get in there somehow. The first thing most of us heard that morning on *Canberra* was the gun-line in San Carlos opening up, saturating the area with shells.

Things just developed with a rush. Unfortunately Lady Luck deserted us because it was good flying weather. It's important to draw a distinction between 'Bomb Alley' in San Carlos Water, where the 'ducks' in the 'duck pond' were the amphibious ships containing troops and combat supplies, and the water-filled 'ditch' of Falkland Sound, which separates East and West Falkland. This varied from a mile wide at the top to fifteen miles wide at Grantham Sound where HMS *Ardent* was. In that ditch there was a defensive line, a picket of six frigates and a destroyer. There was a lot of water in between as these frigates tried to cover the approach routes along which the Argentine air force would come. There was an early attack on HMS *Argonaut* which was perhaps a little hasty, but it indicated the determination of their pilots which they confirmed later on in the day.

Initially I flew in a casualty evacuation helicopter to *Argonaut*. We were told to go away because they were about to come under air attack, and watched as A4 Skyhawks came in, then a flight of Mirages. Four attacked *Antrim*. We saw *Broadsword* shoot down a Mirage. Then we saw *Ardent* hit. We thought at first another aircraft had gone down, but the smoke stayed and I heard on the radio the call-sign of the ship and it was *Ardent*. We immediately decided to go and help her. We went to refuel in San Carlos Water, grabbed two stretchers and arrived off the ship. We were the first helicopter on the scene. The pilot, Mike Crabtree, just went very silent as we came down over the hill and flew through the smoke. In the back we couldn't see what was happening. We could smell the smoke and then we came to the [stationary] hover off the port quarter and looked out. It's a sight I shall never forget. The fires of hell were burning in that ship. She was at anchor, the gun pointing straight up at the sky. All the hydraulic power had gone, the flight-deck was just smashed in and looked as if it had been opened up with a can-opener. We had this terrible feeling of being helpless. HMS *Yarmouth* had come in and put her bows on to *Ardent*. The crew had been told to abandon ship and were in their orange once-only life preservation suits and coming across on to the *Yarmouth*.

Then we saw two survivors in the water and lowered the strop to them. To cut a long story short, someone had to go down and get them. It's been made quite a lot of from my point of view but it was very much a crew effort. I was basically just the hook on the end of the winch-wire. The credit belongs as much to the aircrewman who was actually gently operating the winch-motor so that neither of the survivors was jerked out of my hands or off the hook. Plus there was the steady flying of the pilot who made the decision to go for them and positioned his Wessex in the line of any subsequent attack.

The first survivor in the water was flapping his hands. We thought it was to draw attention and I suddenly realised he was drowning. He couldn't reach the strop that was lowered to him on the end of the hook. It was obvious someone was going to have to go down and gather him. I volunteered because it seemed the right thing to do, and it was only when I was in the strop that I realised I wasn't dressed for it. I still had my camera in my pocket and the water was going to be extremely cold. There was a shock of static electricity discharging as I touched the water. I went in and it was cold and I was gasping for breath. I was towed across to the survivor, grabbed him and was lifted up. I was determined that nothing on earth was going to make me let go. It was very difficult for the crewman to manipulate the winch-wires in such a way as to drag five hundred pounds of sea-water-soaked bodies into the aircraft. But he did it. I was exhausted and then got a thumbs-up from the crewman and a tap on the shoulder. He was pointing down again. This time we went for Ken Enticknab. On the way down I prepared myself to slip the strop from around my shoulders and put it around this injured chief [petty officer]. He was very weak and his lifejacket was torn. I didn't have the strength to hold him. I hooked on to the man's lifejacket and we were hauled up.

There was still an hour of daylight left and we took the two survivors to *Canberra* and then came back for more. By this time *Ardent* had been abandoned so I winched down to *Yarmouth* to see what we could do to help. The young naval surgeon was very busy. I just walked around the ship looking at these stained and battered young men. They were exhausted. They had been at it all day. What these boys had done was place themselves between a well handled and hostile air force and our soldiers, who were trying to land on the shore. I think some of the ship's company were slightly anxious that there was no one around to recognise just what they had achieved. All the journalists were ashore with the Brigade commander and had missed all this.

On *Canberra* a tribute was paid by the Marines still on board. As we brought casualties through the gun port door these chaps from 42 Commando bent down under their loads of ammunition. Their faces were covered in camouflage cream, and they very quietly applauded in the darkness.

I never thought in my lifetime I would see ships being attacked by low-flying aircraft with iron bombs, and clouds of tracer having to be put up by determined anti-aircraft gunners; or experience the sudden speed with which these jets move. When you see enemy aircraft coming at you it slows you down. It's like moving in a nightmare, you can't urge yourself to move fast enough. I was frightened. I think it would be fair to say that anyone who says he was in the Falklands and wasn't frightened is either a liar or he wasn't there.

On 27 May – the night before 2 Para fought for Goose Green – we were attacked at Ajax Bay, where the field hospital had been established, by a pair of Skyhawks which dropped a total of eight bombs. There were a lot of casualties to work on. The bomb that had fallen in the slaughterhouse at the back of the old mutton-packing plant had sadly converted it back into a slaughterhouse. There were five dead and twenty-seven injured and an awful lot of work to do.

In the middle of the evening I was asked by Alan Swann, the resident RAF bomb disposal expert, to come and have a look at what he'd found in the refrigeration room at the back. There was this large 900-pound parachute-retarded bomb stuck in there.* My first reaction was to turn and run. He laughed and said: 'I shouldn't bother sir, there's another above your head.' And there was another of these things, fifteen yards away, with a parachute torn off.

There were some difficult decisions to be taken. We knew this was the first time they had used those bombs. This was a new kind of bomb rather than the American or British Mk 82. There was a possibility of time-delayed fuses in these new devices. We worked out that as it was the first time they probably wouldn't have bothered with anything other than impact fuses. So we basically forgot about them and got on with the work, because we couldn't have moved anywhere else. The blokes all photographed the bombs and frightened themselves with the flash guns going off in the darkness. But they stuck at it, and for the next two weeks continued to operate even when the air-raid warning blew 'Red'. The irony was that we had one of the Argentine pilots as a patient in the field hospital with us. It was one of his mates from the same squadron, a chap called Mario Valasco, who dropped the bombs on to the hospital.

Medically speaking, I think our injured were treated a little better. Our battle surgeons were a little more aware of the mechanism by

---

* Argentine pilots would fly low over their targets to give them greater accuracy when bomb-aiming but more especially to avoid anti-aircraft fire. At such short range, the parachute retard slowed the descent of the bomb enough to allow the pilot time to clear the explosion as it hit its target.

which modern ammunition actually causes wounds. The treatment for it is very simple, very basic and very crude. It involves the wide clearing of dead muscle and leaving the wounds open to prevent the development of gangrene and tetanus. We treated all our patients that way and a third of them were, of course, Argentinians. At the surrender, we captured their field hospital and then reoperated on all their patients because the Argentine surgeons seemed to have just done a bit of fancy work, trimming the outside, the outer appearance of the wound, putting a metal clip in, and just leaving the rotten insides to fester. I think we saved their lives by capturing them and operating on them again.

There were two bad moments. The first was the night when HMS *Coventry* and *Atlantic Conveyor* were hit and we realised there was a real fight going on out to sea. It was a question of whether they would run out of aircraft before we ran out of ships to defend us. Morale was a bit low that night. The other bad night was when we got to Port Stanley, were relieved of our duties and the ships took the Argentine prisoners back to the mainland. Morale was very low then because we were exhausted, filthy, very tired and had nothing to do except to put up with the galloping trots we were all suffering from. However, that bad moment has led to a feeling of great pride. For the first time in the history of war the losers went home first. We were acting in the tradition of Lord Nelson, who said in his prayer before Trafalgar: 'Let humanity after victory be the predominant feature of the British Fleet.' I'm sure, gazing down from some heavenly quarter-deck, he was well pleased with what he saw.

Reflecting on it all, I'm disappointed that a lot of people in this country take the privileges that we have for granted. Everything in society that we enjoy – the ability to criticise our government, to go sick, to take a day off, go where you want, have a car, the openness and the freedom that we have – has been fought for in our history. Because we have had forty years of peace, people talk about rights without realising that they have responsibilities to maintain our society. War sharpens those feelings very closely. I'm proud to be in the services and I hope to retire at sixty a happy and contented man.

MARION STOCK

Marion Stock served in the Royal Navy as a member of Queen Alexandra's Royal Naval Nursing Service. She was a staff nurse aboard the hospital ship SS *Uganda*, which patrolled in the Falklands war-zone, protected under the articles of the Geneva Convention, like the Argentinian *Bahia Paraiso*. These vessels were allowed to enter a neutral zone to pick up wounded men. Among the *Uganda*'s patients were the Welsh Guardsmen badly wounded when *Sir Galahad* was bombed.

At first it was something new. As nurses we had never been to sea before; most of us were sick. You hear about the aft of the ship and the starboard part, but they were just naval terms and we had never bothered to find out what they really meant. We soon found out. The first couple of weeks we had to work hard storing the ship, but we didn't think anything was going to happen. We thought: When we get down there they'll say: 'You can go home now.' It wasn't until the *Sheffield* was actually sunk that the reality hit home. It was a very hard time. Most of us knew the medical staff on the *Sheffield* and we also had flight crews and radar staff who knew people. We had been at sea four weeks and we were not going home. Inside I think all of us thought that we wouldn't be able to cope. None of us quite knew who was going to come on board, whether they were going to have bad or just minor injuries. We wondered whether as individuals we were equipped to cope with what we might receive. You really questioned your abilities.

I was working on 'Sea View' ward, the main general surgical ward which dealt with all types of medical cases. On the day the *Galahad* was sunk I and another staff nurse called Sally turned up for our shift at eight o'clock. We were told to go to the officers' mess, which had been turned into another ward to receive these casualties. Just before we got to the door there was this awful stench of burning. Quite close to the mess was a very tiny galley and it smelled as if someone had burned the toast. We opened the doors and there were about forty beds of black faces. It was a feeling of horror. You wanted to close the doors and run. Then you thought: God, you've got to hide this horror you have on your face because of the patients. We walked in and tried to smile and get on with our job, but it was very difficult.

Their eyes were so swollen, at first I thought they were Chinamen. The heat from the flames had caused their eyes to slant upwards. Their faces were so badly swollen they couldn't see, they had very little hair, no eyelashes and no eyebrows. Their hands had been put into flamazine bags. Special cream which we use for very bad burns had been applied and you couldn't really tell where the nails started or ended. It was the same with the fingers. It was very upsetting for all the nurses and the medical staff to see and hear the patients crying in pain. Some of them had bad nightmares about when they had been trapped. Others had seen their colleagues being badly burned and had tried to help or couldn't help. Their frustration came out and the only thing you could really do was sit and listen. You wanted to go back to your room and cry your eyes out because you felt desperately sorry for these people.

We had to take off the cream that had already been applied and start the process all over again. It was very time-consuming. You can't hurry because the skin is very raw. You had to be very gentle and would spend up to half an hour on one patient taking off what was there and re-applying the cream. As the days and weeks went by, though, you could see slight improvement. The hair on some of them started to grow back and you could begin to identify them individually. It was very rewarding for us and for the patients. When some of them started asking for mirrors we had to make a decision. The doctors said it might not be a good idea for them to see themselves. Some of the patients wondered how their wives and girlfriends might react when they got home: Is she really going to love me? How are my children going to react when they see me looking like this? All the things which went through their minds were understandable. But they never complained. They were very brave men – they were marvellous.

The lads tried to keep their own morale high. There might be

84

one young boy of eighteen or nineteen who had lost his legs or had other bad injuries, so the others would try to jolly him along. They did their utmost to keep a smiling face because they didn't want to let their colleagues down. If they saw one of the others depressed they would think: I mustn't get depressed, I have to get on with this life. What they really wanted was to sit and talk about what had happened. We had a psychiatrist on board and a couple of trained mental nurses. I'm sure that helped tremendously, especially during the initial stages of accepting their injuries, trying to help them with the fact that they were alive.

In the beginning we all coped to the best of our ability, but the longer it went on the more tired we became, mentally and physically. You just wanted to go home. Not that you wanted to turn your back on it, but there were times when it seemed one big bad nightmare and you wanted to wake up and be back home with your family or your husband. Luckily we all got on very well together. We became one big happy family really. You couldn't bottle it all up inside. We got together in the evening and talked about what had happened on the ward to the other nurses who worked in different areas of the ship. You felt better just by talking to somebody else, but there were still times when you went back to your cabin and cried in sheer frustration because you felt so helpless towards the patients you were caring for.

It felt claustrophobic because you couldn't get off the ship and go anywhere. We spent four months with the same people, you never saw any different faces. It wasn't like a training exercise. As nurses we didn't have that kind of training. We don't normally go on a warship. We go through nursing training and that's it. You're not taught how to cope on a ship 8,000 miles away from home, not being able to escape or get in contact with your family.

Most of the time when we were down there we didn't know where we were. We knew we were in a little red box [a neutral zone, north of the Falkland Islands] and that didn't mean very much at all. They used to put a little cross on the map but that could have been anywhere. Things started to go through your mind: What if we lose – what will happen? The subject was never talked about but it still went through your mind. You wanted to see your family because you didn't feel safe down there.

*

There was a little shop on board where we used to get personal supplies but they were running out of deodorants and the things every woman needs, things you take for granted at home, which you could nip down to the corner shop and buy. The girls started to panic a little bit. You couldn't do that down there. We began running short of medical equipment, especially medical dressings. I don't know how long we would have lasted on the supplies we had.

There were Argentine patients on board. An Argentine hospital ship [*Bahia Paraiso*] came alongside and picked up their patients. Rumour had it that they even offered us supplies. I don't think they were taken up on it but the offer was apparently made.

At first we tried to keep the Argentines and the British separate, but as time went on we had to mix them because of the shortage of space. It was something we didn't particularly want to do for obvious reasons. Most nurses felt they were simply there to do a job and tried to remain impartial. But when you saw these Argentine boys, some of them seventeen years old, you couldn't help but feel a little bit sorry for them. There was very little bitterness from our lads because they all felt they were down there for a reason and they were all injured in one way or another. If an Argentine couldn't feed himself the British patients would help. They helped to wash them and helped with their bodily functions. They would try and communicate with each other. We had a padre who spoke Spanish.

We had to stay down in the South Atlantic a little bit longer than the other ships. Quite a few bombs and landmines had been left and sadly we had a few young lads with their feet blown off. When everyone else except us had gone home we got a little bit cheesed off. Finally the signal came. There were mixed feelings. We definitely wanted to come home but a lot of us felt we couldn't go home and talk to our families about it. We didn't think they'd understand. I don't think you could have really expected them to understand what we'd been through, what we'd seen, how we had coped and the times that we felt we couldn't cope.

When we got home it was an anticlimax. You had spent four months on board a ship living very closely with people who had become very good friends. Then you were parted. You felt glad to be home but at the same time sad because you couldn't talk to your family about what you'd been through. There is still that kinship even now between people who were down there. You can talk to them and you know they will understand.

PILOTS

IAN MORTIMER

Flight-Lieutenant (now Squadron Leader) Ian Mortimer, RAF, was a member of 801 Squadron aboard the aircraft carrier *Invincible*. He flew a Harrier aircraft during the campaign. On one sortie he was shot down and had to bale out into the sea.

We were told we were going to the Falklands at about 4 a.m. on the first morning of my Easter leave. I had been expecting to spend some time at home. We had just come back from Norway after being at sea quite a while.

We went into work on a daily basis, waiting to see when we would go. Every day we hung around a while and were told to go home again. I never believed it would happen.

Flying is superb, but I don't like life at sea. Ships are great but you just can't get away from them. It's twenty-four hours a day. You can't go home, you don't see green fields and trees. My job involves a lot of planning of tactics. We trained a lot, planned attacks on various targets like vessels and airfields. We dropped a few bombs and did lots of intercept work. Off-duty hours were spent in the way you always do on a ship – in the bar.

The night before we went into action, May 1st, the Commander (Wings) had us all in and told us that we were all about to experience something totally new. I still didn't believe it was going to happen, not until we were launched and were actually being vectored into flights. I listened on my radio to one dog fight as it developed and that was the first time I actually realised we were going to try and kill people and I didn't enjoy one minute of it.

The experience of fear had never been part of my tactical training.

We are very highly trained but the element that is just not there is the fear. It changes our tactical thinking. I concentrated on getting the job done because for the first time there was a chance that if I didn't get it right I might not be coming back.

In our task of ground attack we are trying to get to a target, so if we are bounced by enemy fighters we try and run away. I now believe that's totally wrong. I believe we have to stay and fight because we've got to put the fear of God into them as well. They've got to know that they might die, and that's a very important part of tactical thinking. If they think they can just come and pick off a guy who is not going to shoot them back, it's like shooting ducks in a barrel. That's a little bit what it was like for us with the Argentinians after 1 May. I wasn't in the ground-attack role that day, I was on air defence, and the only thing it changes is the need to be aggressive, the need to make that guy know that if he's not very good he's going to die rather than you.

An awful lot of trade [enemy planes] came our way that day. The majority of it turned around and went back again. We turned back three out of every four raids. The ones that got through I didn't see but some of my colleagues did. We thought seven missiles were actually fired against us, then we found out that some of them weren't missiles at all but fuel tanks being jettisoned. One or two guys came back and talked about missiles passing within 200 yards of the cockpit.

At the end of that first day I think we were all frightened. We all got together and we all talked about it and decided that if it kept on going like that sooner or later one of those missiles would hit us. The Argentine pilots did not come back again in that attack role. It wasn't until about May 3rd that we realised that we'd done enough as far as the fighter role was concerned and we'd already won. We had it sewn up in one day. We shot down two Mirages and a Canberra that day and I think the Argentines actually believed that they couldn't meet us head-on. If they did they would lose and lose heavily, so they changed their tactics and decided not to come back in medium-level air space again. From then on they just went straight for the ships. I don't think there was a single combat thereafter, it was just a question of intercepting them.

When we realised they had changed tactics our fear went straight away. It became more a case of 'Let's go out and shoot the ducks in a barrel.' I can understand their thinking but it's not the way I would have reacted. The one thing they were not was cowardly. They were incredibly brave. They took a lot of hits, they had a lot of losses. We really did make quite a mess of them and they kept coming back. If you come back and your best friend doesn't, you have to think that next time it might be you. They were very brave to keep returning like that. Their Hercules pilots were fantastic. We never stopped them getting into Port Stanley.

The day that the HMS *Sheffield* was hit I was on deck alert, which means we're actually chained to the deck, sitting in the cockpit ready to go – five minutes to get airborne. I was told to scramble and we were given a heading that was totally contrary to everything else we'd done. It clearly wasn't towards the Islands. We flew about fifty miles south and we were given the call sign of a ship. At that stage I didn't realise it was the *Sheffield*. We were told she'd been torpedoed. Even from straight off the deck [of the aircraft carrier] I could see the smoke from fifty miles away.

When we got there I could see this very, very large hole in the side above the water-line, so quite clearly she hadn't been torpedoed. She was just sitting there in the water smoking like mad. Some of the guys had taken to the lifeboats – a lot of them were out on the deck just watching us. For the next hour I chased everything, from surface contacts to submarines to aircraft. Everyone was calling 'Contact' all over the place. That's the element of fear again. It's people seeing things that weren't there. Every trace of a blip on a radar screen suddenly became some kind of threat.

To actually see ships going down was a big shock. It made me realise that going back home to *Invincible* and getting into a comfy bed was not the end of the war. It was all around me, all the time. I was concerned for the people below deck. If a ship is in danger they batten down the hatches. The Navy go down, the Crabs [RAF] go up – they go for the fresh air. No matter what's happening around me, if I was on deck I would think: At least I can dive over the side or something. But below decks? I can't stand it down there, I find it extremely claustrophobic. I can imagine those people who were below decks must have been very frightened.

I had felt we were invincible. We had been trained for all those mega-tactics against this mega-enemy [the Soviet Union]. I think we got a bit complacent. We didn't think the enemy would be as good as he was.

On June 1st I was on CAP [combat air patrol] south of Stanley trying to see if their Hercules were trying to get in. I was running up and down the road from the Darwin and Goose Green area. The Paras had just taken Goose Green and one of the things we were concerned about was that the Argentine Pucaras might be trying to get airborne and hit the army as they came along the road. The plan was to look out for Pucaras and see if I could take some of them out.

I had been up and down the road twice, a good way south and at a good height as well. On the third occasion as I went by Port Stanley airfield I thought I saw something taxi-ing. Just at that moment a cloud got in the way, so I dropped down to about 10,000 feet and moved in quite a bit, convinced that I was out of the way of their Roland missiles [Argentine anti-aircraft defences based at Stanley airfield]. I must have been wrong. The first thing I saw was a tremendous flash. It was just as though somebody had shone a mirror, a huge mirror, into my eyes. There was nothing for a couple of seconds and then I picked up the missile. They were on a perfect 90° intercept, with me flying one way and the missile coming on at 90°. I just watched the smoke trail all the way and I was still quite convinced that I was out of range. I had been cruising at that stage. Rather than try to defeat the missile by increasing speed, I turned away from it and tried to climb to increase the range. At about 10,000 feet the missile started to level off, and I thought that was it: no problem. I wasn't in the least bit worried. I was looking out of my right-hand window, it disappeared underneath, so I transferred my gaze out of the left-hand window expecting to see the missile falling away into the water.

There was an almighty explosion, the aircraft went head over heels and, being a bright lad, I guessed what had happened. It was a phenomenally violent explosion which really surprised me. It took the tailplane off. Even though I wasn't going very fast – we're probably talking about 350 to 400 mph – to suddenly go head over heels at that speed is incredibly violent. I was being thrown around a lot and I couldn't see anything. I suspect I closed my eyes and kept my head well down. I ejected immediately – just about as fast as I could. The violence of the ejection was exactly the same as the violence of being thrown around.

There was a horrible second when I thought the ejector seat hadn't worked and I was still in there. The next thing I know I'm hanging on to this silk. The adrenalin was flowing, needless to say. The parachute was going round in lovely little circles. I was spiralling downwards about 13,000 feet, at 25 feet a second, quite a long time in a parachute. Funnily enough I was even aware of enjoying parachuting, it was very peaceful.

I drifted quite a few miles, which did me a lot of favours because shortly after I hit the water and climbed into the dinghy the Argentinians came looking for me. They had a Chinook out searching around the spot where I had been hit. The wind was about twenty to twenty-five knots and I'd gone a long way in those six minutes. The helicopter was looking in the wrong place. After about half an hour they found me. Another helicopter flew right over the top, then broke away hard. Then a Chinook pointed straight at me, got to within 200 yards before he turned and they both beat it back to Stanley. I speculated that there had been a radar contact on the screen and they wanted to get their guys back to Stanley, which is what the Islanders told me afterwards. There were a couple of Sea Harriers airborne. They weren't coming anywhere near me, but then the Argentinians didn't know that; they left and fortunately didn't find me again.

There are a lot of things to do in a dinghy. We've all trained at baling out the dinghy, inflating it and getting all the survival aids ready for use. That doesn't take long, and I was in the dinghy at sea for about nine hours – three in daylight and six in darkness. It was freezing cold and I was never going to be able to sleep for more than a few minutes at a time so I wasn't worried about that.

You do a lot of thinking in nine hours in a dinghy. My policy was to be completely quiet, completely silent, no lights or anything, which is totally contrary to our training. Normally we try to be found and picked up. Until it got dark I didn't do anything. After dark I would put on my SARBE [search and rescue] beacon, which means an aircraft can home in on you for two minutes. It has a speech facility, so I spoke into it to see if I could get a reply. If I didn't I would shut down for half an hour. I did that throughout the six hours of darkness. I was close to the Islands, which were about two miles away. I was concerned that they might come out looking for me in a boat by homing in on my signals or any lights I might be showing.

But water got in the lead of the aerial and the signal wasn't going out at all.

Helicopters from 820 Squadron had been looking for me from the moment it got dark. They were also from the *Invincible*, so they were good friends of mine. Every now and then I thought I could hear something. There was a twenty-foot sea running and so there was water all around me. It was difficult to tell.

I still had my helmet on, and every time I thought I heard something I had to clear the dinghy canopy out of the way and then try and pull my helmet away from my ears so as to be able to listen. The last time I thought I heard something, sure enough there was a helicopter. They'd actually seen me before I saw them. They had gone by, seen a shape in the water and were coming back for another run-by when I pitched up on the beacon. It worked on this occasion and I got a reply. I don't know what on earth they said, I wasn't too fussed about it by that stage. They put on a strobe light and homed in on me. It took about two minutes and then this grinning Irishman called Mark Finucane came down the wire. I don't know who was grinning most – him or me.

It occurred to me that it might have been an Argentine helicopter. I was drifting due east on my way to South Africa. After nine hours of being incredibly cold with not too many chances I didn't honestly think I'd make it at that stage. I thought the possibility of being a prisoner of war was a better deal than staying in the dinghy. But I was reasonably confident it would be my guys rather than the Argentines. I didn't think they'd bother looking for me in the dark.

I flew again six days later and carried on flying until 14 June [the day of the Argentine surrender]. The end of the war was a big anticlimax because we weren't going home. One of the aircraft carriers had to stay. I think at a very early stage we knew it would be *Invincible*. We sailed north and got into warmer weather for a while and then headed back south and stayed for another few months. We didn't arrive back home until September 19th.

It took me about thirty seconds to adapt to being back at home again. You learn an awful lot about yourself in a war, what you're capable of, what you can do. You learn a tremendous lot about other people too. If people ask me about the war I talk about it. If people don't ask, I don't talk about it. It's almost like it never happened. It's like a dream.

JEFF GLOVER

Flight-Lieutenant Jeff Glover flew a Harrier with No. 1 Squadron. He was the only member of the British Task Force taken prisoner. He was flown to Argentina and held until hostilities ceased, when he returned to Britain and his squadron. Promoted to Squadron Leader, he now flies with the RAF aerobatic team, the Red Arrows.

At the time the crisis in the South Atlantic arose I was in Germany on a flying course. I suddenly had a recall to fetch myself and my Harrier back to the squadron. When I landed I was greeted by my flight commander, who said that all the happenings in the Falklands might involve No. 1 Squadron and that it was preparing itself for war. It took me by surprise somewhat because the Islands were so far away. I didn't actually think we would fly in earnest in that way. We were trained for aggression by the Warsaw Pact. That's the theatre of war for which we prepared, so something like the Falklands took me, and I'm sure the rest of the guys, completely by surprise. To be honest I had never really thought I'd be likely to go to war.

I flew my Harrier from St Mawgan in Cornwall down to Ascension Island. It took about nine hours and I refuelled from Victor tankers. From Ascension I embarked on the *Norland**, which took us down to the Falkland Islands en route to [the aircraft carrier] *Hermes*. We were in company with *Atlantic Conveyor*, on which the RAF Harriers were embarked. The journey down took a fortnight, it was really slow.

2 Para were also on *Norland*. We attended their briefings and gave

---

* *Norland* is a P&O roll-on roll-off passenger and car ferry which operates from Hull across the North Sea to Holland.

some of our own. Watching them train on the ship was quite an insight. They were off land, completely out of their normal theatre, and were racing up and down the decks with packs on their backs, drilling quite hard. At one briefing I came to a deal with a platoon and promised I wouldn't bomb them if they promised not to shoot me down. They seemed to think that was a fair agreement. Otherwise all we did was play cards and drink a bit. I wasn't nervous because we were still a long way from the action. It was only when we were two or three days out from the Falklands that I started to get a little more apprehensive, but I knew I was part of a good team and was quite confident.

For my first sortie I was briefed after breakfast by the boss, Pete Squire. It was the second squadron sortie of the day. It was to be a two-ship, close air-support for the amphibious forces which were doing the landings that day. We went on deck and waited for quite a while before we actually launched. After we took off the boss's aircraft went U.S. [up-the-spout], so he sent me on by myself. I spoke to our people on board HMS *Antrim* who were co-ordinating the air support. Initially they hadn't any targets for me in the area of the amphibious operations so I held off at about 20,000 feet to see if anything came up.·

Eventually they gave me some targets down in the Port Howard area. It wasn't on my map but I knew approximately where it was. From my height I could pick out Port Howard settlement because it was a really glorious day with amazing visibility and no cloud. Instead of plotting a route on a map, I was able to eyeball it from 20,000 feet. I let down about twenty miles away, navigated my way and then rushed in over the targets at low level and quite a high speed. They gave me a range and a bearing of my target from a small jetty and as I overflew I realised that the targets were going to be very close to the edge of town. I was unable to pick them out. I wasn't going to start dropping my bombs close to town, so I flew through without dropping a bomb, climbed again and spoke to *Antrim*.

I suggested I go through once more and use the Harrier's recce camera to take pictures of the target area so that a subsequent mission would know what they were looking for when they went in to attack. *Antrim* had no other trade for me and seemed to think this was a good idea.

About fifteen minutes after the first run I found myself in the

Port Howard area again. I rushed in low and fast, having picked a different direction of attack. Just as I was about to start taking pictures there were three loud bangs and the aircraft went out of control. It rolled very rapidly to the right, almost through 360°. I looked down, saw my right hand and pulled the ejection seat handle. I heard the bang of the canopy exploding above my head, which is the normal way of ejecting. You get rid of the canopy and then out goes the seat. At that point I blacked out and was unconscious. Later on I spoke to a chap from Port Howard who had seen it. He said half or three-quarters of the right wing came off. The plane must have rolled very rapidly, yet somehow it seemed to be in slow time; it was having no effect. I remember being upside-down, seeing the sea very close and thinking: You've got to time it correctly otherwise you won't go out vertically. It must have been very rapid but at the same time all these thoughts went through my mind.

I came to a little while later. I was under water and sort of drowning. I realised that it was light that way up, so I swam to the surface and everything got better again. It was a nice day, except that I was in a certain amount of pain. I couldn't see properly out of one eye and was generally feeling pretty groggy.

I saw the coast and started to swim towards it, which was absolutely stupid really because I was dragging the parachute. I was also dragging the dinghy which was beneath me and I was getting nowhere fast. I think I was in shock. Then I started to get my act together, got rid of the parachute and started to think about inflating the dinghy. I heard voices, turned round and there was a rowing boat full of Argentine soldiers coming towards me. So I thought: What's the point? They were pointing rifles at me. Eventually they dragged me on board and rowed me ashore. Most of my safety equipment was removed and I was taken to their medical centre, which was somewhat makeshift and sited at the Port Howard social club. There were a few beds already occupied by some of their blokes.

My major problem was my left shoulder. Because I had to eject so quickly, instead of using two hands I still had my left hand on the throttle. I pulled the handle with one hand and got what is called a flail injury. I had effectively jumped out in a 600-mph wind up into the free airstream with my left arm still out. It flailed backwards and pretty well broke my arm, my left shoulder-blade in two places and my collarbone.

My face was badly bruised through wind blast and possibly the speed at which I had hit the water. I don't know how long the parachute had been deployed before I hit the water because I was unconscious. I was put on a camp bed and a doctor/medico came up and looked me over. I gave him my Geneva Convention ID card and took the rest of my immersion suit off. He gave me a quick look-over, put my arm in a makeshift sling, gave me an injection and put me to sleep for about eight to ten hours, which was fine by me. Basically I was in a state of shock. I was just being led by the nose; I didn't think about the fact that the people who had almost killed me were now being nice to me. On reflection they were pretty decent and certainly I'm thankful for that.

When I subsequently left Port Howard by helicopter I was introduced to the platoon Blowpipe [hand-held surface-to-air missile] operator. They obviously credited him with having shot me down. I shook him by the hand and said: 'Well done mate.' At the same time I was not necessarily convinced it was a Blowpipe which hit me – it could well have been a triple 'A' they had at Port Howard, a radar-controlled 20 mm Oerlikon. But they seemed to think it was a Blowpipe, so fair enough.

I was not interrogated at all. When I got back to the Argentine mainland after a period of four or five days an air force major came to my bedside and started trying to chat me up. He brought the conversation round to war and military matters, at which point I said: 'I don't wish to continue the conversation.' But I was amazed there wasn't a tactical interrogation, an immediate interrogation. Someone who has just ejected and is in stress, maybe injured, is probably an ideal candidate to interrogate, but fortunately that didn't happen. If they had done I would have tried to stick to the basic four: name, rank, number and date of birth.

I spent about thirty-six hours in Port Howard. Then I was moved by helicopter to Goose Green, where I spent a night, I'm not quite sure why. The following evening we went on to Port Stanley, where I spent a couple of nights in a large medical centre. I was then put on board a Hercules on one of the night missions they were running in and out of the Islands. I was flown to Comodoro Rivadavia. They took me to a large hospital which was part of the air base and I spent a couple of nights locked up under guard in their officers' mess. Then I was flown a long way, for about four hours, and ended up in a place about 1,000 miles north-west of Buenos Aires where I was to spend the next five weeks. It was well out of the way.

Medically they did a reasonable job on me. The doctors in Port Howard and Stanley had fitted me up with a loose sling to suppport my shoulder. And at Comodoro Rivadavia the doctor thought it would be a good idea to put on a heavy plaster cast, a big body cast which encased my arm, shoulder and body, just keeping my right arm free. At the time I didn't think it was such a good idea because it really immobilised me. I had the impression that maybe it was the immobility they quite liked. They had me under close guard all the time but their attitude towards me and the food was quite reasonable. There was certainly no aggro. When I was in the officers' mess I was visited by ten or twelve Argentine pilots who would come in and say hello and ask me how I was feeling. One chap came in and gave me a bottle of wine. Another said he would shake me by the hand because I was a pilot but he didn't agree with what I was doing. I said: 'Fair enough,' and that was it.

At the time I didn't realise I was their only PoW. They claimed they had several dotted around the base, which I didn't somehow believe but it could have been true. It wasn't until I got to Uruguay that I realised I was the only one.

I was quite depressed to have been shot down, when I was first held prisoner. I felt I had let the squadron down, let the boss down. It was my first sortie, we'd only taken six planes down with us. I lost one of them almost immediately so I was pretty fed up. The number of times that I relived that sortie . . . trying to work out what I'd done wrong.

I was worried about my family and whether anyone might not have realised I had survived. When I first got to the place north of Buenos Aires I had a visit by an International Red Cross man, but that was ten days after I was shot down. He said that he would inform my relatives that he had seen me and that I was all right.

I was in virtual solitary confinement for five weeks. I had not done the escape-and-evasion and combat survival courses which most pilots do in their time, certainly within the first year on an operational squadron. I had attended briefings, so I knew roughly the right sort of things to be doing. But then once you're stuck in a room on your own for five weeks I'm not sure what training can necessarily prepare you for. By the end of the five weeks I'd got a routine going and I think that was the key: to pass the time, to have some kind of routine, no matter how boring or how tedious it was. The Red Cross man had left me a certain number of books, but he said he wouldn't see me for two or three weeks. So I used to allow myself about three-quarters of an hour a day reading the book, because I didn't have a watch. He left me some paper, pen and envelopes, and so every other day I would write a letter to my wife using one piece of paper. The next day I would give them to the Argentinian blokes to post. This was a mistake because on the last day, when I was released, they handed me ten of the letters which I thought had been sent off.

In the mornings, just before lunch, I would have three-quarters of an hour to an hour outside in a small courtyard, to wander around. The rest of the time it was just very boring, with nothing to do. I couldn't exercise because I still had on this stupid plaster cast. I'd lie down or sit and watch the room go by, performing mental exercises. I'd try and pick out a day, say 1 March 1961, and try and work out what I had been doing on that day. I'd try and work out whether it was a weekday, which school I was at and who the teacher was, and so on.

On my last visit by the Red Cross man, about a week before I was eventually released, he said that there were no real signs of me being released and that I could be there for some while. I was adjusting already to the thought. I managed to see the odd snippet of an Argentine magazine or newspaper, in which they were really thrashing the Brits with overwhelming victories. I remember a glossy magazine had a line-up of Argentine versus British forces. Almost half the British ships had red crosses through them and three-quarters of the Harriers too. I thought: No way. That is a joke.

Eventually I was flown to Buenos Aires, where I spent another three or four days in hospital and had the big plaster cast taken off. I was given some nice meals and was quite well looked after. Then I was flown to Montevideo, where I was met by the military attaché and some of the embassy staff and driven to the ambassador's residence, where I had a nice lunch.

Flying home I was very excited. Looking back on it all, I felt cheated at missing out on the war, not staying with the rest of the squadron on *Hermes* and continuing the operations, and at having to sit it out in Argentina. It was very disappointing.

NIGEL WARD

Lieutenant-Commander Nigel 'Sharkey' Ward, now retired from the Royal Navy's fleet air arm, is managing director of his own consultancy, Defence Analysts Ltd. In the Falklands he flew combat air patrols as leader of 801 Squadron aboard HMS *Invincible*. He is credited with three confirmed 'kills'.

About two weeks before [the Argentines invaded] we were formally warned that there was something going on in the South Atlantic. Because I was in command of my squadron, I was warned by my superiors that we had to be prepared and ready to go into action seriously. Although we had been at sea for a year and had our leave due, the boys were told they had to be able to get back to the base and be ready to embark within twenty-four hours of me calling them. Within six hours of me being called and being told: 'Get your squadron ready to go', we had ninety per cent of our men at Yeovilton, and all our aircraft on the line ready to take off and get on board.

Going down to the South Atlantic there was a little bit of artificiality about our confidence. All of us knew we were going to fight, or we hoped we were going to fight. We knew there was a considerable amount of danger in real combat: you don't come back from it sometimes. But you had to forget that, just as in peacetime you have to forget when someone's killed flying or in operational training. When we lose somebody we have to get over it as fast as we can and keep our confidence up. If we started to worry it would affect our ability in the air. If it happens we go to the bar as soon as possible and drink on the unfortunate man's mess number for the evening and make up a song about him, or at least a verse of a song. It's a very soul-searching event, but the last thing one can do as a fighter pilot in peace or war is get too upset or adversely affected by death. It's been with us since the [Second World] War. We lost more Sea Vixen crews [in peacetime in the 1960s and 70s] than they ever lost other fighter pilots. And it's on the blood, sweat and tears of those people that our expertise for the Falklands was built. It only came from a lot of work, hard flying and, sadly, a lot of casualties.

Two of my close friends from my squadron down in the Falklands were lost very early on in the war. It was extremely sad. I was on deck in my aircraft when I heard the news and I made up a song immediately, on my knee-pad, thinking the boys in the crew room were going to be very upset. I got back and said: 'Listen fellas, I know it's sad but how does this sound?' and stood there and recited this little song. And they told me where to go. They said: 'Get lost boss.' I went down in my cabin, thought about it and went back up two hours later. They were all happy and said: 'Well it wasn't that bad a song boss, we're just a little sort of nervy and apprehensive today.' The aim of the game was to get them back on top pitch, to give them something to get angry with, perhaps to recover from, to get on with the game. There cannot be the slightest element of self-doubt when you are flying combat missions. You need every bit of concentration, nerve and confidence if you're going to win.

We were trying to keep the enemy awake every night by bombing Stanley, but on one occasion we decided to mount an operation to make the enemy think we were invading. The plan was to fly across to Goose Green and Fox Bay – which was 300 nautical miles from the *Invincible* – drop flares on each location and then come back to the ship. Before I left to do the job I told the Admiral's staff what was going on, and said: 'Please tell all the ships that I'm doing this. I'm going to be a lone aircraft coming back in the middle of the night, and I don't want to be shot down.' In the last war we lost a fair number of aircraft to our own fire.

Everything went off as planned and I dropped my flares on the right place – 11 May I think it was. The Argentine radio broadcast that the invasion had started, so I heard later.* I came back towards the ship and was about ninety miles from *Invincible* when I heard on my little electronic gadget that someone had locked on to me

---

* In fact, Ward's mission was part of a deception plan to cover the SAS raid on Pebble Island on 14 May.

from down below with an acquisition radar. I was liable to be shot at.

I immediately peeled away to the south, which meant that life was going to be tight for me because I was quite short on fuel. I then realised what was happening and started to interrogate people on the ground in rather caustic and severe language as to what was going on. One of our own frigates was illuminating me with radar and was going to have a go. They obviously hadn't been told by the command what I'd been doing. It took a lot of angry language – which they responded to with a certain amount of laughter – to resolve the situation and make it safe for me to return to the ship. But that wasn't the end of the sortie . . .

Imagine being in a tiny jet, everything black everywhere, with a ship somewhere ahead but with no lights on and in quite rough seas with snow clouds around. Your ship is one of about thirty. Now you've got to pick it out. It's like finding a needle in a haystack. You've got to approach it and land on board. I came down the approach but it meant I could make one pass only because I didn't have the fuel to go round again. If I had got the wrong ship I was in trouble.

Fortunately I found the right ship – but because of a snow storm they didn't see me on radar until I was almost on the deck. So really it was 'Help yourself lad or you're in trouble.'

Eventually they came up on the radio and said: 'Sharkey we can see you now, you're about three miles on the approach.' This was actually when I was about 300 yards from the deck – halfway between free flight and the hover, which in itself is very difficult. I apprised them of the information and said: 'No I'm not, I'm 300 yards, 250 now, can I have some lights please.' You can just imagine everything black, literally very very black, and you're doing all your work from a cockpit, looking in the radar screen, trying to work out the attitude of the aeroplane. It's quite a dangerous old business. And then you find out that nobody really knows where you are except yourself. There's a lot of workload involved there too and you get excited. They put the lights on and I came over the deck. Fortunately it was the right ship. I was very short of fuel and as I came over the end of the deck, the wind changed through forty-five degrees and it was something like a forty-knot wind.

In a Harrier, if you get the wind off the nose and you're doing more than thirty knots the aeroplane can turn upside-down. So that added to the excitement. I called out in a sort of high-pitched voice: 'Is there anybody on the deck?' Because I thought we were going to crash the aeroplane, it was quite a handful with the ship heaving all over the place. As I put the aeroplane over the deck I put it down. As soon as my wheels hit the ground, my anger dissipated and I thought: 'Well, I'm back. Thank goodness for that.' Many people had that sort of experience.

We heard on our radio on board the ship the Argentine news broadcasts saying that we had been christened 'The Black Death' – because of their paint scheme our aeroplanes looked very dark. On hearing this I thought we could take advantage and tease them a little in the air by calling ourselves the Black Death to them. In Spanish that is *La Muerta Negra*. It sounded really good, so I instructed all my boys to get airborne and when they were going out on to combat air patrol, to call up the Argentine safety frequency: '*La Muerta Negra* is-a-coming.' It was a bit like the cartoons, all part and parcel of the confidence-building, propaganda almost. I've since heard that they thought it was a fair trick to play. They didn't think it was dishonourable, and to them honour is everything. It was war and it was a great wheeze.

My overall impression of the Argentine fighter pilots, whether navy or air force, is very high. They were brave pilots doing a job that they weren't conversant with, and with much poorer training. They hadn't fought a war since they first had aeroplanes. We had all the experience of the Second World War and action since then, so we were in a very fortunate position. They came out over the sea from a land-based environment to fight what they had heard were a group of very good fighter pilots. They were very brave and they never stopped coming. They lost a lot of aeroplanes and we had nothing but the highest respect for their courage.

Every day they had a Hercules transport plane taking stores in to the Falklands, mainly at night or early dusk. We wanted to stop it, so we often flew way beyond West Falkland to try and shoot down a Hercules or at least intercept one. On the way back from a sortie with my number two, Steve Thomas, we were called by HMS *Minerva* from San Carlos: 'Contact north-west forty miles. Do you want to have a look?' It was like a red rag to a bull. We were already pointing north-west and, going for it, picked up the man on radar and chased him. He knew we were coming and he turned for home and ran as fast as he could, about 350 knots, descending down through the cloud to low level. So we had to make up the forty miles he was ahead of us, get down through the clouds, identify him and do something with him.

In principle we didn't really want to shoot a Hercules down. We would have liked to have given him a chance, flown alongside the cockpit and said: 'Sorry boys it's all over, either bale out or ditch it or land it on a beach but you're not going anywhere.' We talked about it quite a lot in the crew room. But sadly we had almost too little fuel to get back to the ship. It was very marginal. There was no time to mess around with courtesies, so as I was leading the pair I shot two missiles into the aeroplane and all my guns to bring him down quickly. It was a choice of losing one Hercules or perhaps two Sea Harriers through lack of fuel. It was sad to think that the occupants had to die. But on the other hand I didn't think much about that problem at the time. We were delighted to have taken a Hercules out because they were bringing ammunition and supplies to their boys and supporting their war effort. It's no different from shooting down a fighter pilot, it just does a different job. In the cold light of day afterwards we were sad there wasn't time to give them warning, but that's the way it goes.

May 21st [the day of the British landings at San Carlos] was the day it all came together for us as fighter pilots working with the fleet, the boys down below. Falkland Sound looked the most wonderful technicolour that you've ever seen on a cinema screen. There were beautiful hues of blue and green in the water, you could see the kelpweed underneath. It was like the Scottish highlands on the land and below us were seven small grey frigates making a ring of steel around San Carlos Water. They were there to take the punishment that was about to come from the Argentine air force and navy pilots. It was very moving. I thought of those chaps down there in the ships, practically indefensible; they were in a sense sacrificial lambs so that the boys in the *Canberra* and the other assault ships could get ashore unscathed. It was a brilliant plan and it worked.

There was nothing we would not have done to shoot down Mirages and A4s, to protect those fellows in the frigates. It was very exciting. Never ever before in my career have we been so much together and they felt it down below as well. You could tell from the comments to us from their ops rooms. When we shot down a couple of Mirages I called the ops room and said: 'More trade?', which means 'Anything more for us to do?'

The fellow at the other end said: 'Wait.'

I said: 'What do you mean wait?'

He said: 'Well, we've just had our ops room strafed with gunfire, with 30 mm cannon. The man across the desk from me has lost the top of his head and I've been hit in the arm and I'm just collecting myself.'

I felt awful. I said: 'Okay – sorry about that,' and within seven seconds he was back on the line saying: 'Right, we think we've got trade for you, up to the north.' It happened just like that, quite amazing.

On another occasion HMS *Minerva* called us up and said: 'We've got some slow-moving targets down over the southern part of East Falkland, can you go and have a look?' We were delighted to do that. I had two wingmen that day – Steve Thomas and Alastair Craig – and we shot off down to the south from 15,000 feet looking for what we thought would be helicopters or Pucaras. All we saw was one Pucara – it was flown, we found out later, by a Major Tomba – at very low level over the land. So my wingmen attacked him from the beam, that is from the side of the aeroplane, using guns. I watched them firing on the first pass and they were killing a lot of sheep and digging up the peat but they weren't hitting him. I thought that as I was a bit astern of them on the run-in, I'd shoot him from behind, in the conventional position. On my first run-in I fired at him, shooting half his left aileron off and setting his right engine on fire. So I was hitting all right. I pulled away and thought he was going into the ground. Not a bit of it. My wingmen came back in from the other side, firing again, killing a lot more sheep, and I had time to come in again from the stern.

This time I came in slower – first pass I was at about 350 to 400 knots. I put my flaps down to bring my nose down so I could aim more easily. I was flying along between ten and sixty feet above the deck on my radio altimeter, noticing the height in my head-up display quite carefully, but tracking nice and smooth. I fired a long burst into him, set the port engine on fire and knocked bits off the rear fuselage, and the canopy shattered.

As I pulled off I thought: Well, that's that. But he was still weaving away, and wasn't going to give up. So my wingmen came in again, killed some more sheep. I had a final pass and emptied my guns into this character. It was a bit like a Second World War movie going through the explosion, bits and pieces flying all over the place, still at very low level. As I pulled off I saw an ejection seat go out of the aeroplane, a parachute open, and a man settle on the ground.

I thought: What a character. He should have got out after the first pass. He stayed with it until it just wouldn't fly and got out just before it hit the ground, and apparently walked back to Goose Green. He was later captured, and I have nothing but the highest respect for him. That was real bravery.

CARLOS TOMBA

Major Carlos Antonio Tomba served as a Pucara ground-attack pilot with Attack Group 3, based at Goose Green. He was shot down by 'Sharkey' Ward shortly after the British forces landed on the Islands. He baled out and was able to walk back to his base, but was captured when the Paras took the settlement a few days later.

We were returning to base that day when we were attacked. I saw two anti-aircraft missiles flying by, so we swerved away and started evasive manoeuvres. We thought we had escaped and our controllers assigned another mission to us. As we flew over San Carlos my wingman said that he saw Harriers, but I couldn't see them. We started circling and after two or three circuits I felt an impact on my plane. I looked at the wings and saw a pretty large hole, like a rose with open petals. Above me I could see two Harriers. The aircraft was still under control although it was shaking violently. The engine and controls seemed to be working properly so I went down very low, hugging the terrain to evade my pursuer.

I was then hit by another burst of machine-gun fire and once more the machine shook violently. This time one engine caught fire and the controls were responding very weakly. I lost control of the aircraft altogether. Soon the whole plane appeared to be on fire and that was when I decided to eject. The aircraft and I practically fell together. I was not prepared to eject until the plane was completely useless and totally out of control because a pilot always stays with his plane until the last moment.

After the first impact I thought I could handle the aircraft and it was only when I had no chance that I baled out. I didn't think I was being suicidal hanging on until the last minute. I knew what I was doing because of all the training I had received. You react instinctively – there is no time to think really.

When I landed in my parachute the first thing I felt was great anger because I had lost my plane. I had lost my weapon and my way of fighting without even catching a glimpse of the enemy. I thought about my family, my wife and my children. I thanked God that I was still alive. Then I thought that I had to recover and continue the fight. Afterwards I had to walk back to my base. It took about six or seven hours but my duty was to return to my comrades.

I never thought that I would have to fight as an infantryman, but at that point we had to fight with everything we had. We could not use the planes because of naval shelling, so we used other weapons to fight the enemy on the land. We had to defend the airport [at Goose Green when the British Paras attacked]. We used the aircraft cannon and machine guns because that was all we had.

We don't know how effective these weapons were because we were too far away from the British troops. My greatest pain in the war was surrendering. For a soldier the worst thing that can happen in his life is to surrender his weapon; our duty is to fight until death. Our CO called us all together before the surrender of Goose Green and with tears in his eyes made us sing the National Anthem as a way of showing that in our hearts we were not giving up. We had been materially defeated: spiritually we would never surrender.

I know that my flying helmet is at the Fleet Air Arm Museum at Yeovilton in England. I'd like to get it back some day. I would be glad to go back and fight in the Malvinas as many times as I am needed.

RICARDO LUCERO

Lieutenant Ricardo Lucero was an Argentine air force fighter pilot who flew an A4 Skyhawk jet with Attack Group 4, based at Rio Grande. Shot down on 25 May 1982 after attacking the British Task Force in Falkland Sound, he was treated by British surgeons. He remains a pilot on active duty with the Fuerza Aerea.

The attack on 25 May had a special significance because it is Argentina's national independence day. We had not been given any special orders but we all knew it was important for morale to produce something extraordinary. From my cockpit I could see as I came over the bay that there were seven ships there. We flew in from the south. There were four aircraft in our flight and we had to pick our targets individually. In the middle of the bay I saw a ship I recognised as HMS *Fearless*. It started to move to port and I was about to release the bombs when I felt a great explosion and the plane lurched forward. I don't know exactly what hit me but I saw explosions around all our four aircraft. I tried to tell my squadron leader that I had been hit but the radio was out and the controls of the plane were not working. Smoke was filling the cockpit so I decided to eject.

I felt I was spinning backwards but I never lost consciousness. I thought I was going to die. I thought of my friends and relatives but I felt at peace because I knew I had done my duty. Then something exploded under me and suddenly I was floating down under an open parachute. I sank into the water and tried to go through the emergency procedures but I could not get rid of the parachute.

When I surfaced I felt great pain in my legs. I saw a few dinghies around with soldiers pointing their rifles at me, so I held up my hands

113

and they tried to lift me up into one of their boats, but it was difficult because I had my survival suit on. I couldn't help them much because my hands were half-frozen. Then a landing craft approached and tried to lift me on to its ramp, but that didn't work either and I came under the ramp. Finally I had to take a deep breath and go under the ramp to the other side of the craft and they then managed to drag me aboard.

They took my survival suit off and pointed at me with their rifles and I felt great relief because I was saved. I still could feel this great pain in my legs and when I looked down I noticed that my left leg was bent at a strange angle and knew I must have dislocated it. I was taken on board a frigate and there they gave me first aid and morphine and painted an 'M' on my face so that the doctors who treated me would know that I had been injected with morphine. The morphine helped my pain and then a doctor told me that I had broken ligaments in my left leg and that I had pulled the ligaments in my right leg. He put my leg in place and they wrapped my leg so that I couldn't move it.

Then I was questioned, but there was no pressure on me to answer. They took me on deck and I thought: This is it, they are going to throw me overboard now. I suppose when you are a prisoner at first you tend to be a bit paranoid and your moods can change suddenly. One moment I felt relief because I was saved, and I had fallen in the right place, and the next I thought it was all for the worse. Then I heard a helicopter and they put me on it and took me to the hospital at Ajax Bay.

When I arrived, Surgeon Commander Jolly told me: 'Here you are just one more among our wounded.' And that is how I felt from then on. I never really felt like a prisoner because I was treated very well and given all possible help. In the operation he fixed my leg as best he could but he did tell me that I would never manage to bend it properly in future. Initially I had been told that the war was over for me and that I had a very serious injury and that they didn't think I would be able to fly again. It was only when I returned to Argentina that I had several operations and after a long period of rehabilitation, approximately ten months, I was able to fly again on A4s. About two years later I received a letter from Dr Jolly asking me how I was recovering from the injury. I haven't replied to that letter but I am fully recovered.

GUILLERMO OWEN CRIPPA

Lieutenant Guillermo Owen Crippa piloted an Aermacchi ground attack aircraft with the Argentine fleet air arm 1st Attack Squadron, a small unit based at Puerto Argentino (Port Stanley). He was the first pilot to engage the British Task Force when it landed on 21 May 1982, and gave the first full report on the enemy invasion.

Once the Malvinas were taken I thought war would be inevitable. I couldn't imagine the British government remaining impassive after our occupation. So we had to prepare ourselves for war. It is true that Great Britain was an unexpected enemy for us, but this didn't worry me. I knew of the Harrier's capability for air combat and obviously I realised it was a good aircraft, but we were well prepared for combat. We studied British air strategy: nothing that they could do would surprise us. Our problem was that we had no possibility of keeping combat air patrols over the Islands to give us protection. This was obviously a major factor in the war.

I was so keen on taking part in this conflict that I put myself forward although I was not initially chosen. I was a professional pilot in our fleet air arm and I thought that if my country had spent all that money training me, it was my duty to come forward and perform now. There was a sentimental reason too. The Malvinas had been occupied by the British, and as an Argentine this bothered me because I considered the Islands my territory.

The first and only PoW I saw was Jeff Glover, who was brought to Puerto Argentino after he was shot down. I am not fluent in English but we managed to communicate. He didn't understand the reasons for the war and he didn't think we did either. I said that in my case the reason was that I was defending my own territory, because I had been taught ever since I was a child that the Malvinas are Argentine. I said that I admired his courage in fighting for something he didn't understand, but in my case it was different.

This of course is the difference between the Argentines and the British. A British pilot or infantryman fought in the Malvinas because he was following orders and he had been prepared for this sort of mission. I was fighting for other reasons.

When a colleague went out on a mission we would wave him goodbye thinking that perhaps that was the last time we would see him, but I think the pilot was not necessarily thinking that way. Sometimes it was even funny to see the faces around me when I went out on a mission. They looked as though they were saying a final goodbye. It nagged me and I felt like saying: 'Hold it – I'll be back in a short while.'

When a fellow pilot failed to return we thought initially that he might have survived anyway and that it was part of the risk that we were taking. Normally we would calculate his possibilities of survival in the mission he had been given and would draw our own conclusions.

The one single incident that really surprised and shocked me in the war was the sinking of the *Belgrano*. At first I thought, given the area where the ship had been sunk and the weather conditions, that none of them would survive, and I was very happy to be able to meet my friends among the survivors again.

In those circumstances you were forced to come to terms with the death of your friends. No one death is more shocking than any other. Somebody is there one day and gone the next. Some hit you not because the circumstances are more or less tragic but because you knew that person very well and you miss him. You also think: Christ I was just having a chat with him a few minutes ago! But you learn to accept it.

On 21 May there were reports of British ships in the straits of San Carlos. We went on alert very early that morning and set out to recce the zone. I chose to take off with one other plane and told the rest to prepare their own planes. We were briefed and we prepared to take off, but the other plane had technical difficulties and I flew off on my own. This wasn't very safe but we needed to check urgently what was happening. I followed my course towards San Carlos and I saw two Harriers shooting down one of our helicopters. I saw it fall heavily to

116

the ground, it exploded and its crew members ran out. When I reached San Carlos the whole area was covered in mist so I couldn't see at all. Then I went out to sea thinking that this was where the British ships were likely to be. But I didn't see a single ship, and that surprised me. When I headed inland again I saw first one ship, then two. As I came over San Carlos itself I came face to face with a Sea Lynx helicopter. I was going to attack it when I saw the ships in the distance.

I decided to forget about the helicopter and go for the other targets. I banked away from the helicopter when I was only a few yards from it and at that moment the pilot must have seen me because he dived down. I had to laugh and thought to myself: It's your lucky day today. Obviously I couldn't have missed him from that range.

I flew straight to the first ship which was lying at anchor, landing troops. I don't know which of us was more surprised. I came in for the attack and they started firing at me. I was taken aback by the number of ships there were in the area and I thought to myself: If I go back and tell them there are so many ships they'll never believe me. I circled and came back trying to hug the terrain and I drew a little map on my knee-pad before I returned to Puerto Argentino.

It was strange because it was a beautiful day, very peaceful, and the Islands looked lovely. It was incredible to think there was a war going on. It all looked so bucolic that any thoughts of aggression and violence seemed out of the question. The seagulls were flying, the sea was calm, there was a light breeze and it was very sunny. Not your normal Malvinas weather at all. At first it was a shock and then quite exciting to find all those ships. It may seem odd but I had often been on missions without finding anything at all. So this time I thought: Here they are – I can do something. I was surprised to see all those ships in such a small space. It made it hard for the planes to attack them but it also restricted them.

When you fly very low you take risks, but we were well trained and we did it for our own protection. It doesn't happen like you see in the films because in the films every shot counts, you have to make it look as dramatic as possible. In real combat people make a lot of mistakes. You miss shots. You go on percentages.

ALBERTO PHILIPPI

Captain Alberto Philippi of the Argentine fleet air arm flew A4 Skyhawk missions against the British Task Force from the air base at Rio Grande. He was one of the pilots who made the low-level bombing attack which sank HMS *Ardent*. He currently works on a project developing ground-support capability with the Argentine army.

When I heard the Malvinas had been occupied on 2 April it made me very happy but I didn't think it would come to an armed clash with Great Britain. I thought there would be some tension and then we would find a diplomatic solution. Right up to the day when I carried out my first mission I thought that diplomacy would prevent war. Unfortunately that didn't happen. It didn't matter that we were flying against British ships because when you get into the cockpit of your plane you forget about everything else and concentrate on the mission you have been given.

The mission was: 'Attack ships off the Malvinas.' Then I had to get my men home. We navy pilots are constantly being trained to attack ships. The difference this time was that our bombs were real. What happens when you go into combat is that your pulse-rate increases, the adrenalin flows much quicker and keeps you in a state of tension that you wouldn't have on practice manoeuvres. The brain works two or three times quicker than normal. The first actual combat mission is difficult but when you fly the second one you know more or less what you are going to find. However, the very first time you keep asking yourself: What's the enemy going to be like? That is what happened to me on 21 May.

We took off in two sections, a total of six planes, and headed for the islands at 27,000 feet. As soon as we approached enemy radar range we dipped down to sea level and headed for the south-western entrance to San Carlos Bay. We were flying very low and the weather was breaking. This situation became critical when we reached Cape Belgrano* because we had to turn into the entrance of the strait where the visibility was so reduced that my wingman had to pull up very close beside me. This is something you should never do, because it produces a bigger signature on the enemy radar and therefore you are an easier target. Visibility was down to a mile, which is also dangerous because a frigate on picket-duty would detect us at about fifteen miles, launch its missiles at a distance of about five miles, and still we would not be able to see her.

So that day everything was against us, but we decided to proceed. As we came in from the south there was no ship there to attack so we continued towards the designated alternative target, which was the ships in the port of San Carlos itself. We swerved in at maximum speed and minimum height and at that moment we saw a frigate and immediately deployed into an attack formation. Normally we wouldn't fly so low because it is quite dangerous – you feel a sort of vertigo when you are flying at fifty feet. I had my altimeter set at thirty feet and the alarm went off several times. When you are doing all this at 450 knots you feel you're on the edge.

That's how we were going in to attack the frigate. She began to move at high speed so we knew that she had detected us. This meant that a direct attack was no longer possible, so we circled to the right hugging the terrain as much as possible, to attack the ship from behind. We attacked diagonally from starboard.

We each carried four bombs and as we started on the run-in we fired at the frigate with everything we had to reduce its anti-aircraft fire. We had studied silhouettes of all the British ships so we were quite familiar with them. I knew exactly which kind of ship it was; the difference was that this particular one I had to sink. The frigate was reacting very well. She had increased speed, which I could see by her wake. She was trying to reach open waters. As I came over her I swerved to the right as I dropped my bombs and started my evasive manoeuvres. There is no doubt that the skipper underneath me knew his job.

* Cape Belgrano is the Argentinian name for the southernmost tip of West Falkland, Cape Meredith.

As I escaped I heard my wingman saying over the radio: 'Very good sir,' which meant at least one of my bombs had exploded, so I could forget about everything else and concentrate on the evasive manoeuvre. I thought I might have a missile on my tail. The frigate threw everything at us and I could see little fireballs rushing past my cockpit. They were making it difficult for us. I heard another wingman say: 'Another one has hit,' which told me that we had struck the ship with at least two bombs. That was a good percentage. I instructed the squadron to return home along the same route because there did not seem to be any enemy along that path. It would also be easier to escape at maximum speed and in an open formation.

After about two minutes I was beginning to relax, thinking we were out of danger, when I heard my number three shouting: 'Harriers, Harriers.' I ordered all my pilots to drop their fuel tanks in case it turned into a dogfight. We started evasive manoeuvres to see if we could come face to face with them. I banked to the right and when I turned left again I felt the impact on my tail. A loud explosion shook the whole plane and I tried to push the stick forward with both hands but it seemed welded to the floor. Obviously the rudders were not working. The plane was out of control. I looked right and saw another Harrier approaching at about 150 metres, coming in for the kill. I told my men I had been hit but was not wounded and that I was going to eject. I pulled on the ejector handle and after that I lost consciousness.

When I came to I was hanging from a parachute, falling over San Carlos. I had ejected at too fast a speed and the impact had knocked me out. I followed the emergency procedures. The first was to check your lifejacket is fully inflated and then inflate the dinghy. Something had gone wrong, the dinghy stayed flat. I had to swim for the coast, which was about 200 metres away. When I reached the shore I was completely exhausted. I could not stand up. I had to crawl on to the beach and just stayed on the sand for about half an hour getting my breath back. The Harriers came over me a couple of times, looking for my squadron I assume. After that, total silence.

I spent the next four days and three nights walking south, because the enemy was north and I wanted to avoid being taken prisoner. I wanted to reach the Argentine lines. On the fourth day I was resting when I heard engine noises and looked up to see a jeep and two tractors on the coast. I assumed they were Argentine forces so I signalled with my emergency mirror and they soon came over to where I was. A man came over to me smiling and he introduced himself as Tony Blake, the manager of the local estate. I told him I was an Argentine pilot trying to return to my lines. From that moment the man behaved nobly and gave me all the food he had, which was wonderful because I had not had a hot meal in four days. He took me home and then let me have a hot bath and call the Argentine forces to tell them where I was.*

I'll never forget how Tony Blake behaved. I wanted to present him with my survival knife but the war was still on and I didn't know if I would need it again. I told him I would give him the knife when we saw each other again.

We are skilled professionals but we don't really want to go to war because we know of the tragic consequences. Unfortunately this time we had to go to war and we tried to do our duty as best we could. We have been described as 'suicidal kamikazes' for what we did but nothing could be further from the truth. We are motivated, we have a patriotic pride, but we love our families, we love our fellow human beings and, above all, we do want to live. The missions we were given were dangerous but we had to carry them out. If some people thought that we were acting suicidally that is not the impression we had of ourselves. We had not been ordered to kill ourselves in battle against the enemy. The mission was to neutralise the enemy ships. When I dropped my bombs I didn't want to kill the *Ardent* crew, I was just trying to stop the ship. I would have preferred it if all the crew escaped unharmed. That's what I felt during the war and that is what all my colleagues felt. I want to tell Captain West [HMS *Ardent*'s skipper] that I am very sorry about the damage I caused to his ship. Above all I am really, really sorry that men lost their lives in that attack. I was doing my duty as he was doing his, and I just hope that one day our two countries will resolve this conflict. We will then be able to have a whisky together and drink to the memory of my late and very good friend Captain Marquez and all the sailors of *Ardent* who died in the attack.

---

* This call was intercepted by British Signals Intelligence. An attempt was made to get an SAS team to capture Philippi but it was cancelled at the last minute.

JOSÉ CESAR ARCA

Lieutenant (now Captain) José Cesar Arca flew A4 Skyhawks with the 3rd Attack Squadron based at Rio Grande and was involved in the attack on HMS *Ardent* in Falkland Sound. His aircraft was badly damaged in a dogfight with a British Harrier. He ejected near Puerto Argentino and was picked up, injured, by his own side and returned to Argentina.

After dropping my bombs on HMS *Ardent* we were following our escape route back to the mainland when we were intercepted by two British Sea Harriers. I saw one of them on my left firing a Sidewinder [air-to-air missile] at Captain Philippi which exploded right on his tail. I was taking evasive manoeuvres but the cannons were jammed. I couldn't start a dogfight. One of the Harriers [piloted by Lieutenant Clive Morrell] was on my tail so I flew very low over the water trying to lose him. I felt about ten hits on my aircraft and most of my systems were knocked out. I had to fly manually trying to shake him off. Morrell must have run out of ammunition because he stopped shooting at me. I knew I wouldn't be able to reach the mainland, so I tried to land at Puerto Argentino. Morrell had hit one of my fuel tanks and I was losing gas. I had only my reserve tank – about 2,000 lbs – that's why I couldn't get back home.

I approached Puerto Argentino at very low altitude but I couldn't alert the control tower because that would have brought on another British attack if they had intercepted my radio message. I tried to bring down my wheels as I came over the tower but only two wheels came down. I decided to fly over the tower so they could tell me whether or not I was able to land. It so happened that the officer in the control tower

122

was a friend of mine and I told him I would reduce speed to come in for a landing.

He said: 'Do you realise what condition your plane is in? Your plane is so full of holes I can see the sky through it. You don't have any landing wheels – you'll have to bale out.'

I ejected at 2,500 feet with my plane flying at 180 knots. I could only pull the ejector handle with one hand, because my right hand was broken, although I hadn't realised it. Baling out is a strange feeling because it is something you cannot control. You are hurled out of the plane and tumble through the sky until you find yourself gliding down under a parachute. I had left the controls of my plane so that it would stay on a straight line, but it had tipped slightly to the left and started to circle. As it circled it headed straight at me while I was falling down towards the sea.

When it came towards me I thought: This is incredible, I have just come out of combat, I've bombed a frigate, I've been in a dogfight and now my own plane is going to crash into me and kill me!

It was frightening to say the least to see this hunk of metal out of control and coming at you. Thank God the anti-aircraft batteries around Port Stanley managed to shoot it down. I plunged into the water. There were no proper rescue helicopters in the area and an army attack helicopter [without a winch-system] came to pick me up. After thirty minutes in the water with the helicopter so close and yet unable to rescue me I decided to take my survival suit off. I finally managed to cling on to the landing skid of the helicopter. I hung on with my arms and feet while the mechanic held on to me by the head as we flew the 500 metres back to the shore. The helicopter could not land with me underneath it so it had to drop me on the stones of the beach.

SOLDIERS

MANUEL BATISTA

Sergeant Manuel Batista is a career NCO and Marine instructor at the Puerto Belgrano naval base, near Bahia Blanca, 500 miles from Buenos Aires. He was part of the contingent of commandos who landed at Port Stanley on 2 April 1982, and was involved in the final stages of the battle against the British Royal Marines at Government House.

We were told what our objective was when we were on the ship going to the Islands and they told us our individual tasks. I was to be on the lead boat in the initial landing. This covert force of Argentine commandos had gone ahead of the main force to attack and capture Government House. Our mission was to recover the Malvinas, and the operation had to take place causing a minimum of casualties to the British Marines. We had initial doubts about this because commandos are not trained for this type of operation. It's a bit like surgery without cutting the flesh. But we were very confident and enthusiastic as we planned the operation on the ship. As an Argentine and as a professional soldier I was thrilled, because to be a protagonist in the recovery of the Malvinas, which had for so long been in British hands, was a great source of pride. It was the climax, the high point of my career. I was being assigned an important role in the operation. I felt very confident because I knew the other soldiers and officers, and how good they were. We are a small corps.

As we sighted the Islands I was one of the first on deck. I saw headlights moving around as though they were expecting us, they seemed very close to the beach where we were supposed to land. As we approached I saw the signal that was supposed to guide us in. A small commando unit went ahead of the main force to signal

127

us where to land. I had to make a decision and I decided to land on a beach to the right. As we approached our rudder got stuck in the weeds but we reached the beach with our oars and the engine. We regrouped and on the way to our objective I saw a machine-gun nest on the beach where we were meant to land. We deliberately did not engage the British machine gun because we had been ordered not to cause casualties. So we by-passed them. I was about 100 metres in front of the unit. As we approached Government House I searched a few houses and took several members of the Civil Defence Force prisoner. I carried on and took two Royal Marines by surprise. Another British Marine was trying to get to a hedge in front of Government House so I covered him with my gun and handed him over to my unit.

British Marines were around the outside of the building. I told them to put their hands up. After some hesitation someone spoke in English and they advanced towards me. Other British Marines also laid down their weapons and surrendered. I knew someone was taking photographs but I didn't think it was very important. As I went on to the patio of Government House I found Captain Giachino, and two of our other commandos who had been wounded in the fire-fight with the British soldiers. When I was later told that Giachino had been killed I was very sad because he was a valuable officer. It was a terrible loss.

When I saw the Argentine flag flying over Puerto Argentino for the first time in 150 years I felt a great thrill and great happiness because I had been of service to the Fatherland. The fact that we had completed the mission filled me with pride. I see a fundamental difference between ourselves and the British Marines who were there. This is caused by different types of motivation. We felt that we were defending our territory, while the British as professional soldiers were defending what they were ordered to defend. They are very professional but they are cold; they lacked our motivation.

I returned to the mainland on 3 April and I was sorry that I was not sent back. I envied the men who went there and I would have liked to have stayed on to be involved in defending the Islands when the British attacked.

BARRY NORMAN

Sergeant-Major Barry Norman is a career Paratrooper. In the Falklands War he served with the 2nd Battalion, the Parachute Regiment (2 Para). He was bodyguard to the commanding officer, Lieutenant-Colonel 'H' Jones, and was with him when he was shot and killed at the battle of Goose Green on 28 May 1982.

I actually left for the Falklands three times. After the first signal arrived I went back to Aldershot and took all my kit into work, said farewell to my wife and kids and promptly got told to go home. We weren't going that day. I went into work the next day and they said: 'Oh you're going to Hull in about an hour's time.' I immediately went home, got the kit again, got on a coach and went to Hull where we loaded the *Norland* * with ammunition, rations and everything else you need to go to war. When we finished we sat waiting for the rest of the battalion to arrive.

They then said: 'They're not coming to Hull, we are going to Portsmouth to pick the battalion up.' We sailed to Portsmouth and they said: 'You can go home tonight if you wish.'

I went home, knocked at the door, and the wife said: 'What are you doing home? I thought you'd gone.'

I said: 'No, they've given me a couple of nights off.'

I went to work the next day, having upset the kids again saying farewell, and got on the coach to Portsmouth. The wife thought I was coming home that night. I rang her from Portsmouth saying I wouldn't be home.

* The North Sea car ferry.

When the battalion arrived and got on board we got the sailing orders. Our band was on the quayside, playing the regimental march and 'Rule Britannia'. I thought the band should have been on the boat playing the same tunes and sailing with us. I didn't have anybody to wave to on the quayside, but I still stood there. A lump came in my throat because military music does that to me. We didn't think we were going to war or even very far, although all the intention was there and the preparation had been done. Many of us thought the Argentines would back down long before we got there and that the threat of war would be enough. So we thought we were going on a little cruise.

I am an instructor in armour. On the way down I had to teach the whole battalion, at different intervals throughout the day, armour and aircraft recognition. I had to do training myself – medical, fitness and weapon training – so I didn't have time during the day to think about much other than work. In the evenings we had the usual mess facilities – a sergeants' mess will be a sergeants' mess.

Up until the *Sheffield* got hit nobody had the impression we were actually going to war. It was still the atmosphere you get on an exercise. The news about the *Sheffield* was a shock. It then came home that this was a war situation. Lives had been lost and we realised the full implications of that. Everybody knew we were actually going ashore.

(The Norland *arrived off San Carlos Water on the night of 20 May.)*

We moved from the hold of the ship into the landing craft. Our bergens [packs] containing kit weighed upwards of 100 lbs to 120 lbs, with full scales of ammunition plus two mortar bombs. Getting across into the landing craft was very difficult. One guy fell between the two and badly injured himself and that was as much as he saw of the war unfortunately. Crammed into the landing craft we headed for the beach. It was cold and dark and they said: 'You'll see a flashing light on the beach given by the SAS or SBS to say the beach is clear.' We headed for the beach – no flashing light. Our guide was round the corner busily flashing away his light, but we couldn't actually see him. Everybody was expecting to see the light. The adrenalin had built up in the blokes. There were about 100 people in the landing craft, and eventually it was as if 500 to 600 ants were weaving around. Commanders were shouting and screaming for their blokes.

It was still dark when we hit the beach; in fact we missed it. The Royal Marine coxswain in charge of the landing craft decided he was close enough, so we stepped off on to what we thought was the beach. We went straight up nearly to the waist in water which, being the South Atlantic, was quite cold. I was not amused. Even at this stage people thought it was like an exercise: 'We're wet; we get wet when we are on exercise.'

It was a bit farcical. We thought we were going to war but there was no opposition. You had 500 or 600 screaming Paratroopers coming off a landing craft on to a beach, never having done that sort of thing before. We were so used to going to war or exercise by parachute. Chaos reigned for some little time; companies had to regroup and go off to do their own individual tasks. If the landing had been opposed I think we would have been in a little bit of trouble in the early stages.

We regrouped, picked up our packs and sagged at the knees. The battalion 'snake' wound its way up Sussex Mountain, a long hard climb which we were prepared for, but it was slightly slippery underfoot, and on a couple of occasions I fell over because the pack was so heavy. I was like a dead turtle with the pack on the ground and my two feet in the air. I had to get two blokes to roll me over and stand me back on my feet before I could actually proceed up the hill.

I saw this little blip of an aircraft heading towards us. All of a sudden this thing – which I found out afterwards was a missile – leapt out of the ground and knocked it out of the sky. And I thought: 'Quite realistic really. Good exercise this.' The pilot baled out and came down on the ground. This was our first experience of war. Until then we had only heard it: the naval bombardment, the Marines taking out an Argentine observation post, they were like good special effects.

The commanding officer of the battalion has his own 'tactical head-quarters' [Tac HQ] to help him run the battle. It consists of key personnel: the battery commander who controls the guns, the mortar commander, signallers, plus his protection party. He chose me on the way down to be in charge of his protection party during the campaign.

Once we hit the beach, wherever the CO went my little band of Indians went with him.

Just before we marched on Goose Green we left a house where we had lain up during daylight. Again it was still unlike war. The battalion snake weaved its way through the tufty grass, just like Dartmoor: undulating, very slippery, dark, misty and wet at times. We had spent a miserable day freezing because we had gone in 'light scales' * with maximum ammunition and very little warm clothing. We approached the start-line† which had been marked out by the patrols, which again is what we practise on exercise. We formed up with two companies up, one company to the back, with the Tactical HQ between the two forward companies. At 'H' hour the naval bombardment should have arrived and didn't because the gun jammed. We relied on our own artillery to start the ball rolling. It was totally dark and the only illumination was provided by our blokes and the mortars. Still this feeling of actual war wasn't there. Although there was firing going on, the opposition was minimal, basic defensive positions in trenches. It led the blokes into a false sense of security because they upped and ran. In the early stages there weren't many casualties. We suffered some with Argentine sniper fire. And then the actual feeling 'This is war and not an exercise' was hammered home to us when you saw your own blokes lying dead and injured.

It was getting light all the time, and in the first phase of the battle 'H' Jones took the Tac HQ over to 'A' Company's position to have a talk with the officer commanding. 'A' Company had deployed one platoon off to Darwin, one of the smaller settlements. Two platoons went to the high ground but when they reached it all hell broke loose. It was perfect killing ground: the trenches of the Argentine positions were on the high ground facing down into a little bowl with water on the left. However, the first burst of every trench that opened up on us went high. It has been proven time and time again that at first light and last light soldiers tend to shoot high. I am quite pleased they did, because

---

* 'Full scales' and 'light scales' refer to the weight of kit a Paratrooper carries. They landed on the Islands carrying full scales, i.e. all their kit. They went into battle with light scales, i.e. carrying only what they needed to fight with, to allow them to carry more ammunition.

† The 'start-line' is a forming-up point where troops gather before going into battle in attack formation.

if they had waited until daylight came they would have slaughtered us. It was chaos.

The amount of fire that came down on us in that first few seconds was thousands of rounds. By firing high in the first burst they gave us time to get to ground. Once they realised their mistake nobody was physically standing up. Again they brought down fire. We were behind little tufties and in an inlet, so the fire never hit anybody. We still had to get to the killing ground with the fire coming down. There was nowhere else to go. Off to the left was the inlet with quite a high bank. We didn't know if it was mined, but looking around it was the only place to go.

The CO got up and said: 'Right, we can't stay here all day,' and went into the inlet and with a mixture of crawling, running, sprinting and diving we all got out of the killing ground and into the inlet and the protection of a bank, which luckily was not mined. 'A' Company's attack started floundering after they cleared up the Argentine first platoon position. The CO got on the radio and told them to get a grip, speed up and continue the movement, which they couldn't. So he said: 'I'm not having any of this' and decided to go up and join 'A' Company. To say he got a little pear-shaped would be an understatement. When he made up his mind that a thing was going to be done, then it was going to be done, and off he went all the way round the edge of the inlet, which still left us about 200 or 300 metres to go to 'A' Company's position. There was a bank of gorse which gave us a bit of protection from view but none from fire. We had to get from the bank which had given us perfect protection to the gorse and then to 'A' Company's position. We got to the gorse and meandered our way through it, which still left about 100 metres of open ground to cover.

I and another sergeant-major threw smoke bombs to give protection and we went through the smoke. It was good to know they couldn't see you. We got to 'A' Company – there were dead and injured lying around. The CO went up to the officer commanding 'A' Company [Major Charles Farrar-Hockley] and asked him what the situation was and why they had got bogged down; what was he going to do about it? When the decision was made, everybody got in a straight line and we called for mortar fire with smoke and went over the top again and started for the Argentine positions. As we got halfway the smoke ran out. It was windy and the smoke didn't stay very long; it was as if we were on a snooker table, flat and no protection at all. We sustained quite a few casualties, some of them fatal, in that initial burst from the Argentine positions.

I saw the trenches being cleared by elements of 'A' Company. There was maximum fire by mortars and smoke to obscure movement. They then rolled the trenches up; you could not do a frontal assault. They started at one end and rolled the trenches up on each other. They were more like huge bunkers with four or five men in each bunker and thousands and thousands of rounds of ammunition. It took courage to get rid of them. The platoon commanders were given areas to clear and they just said to the corporals: 'You will take that trench,' and he and his section went and took the trench.

You try and get to the trench as quickly as you can, firing. Before you go in you put in a hand-grenade or something to disorganise the people in the trench and then, just like on television, you get in, bayonets fixed, automatic fire, to kill the people in the trench. You have fighting men forward, and the aim of the game is to neutralise the trenches – either you kill everybody in the trench or they give up. If he hasn't got a weapon and he has got his hands in the air, we say he is giving up. If he has got a weapon and he hasn't got his hands in the air then we take it he's not going to give up and we shoot him. You are in a very close environment in a trench. The fine line between life and death is either you kill him or he kills you. Once you are in a hand-to-hand fight, unless he is stood there with his hands in the air you have got to assume he is about to kill you and do the necessary. And in that case it's kill him.

If they give up or they are wounded, they are taken back through the chain to the platoon sergeant, who then passes them back to the sergeant-major and the medics, and they are then held in a company cage before being passed back to the battalion cage which is supervised by the regimental sergeant-major.

You don't get time to think in the middle of all this. I am a soldier, and if the CO says you do something, then you do it. You might think: 'Bloody fool' afterwards or during it but you get out and do it. The CO said: 'We're joining "A" Company and we're going over the top.' So we joined 'A' Company and we went over the top. There was more fire when the smoke cleared – the adjutant and the second-in-command of 'A' Company were killed. So we went to ground and again there was nowhere else to go. We could have reversed and got shot in the back. We couldn't go forward because it was too far to go.

The CO said: 'Right, follow me.' He got up and ran to the right, off the feature [high ground], so we had exposed ourselves to the enemy. We were running diagonally across his front, and down to the right. Once we were there we were then in a slightly better position. But when I got behind the CO he didn't stop. He kept running. I thought: Here we go, and I kept up with him. We went round into a re-entrant [valley with a dead-end] between two Argentine positions, one we had cleared and one we had tried to clear. Suddenly somebody behind me shouted: 'Watch out, there's a trench to the left!' Hearing that, instinct took over and instead of running I dived and hit the ground as fast as I could, just as they opened fire on us. The CO had got beyond the next trench and was obscured from the enemy because of the way the land was going. All the fire was coming my way. I fired back, and emptied the magazine straight away, twenty rounds rapid towards the enemy position to keep his head down while I got into the best position I could. Whatever cover there was I found it, and there wasn't much. I changed magazines, which was difficult because I was lying down and the magazines had jammed in the pouch, so I was flapping quite a bit but I did it. I looked out of the corner of my eye as I was firing again and saw the CO take his sub-machine gun and start charging up the hill towards the trench I was firing at. But he was also coming into view of the Argentine trenches behind us. He kept on going. I shouted at him to watch his back because I could see what was going to happen. He ignored me, or didn't hear me – I would think he actually ignored me – and charged up the hill to neutralise the trench that I was firing at.

He got to within six or seven feet of that trench and was shot from the trenches behind. You could see the rounds striking the ground behind him, coming up gradually towards him, and they shot him in the back. The impact of the rounds hitting him pushed him right over the top of the trench he was going for. He lay there and one of the Argentinians tried to lean out to finish him off. He couldn't because I was still firing. Then I had a choice of staying there and firing, or I had a grenade. I thought: If I throw the grenade I'll neutralise the CO at the same time. I continued firing for what seemed like a lifetime. All of a sudden I heard a bang to my rear. It was some of 'A' Company with 66 mm rocket-launchers and M-79 grenade-launchers hitting the Argentinian bunker, which neutralised it completely. An M-79 went into another

135

one and next thing the white flags came out and the hands went up. At that stage I thought: I've survived this one, and ran up to the CO.

Two prisoners from the trench were handed over. I got to the CO, who at that stage was still conscious, although slipping into unconsciousness. I turned him over, he was lying on his back. I got his webbing off, found the wounds and applied shell dressings. What struck me was that there was very little blood, so that meant a lot of internal injuries. He was slipping into shock and we carried a drip containing saline solution for that sort of thing. I administered the drip to try and stop him going into deep shock. He took the whole litre of my drip and then I used his. Sergeant Hastings, one of the platoon sergeants, said we had to get him to the helicopter landing site, which was on the high ground. I kept him warm while Hastings and some of his blokes constructed a stretcher from the corrugated sheeting around the trench. Our first attempt at a stretcher collapsed, with the CO on it. It was one of those sorry states of war; it didn't do him any more harm than the injuries he had, but unfortunately he hit the ground. We reconstructed the stretcher, and carried him to the landing site.

He was completely unconscious and the helicopter didn't arrive. For a few minutes afterwards I stayed there, trying to keep him warm with extra windproofs and his own quilted jacket. He died. I felt slightly numb because COs are not supposed to die. The implication of the commanding officer taking on an enemy position from the front was comic book stuff you read about, you don't think it should happen. My own opinion was that he shouldn't have been there, but being 'H' Jones he was always going to be there because he was that type of CO. Once he died I thought: He's dead, I've survived, but I didn't have long to ponder on it because Major Keeble then took over command of the battalion; 'B' Company were starting their fight and Tac HQ has to go where the fighting is. We left the CO to be dealt with by 'A' company and headed off to rejoin the war.

The decision was taken to stop fighting for the day. We had to regroup in the dark. We had to take stock, see who was missing and organise our defences. The Argentine prisoners were there, moaning all night because they had casualties as well. It was not until later that night and first light in the morning that we could actually start evacuating

136

the casualties. I organised my blokes in a defensive position. We hadn't taken any warm kit with us. I only had windproof trousers and jacket, and a waterproof in one of my pouches. I organised the blokes and did what a sergeant has to do for his men. Then I had to start administering myself, clean the weapon and give myself a meal.

I sat down and thought: I'm lucky. I went numb and then the whole implication of what had happened throughout the day, the people who had died and the casualties I had seen started appearing before me. There was an eerie silence, it was pitch-dark. Freezing. The mind just ran riot and I felt tears trickling down the side of my face when I thought about good blokes who had died that day and the fact that more were likely to die tomorrow. A lump came to my throat and I lay there for a good couple of hours, going through the events of the day. They were the worst hours I ever experienced in my life. During the battle you don't get time to think about what you're doing, you just do what you are told, or what you are supposed to do. You have no time for emotions or any thought of your personal safety or whatever else is going on. You have one aim as a soldier: get to the enemy. It's only when the fighting has stopped and you have done your job for the day that you get to think about people dying and surviving. In my case it was surviving.

The Argentinians had left Goose Green a pigsty. We went into some of the houses and they had deliberately shit in the bath as opposed to the toilet. We made a mistake once they surrendered of letting them go back into the houses to collect their belongings. They did a lot of the damage then that they had not done previously. The homes stank, and I couldn't understand how any army, especially one supposed to be quite good, could allow themselves to degenerate into living in a pigsty. I could not feel less for the officers if I tried. They were contemptible for allowing their men to suffer the way they did. They had a lot of food and comforts whereas the soldiers had very little food, very little comfort. It was a conscript army and they treated their men in the most unprofessional way. The men I felt sorry for after a while, but the officers were contemptible.

We thought they had booby-trapped the settlements. The sheep pens were the prisoner-of-war cage, and next to them was a pile of ammunition that had to be moved. We had a rough idea it was booby-trapped and asked the Argentinian officers if they would move the ammunition for their own safety. They detailed off some men to help move the mortar ammunition and artillery shells. There was a booby trap which went Bang! The soldier next to it was caught in a vacuum of flames and explosives. We could not get to him. He was screaming and one of the soldiers present shot him to put him out of his misery. It was the only thing we could humanely do for him.

We didn't call Stanley 'Stanley', we called it 'Endex'. It's military language for when an exercise ends. Once it was over and we got to Stanley I thought: Let's pack up and go home, because on an exercise, once everything is finished, they get you out of the area as quick as they can, back to normality.

It was a hell of a shock when we got into Stanley. I thought: Bloody hell, was it all worth it? The Falklands being the Falklands and Stanley being where it is, the houses and the actual layout were quite a shock to the system. It took a bit of getting used to. My idea of a town is a European town, especially for the capital of a colony. I thought there would be proper houses but they were just shacks. Because of the occupation by the Argentines it was smelly, dirty, and not my idea of what Stanley was going to be. I walked around the corner and there it was in all its unsplendour.

We were stopped from going into the town because the Marines had to be seen to erect the Union flag above Government House, which was slightly unreal seeing as we were there before them. I was amazed to see Argentinians still walking around. My idea of a prisoner is when he is locked up in a cage, and it was very disturbing and bloody annoying that the Argentinians were walking around. It was some time before they were herded together and taken out to the airport.

Coming home we landed at Brize Norton. The earlier flights had been met by royalty and we all thought we would have a quiet arrival, sneak on the bus and go back to Aldershot. As we got off the aircraft we looked in the lounge and saw it full of people. We thought: Hello, something is up here. I went into the terminal and there was my wife, my daughter and son, my mum and dad, my brothers and mates from Guildford. To say I was choked would be a slight understatement. I don't know who cried first, me or the wife, because it was very emotional. And I still could not quite understand what all the fuss was about. I didn't think crying was a manly thing to do. I didn't sob, it was just sort of tears. They say that's permitted, although Paras don't cry. But emotions are emotions and sometimes you can keep them penned up, and sometimes you cannot. For me that was one time I couldn't. You are supposed to be hard and immune from that type of thing. I found out I was just as vulnerable as everybody else.

CHRIS KEEBLE

Major (now Lieutenant-Colonel ret.) Chris Keeble was second-in-command of the 2nd Battalion, the Parachute Regiment. He led 2 Para to victory at the battle of Goose Green after his CO, 'H' Jones, had been killed. He was awarded the DSO. He left the British army in 1987 and is now developing a leadership centre in Oxfordshire.

We had been working up to go off to Belize in Central America when the Argentines invaded the Falklands. We watched the Task Force sail off while we were held in reserve in preparation for supporting the Falklands operation if we were required. The Parachute Regiment has a great desire to maintain its standards and here was an opportunity to demonstrate them, so the battalion was keen to go. I think we had a fair idea it would come to war. They had captured the Islands and they didn't look as if they were going to remove themselves in a peaceable way, and there wasn't any alternative.

By the time we came to embarking on the *Norland*, we were not totally equipped or prepared for an offensive operation. NATO is a defensive alliance and we concentrate quite a lot on defending terrain. The only way to get the Falklands back was by attack, and we spent a lot of effort, in the week before we sailed, acquiring additional machine guns, M-79 grenade-launchers, and air-defence weapons to improve our ability to take the attack to the enemy. There was a great feeling that here was an opportunity to demonstrate everything that we had trained for in the Parachute Regiment.

There were a thousand people embarked on the ship. There was an atmosphere of frenzied activity, of getting acclimatised to these strange and cramped conditions, of acquiring all the seamanship skills that one

140

needs in case of a disaster at sea, perhaps if we had been torpedoed. We had to maintain our fitness, test-fire our weapons, exercise our command and control system. There was a massive amount to do. And we also had to cross the Equator and that's a serious business. That was one of these splendid affairs where we stopped all the training and played silly games and threw buckets of water over each other and were generally relaxed. Morale was very high indeed.

It was a long time between the sinking of the *Sheffield* and the actual landings. The soldiers felt quite vulnerable on the ship. There was a constant threat from Argentine submarines and we had to hold ourselves in instant readiness to fend off an attack. We had all our air-defence weapons deployed across the top of the ship, and machine-gun posts were welded in around all the corners. The whole ship was darkened at night and blacked out, like during the London blitz. All sound was removed. We sailed along through the darkness as a counter to this threat.

Although we are trained to be Paratroopers, what you're actually training people for is coping with fear. The process of jumping out of an aeroplane is a frightening business. It is a very useful way of getting a body of people collectively and individually to cope with uncertainty. They have to hold themselves in and have the wit and competence to suppress the natural desire to run, and get on with what we were supposed to be doing. And that was the attitude that was applied to the anti-submarine measures.

The day before the landings, there was an amazing sea mist which blanketed the whole area and protected us from Argentine aeroplanes. But one still felt like a fish out of water. After all we were soldiers, we had spent our whole lives training to operate on land. That was our element. So sitting in a floating ferry in the South Atlantic was unusual. It was different. We were anxious to get ashore, to get to grips with the Argentines.

We closed in to the Falklands at night. We had turned this ferry into an amphibious platform. The whole thing had been redesigned so that you could exit from the ship in an orderly and tactical manner at night on to the Royal Marines' assault boats. That was done reasonably efficiently. We had, after all, done our two-hour Royal Marine course round the bay

141

in one of their amphibious landing craft at Ascension Island, which is about all you need to become a Royal Marine. We had the naval guns bombarding Fanning Head, overlooking San Carlos, so there was that background noise. There were the dark red lights, columns of people streaming through the ship, slowly dropping down on to the assault boats. They formed up and then ran down through the darkened waters of San Carlos Harbour and on up to the beach. There was a nervous energy running through the whole thing.

I remember in my particular boat, when we hit the beach, the ramp went down and a naval order, which is part of their drill, I suppose, went out as: 'Troops Out'. And not a soul moved in the boat, because of course when you move Paratroopers collectively you don't shout 'Troops Out', you shout 'Go!'. This Royal Marine shouted again 'Troops Out', and nothing happened. And then a quick-witted sergeant-major shouted 'GO!!' and everybody flooded off the boat.

Our job was to capture Sussex Mountain. Part of Brigadier Julian Thompson's plan was to hold the high ground circling San Carlos Harbour. It was a ridge of land separating San Carlos from the nearby settlement at Goose Green. We had to climb to the top of this hill and secure it. We had about 120 lbs on our backs, we were like snails carrying our houses ashore. We couldn't leave our equipment on board because it could either be sunk or it might disappear over the horizon out of the clutches of the Argentine aeroplanes, so we had to carry it with us. We made this very long, slow and painful crawl up this hill at night. It took us hours of effort, particularly as we hadn't really maintained our fitness on the ship on the way down. Although we'd run round decks, the actual physical effort of carrying heavy loads over difficult country at night was considerable. And when I got up to the top of Sussex Mountain I was knackered.

Our principal task, apart from just occupying this piece of ground to avoid them taking it, was to protect the Rapier air-defence missile systems that were placed out once the landing was secure. And for the next six days we watched the Royal Navy being hammered by the Argentine aeroplanes. The light is very clear in the Falklands, it was very good weather. As you looked down into the Sound – hundreds of feet below you – you could see all the ships. And you then heard this roar of jets go right over us, just clipping the top of the hill, diving down into the harbour. Then you saw the plumes of water as the bombs went off. I was standing next to 'H' Jones on one occasion and he said: 'John Nott wanted a sub-service Navy – by God he's going to get it.' We saw the effect of the bombs against the ships, but we were too far away to actually see ships sinking, apart from the *Antelope*, which exploded with a tremendous ball of fire in the middle of the night and was then left sticking out of the water, burning, for the remainder of the time we were there.

Obviously we were very glad it wasn't us being hammered, but there was a growing frustration that we were sitting on this hill freezing our knackers off. It was cold up there, it was windy. There was snow, we were sitting in trenches half-full of water. Our soldiers were getting trench foot and we were slowly going downhill. We wanted to get off that mountain and get the war over.

We didn't ask to go to Goose Green. An order came through from the Brigadier's staff that we were to make a raid. This was then aborted and twenty-four hours later it was set up again and 'H' Jones made a plan to move the battalion down to Goose Green. But he had to leave a certain number of men up on Sussex Mountain because of the need to defend the Rapier missiles. So we set off in a great long 'Airborne snake' with about 400 men on the sixteen kilometres to Goose Green. 'H' was somewhere in the middle. There is a tactical way of moving across country, you don't have the CO at the front with a flag. 'H' Jones was a warrior, he wasn't a peacetime soldier. He was aggressive, he was determined and a charismatic leader. Everybody knew that he was in charge, and he knew what he wanted to do. He was generally right in what he wanted to do. And he made a plan to capture the place.

We moved down to a place called Camilla Creek, which was a small farm settlement about three or four miles from the actual start-line. We settled in there and acquired the intelligence we would need to make this attack.

We had several sources of intelligence. Brigade HQ had given what knowledge they had of the place and earlier, on the boat, we had studied the topography and the intelligence layout of their forces. The day before the attack we captured an Argentine intelligence officer who had come out in a Land-Rover to get some information about the settlement, and we did a tactical questioning of him. He gave us a fair amount of information. We put out our own patrols and snipers on to the ground to have a look, so we had a fair idea what was going on.

The battlefield at Goose Green was a corridor about five miles long and one mile wide, flat – bare-arsed. There was no cover, and that was the most serious deficiency about it. Halfway down, running across the direction from which we would approach, was a ridge-line where they built a defensive position. It was not an easy battlefield to fight over, very limited opportunity to manoeuvre and you didn't have to be von Clausewitz to work out that you only had two options: either you came from the north or from the south.

'H' wanted to try and capture the settlements of Darwin and Goose Green at night because the battlefield was so bare. He constructed a plan to manoeuvre his three companies of about eighty men each down this corridor, supporting each other, with artillery and naval gunfire from HMS *Arrow* offshore. They would fire us in, and by maintaining momentum and aggression we would get those two settlements before daylight. That was the plan. But plans don't always work out like that, because on your side you have 400 people trying to make it work and, in this case, we had 1,500 people on the other side trying to screw it up. Inevitably it went wrong. We made fairly good progress during the night. The Argentines fought hard. They had had two months to prepare their positions and we didn't know the ground.

This was our first battle and it was confusing; it was dark and very noisy. It was raining and we made slow progress. Come dawn we had only gone a third of the way towards achieving our objective. I had always thought that when you fought a battle, somehow you'd start and you'd go up this graph until you won it. Or you would start and you went sliding down the graph to defeat. It was nothing like that at all. Sometimes you were winning, things were going really well, and you were buoyant; your morale was good and you felt terrific. Other times you heard of casualties, you were under artillery fire, you didn't understand what was happening on the battlefield. You were grovelling in the dirt trying to avoid somebody's machine-gun fire – it could have been your own, it could have been the enemy's. You were losing control of your own fear. It was very confusing, and you lurched from success to apparent failure. And that's how it went all the time.

By dawn the battalion had reached the main enemy defensive position along the ridge, a low line of hills which dominated all the approaches.

The death of HMS Ardent: *'The fires of hell were burning in that ship . . . it looked as if it had been ripped open with a can opener.' Argentine pilots bombed the ship on 21 May 1982 – the morning of the British landings at San Carlos.*

Major Ewan Southby-Tailyour
(Royal Marines).

Guardsman Wayne Trigg
(Welsh Guards).

Lieutenant Alastair Mitchell
(Scots Guards).

Going ashore: Top: *Men of 3 Commando Brigade take the landing craft to San Carlos on 21 May 1982, the day of the British landings.*
Above: *Welsh Guardsmen – survivors from the bombing of* Sir Galahad *– arrive at Bluff Cove.*

'I have a rendezvous with Death
At some disputed barricade,
When spring comes back with rustling shade,
And apple blossoms fill the air –
I have a rendezvous with Death . . .
And I to my pledged word am true,
I shall not fail that rendezvous.'

Alan Seeger, World War One poet, killed in action in 1916.

General Mario Benjamin Menendez, Argentine military governor of the Malvinas, in his command post.

Brigadier Julian Thompson, who led 3 Commando Brigade, arrives back in Britain at Southampton.

The Community Centre at Goose Green, prison for 114 local Islanders kept under armed guard for twenty-nine days by Argentine troops. They waited helpless inside while British paratroopers waged a battle to rescue them.

Two of the liberators from the 2nd Battalion the Parachute Regiment (2 Para):-
Above left: *Sergeant-Major Barry Norman, who served as bodyguard to Lieutenant-Colonel 'H' Jones and who was with him when he died.*
Above right: *The man who led 2 Para to victory after the death of their commanding officer: Major Chris Keeble with his family outside Buckingham Palace after receiving his DSO.*

'J' Company, 42 Commando: the men who were originally captured by the Argentine army when the Falklands were first invaded and who then returned to help recapture the Islands.
Top: *On board* Canberra *on the way back to the Islands.*
Above: *At Government House in Port Stanley shortly after the Argentine surrender on 14 June 1982.*

You couldn't go around because there was water on either side. Two companies were fighting: 'A' Company was on the left around Darwin, 'B' Company was on the right. At dawn they both came to a grinding halt. 'A' Company's battle was a shambles of corporals and toms [privates] fighting individually, trying to make progress yard by yard against the enemy trenches. We had hoped to get artillery support but the wind was blowing at fifty to sixty knots across the ground and it was so great that you couldn't drop the shells where you wanted and so you didn't risk firing them. The mortars had run out of ammunition because we could only carry so much down with us. There were no helicopters to supply more mortar ammunition. We had hoped to get the Harriers to give us a real punch to our progress but they couldn't take off from the carriers because of fog. 'Sod's Law' was operating well that morning.

In order to get the attack going on to the left flank, 'H' took his Tactical HQ forward. He had with him radio operators, minders, another officer to help him with the command and control: about ten to fifteen people in all. He moved them up towards 'A' company to find out what was going on. I was 800 metres back, sitting with my alternative Tactical HQ which we had arranged to cope with the very situation that occurred, which was of course that 'H', in regenerating the attack of 'A' Company, lost his life.

He and I, and the signallers in the HQ, had prepared a phrase, 'Sunray is down', so that I would know that something was wrong with him, which would be the key for me to step into the breach. And in this confusion over the radio came this cry: 'Sunray is down.' I couldn't believe it and I actually asked for verification. Colour Sergeant Blackburn, his signaller, shouted again: ' "Sunray is down" for Christ's sake.' Then the surge of apprehension and fear ran through me: Would I perform well enough? What do I do now? What's the situation up there?

I spent twenty minutes trying to get a clear picture of what was actually happening 800 metres ahead of me. I had one company left – Phil Neame's 'D' Company – and the question was whether to reinforce the shambles of 'A' company or to try and sort out Johnny Crosland and 'B' Company, who were pinned down on a forward slope by the machine guns of the Argentine defensive position at Boca House [on the far right].

All that ran through my mind, and eventually I got a clear picture. It was as clear a picture as I was ever going to get. I then set off towards Johnny Crosland's company. We took with us the Milan anti-tank missiles * and additional ammunition. I also took the Brigade liaison officer, Hector Gullan, who had a direct link to the Brigade commander. As we set off over the hill, in came two Pucara aircraft and strafed the position behind us, but we had to ignore them. In the time that it took me to get up to 'B' Company, Phil Neame – the canny Phil Neame, who commanded 'D' Company – had realised that he could outflank the Boca House position by slipping his company down on to the beach. There was a small wall between the edge of the grassland and the beach. His men crawled the 800 or 900 metres along this little shelf until they were adjacent to the enemy defensive position at Boca House. Brilliant. With a combination of the Milan anti-tank missiles which fire over 2,000 metres and have pin-point accuracy, we were able to destroy the enemy machine guns which were pinning us down. With the application of artillery, the skilful use of 'D' Company, we had outflanked them. The enemy position collapsed and they surrendered. It meant the beginning of the end had started. We had left Sussex Mountain some forty hours earlier, so we had been on the go since then with very little sleep.

We were now towards last light of the day. We were tired. We'd run out of ammunition and there was actually no way we could break into the settlement. We had a lot of casualties. There were prisoners of war all over the place who had to be gathered in. We had run out of steam basically, so it seemed to me the best thing was to consolidate, dig in where we stood. We could redistribute the ammunition, use the ammunition we had captured from the Argentines which was the same calibre, get in some more artillery and reinforcements, and get out our casualties and prisoners of war. That's what we did at night.

But we still hadn't broken their will, and we hadn't got the firepower to do that, not totally . . . they were still fighting from inside the settlement. The pleas we had put through the system to get Harrier air support finally came through. As dusk settled two Harriers came in from the west and dropped cluster bombs on the perimeter defences right next to the settlement at Goose Green. A third Harrier strafed the area

---

* These wire-guided missiles were used in the Falklands to knock out enemy bunkers.

with machine-gun fire. Then a silence fell over the settlement. All their shooting stopped and for the first time I felt: We've won, they've cracked.

I had a feeling that there was a chance that we could take this settlement in the morning so long as we reinforced ourselves. Then as I moved back up into the area of our headquarters in a gully to the back of Darwin Hill, somebody came up to me and said: 'There are 114 civilians locked up in the village hall in the centre of Goose Green.'

There was no way we could attack the place because we would kill the very people we'd come to save. I was by now feeling very tired. I was confident that we could work out a solution but I had no idea how to do it. I prayed. There is nothing in the textbooks which tells you how to solve that problem.

It seemed to me that there were two options: either you offered them a surrender or you reinforced yourself massively and went in there hard and fast and destroyed everything. I spoke to the Brigadier and he agreed to send down another company, with more artillery and ammunition and more firepower in the morning from Harriers.

I sent two captured Argentine officers down into the settlement with a note which explained my two options: surrender or take the military consequences. They took the surrender option and we met in a small hut on the airfield. I met the three military commanders there and they agreed to my terms. They would assemble on the sports field.

Eventually about 150 people in three ranks marched up and formed a hollow square. An officer in an Argentine air force uniform walked up to me and saluted. I asked for his pistol and took it. When we looked closely we saw that all these people weren't soldiers at all. They were airmen. We reckoned there must have been 150 of them in the settlement.

I said: 'Where are the soldiers?'

He indicated the settlement and said: 'They're coming.'

Three or four of us moved forward – there were only about eight of us altogether at the surrender – to look down into the settlement. There, to our amazement, must have been 1,000 men, marching up in three ranks. We just held our breath.

Somebody murmured: 'I hope they don't change their minds.'

They came up and formed a hollow square as well. They took their helmets off and their equipment and laid their weapons down. The military commander handed me his pistol and that was it.

*

I think it is a measure of the soldiers who fought in that campaign, that despite the fatigue, the weather, the fear, despite all the slumps where you bottom out and think you are losing, you still have the will to go on. And the man whose will is sustained the longest is the winner. The reality though is nothing like a rehearsal. It's dark, it's confusing, there is an enormous amount of noise, there's this notion to keep on going in a coherent, balanced way. If you're a 'tom' you're working with three other people in a group of four with a machine gun, and there's another group of four on the right-hand side making a section. And there are three sections and you are moving across ground. You're trying to maintain the balance between the two machine guns. There's incoming fire to you, there's white phosphorus going off to provide smoke and illumination, there's tracer coming towards you and going away from you. There's fear running through you. You've got your bayonet on the end of your rifle. You're moving in short bursts of activity from bits of cover to bits of cover, slowly eating up the ground towards the enemy. You're trying to cover the last crucial, difficult, bloody 300 metres to the enemy and he's fighting you from his trenches. You may have to fight through a minefield, you can't be deterred by that. You may see somebody go down beside you with some awful wound, you may be tempted to stop and bandage him up but you can't. You've got to keep going. You close up towards the trenches. You throw grenades, you fire your weapon, you bayonet. It's savage gutter fighting. Everything you've ever experienced before is nothing like it. It is basic killing.

The hardest bit comes when you have got to close those last 300 metres, when you place your body and your firepower and your ability to manoeuvre at the enemy. You move as hard and as fast as you can against their trenches. You don't piss about. War is about the application of violence.

The philosophy of our soldiers – whether it is our regiment or any other regiment – is that we are a body of people welded together by our traditions, by our regiment, by a feeling of togetherness. We're a family of people and you have to remember that. We all know each other, we know each other's families. This is a body of people who would die for each other. If you run away, you're running away from all that. It's like withdrawing the love of your mother, it's that kind of commitment.

We have to win, the mission is paramount. It is more important than anything else. It's death before dishonour, the old-fashioned values, if you like.

On the way south we had impressed on people continually the importance of winning, of achieving the mission. Now the problem with all that is that we're all human; if you dedicate yourself to the mission, what happens if you get injured, what happens to your morale then? It takes a major plummet. What happens if you see your buddy shot away? – there's a real crisis. So there had to be another measure to sustain morale, and the principal thing that has to be provided is a very efficient and worthwhile casualty care system. Our brilliant doctor, Steve Hughes, on the way down introduced a system where we could take all our equipment with us so that if a man was injured you could give him first-class, almost surgical care, on the battlefield at the site of wounding. They had morphine stashed away inside the linings of their helmets. They had an intravenous fluid pack, maintained at body temperature, inside their shirt which could be knocked up immediately. They had their field dressings, four of them, and some antibiotics. They had this self-care kit on them and felt confident that if they were injured, the trained medics among the troops would look after them. So we were able to maintain this balance between mission and morale. In addition, you have to have this desire to maintain the momentum, to maintain the aggression and provide the self-sacrifice to achieve the objective.

I take no credit for the destruction of the Argentine defences at Goose Green because I didn't do it. I am a commander, I press the buttons. The people who won the battle at Goose Green were the 'toms' and the junior NCOs who converted what I call the 'Chinagraph drawing' into reality. They actually do the dirty gutter business of bringing violence to the enemy to break their will.

We won because we were able to sustain our will longer than they were, they bottled out sooner, even though it often hung in the balance. It would be very interesting to compare the slumps in our battle with how they saw it at the time. If they had counter-attacked at dawn they would have thrown us off the battlefield because we were totally outgunned and wrong-footed. But maybe they didn't perceive what was actually happening; maybe our momentum was so fast that we didn't give them time to react to what we were doing.

When we liberated Goose Green itself I was expecting a hero's welcome – you know, the garlands of flowers, hugs and kisses. But they're a pretty dour people. They cope with many misadventures in their lives, with the weather and other disasters. They were jubilant obviously to begin with. They were crying because they'd been locked up for twenty-nine days in the settlement, in this little village hall. Once they were liberated out in the daylight their emotions ran free. The children ran around. But it quickly wore off. Nevertheless, there was enough of an emotion to realise that we had done what we said we would do. We had come and liberated these people who had their freedom taken away by the Argentine invasion and that's what made it all worth while for me. After Goose Green I insisted that we bury our dead and give the soldiers time to grieve. It's important. A hole was dug by a bulldozer on the side of a hill and we literally carried each of our friends and put them down side by side and we said our prayers and cried. It was a pretty bad moment. Then we left and got on with the war.

When we got to Stanley we had a mixture of relief at being alive, and sorrow that we hadn't got everybody with us, coupled with thoughts about the futility of war and how important it is to prevent it ever happening again. I don't think there were any best moments. The whole affair is one of tragedy. War is a messy, dirty business. We should never ever allow ourselves to go to war.

ERNESTO ORLANDO PELUFO

Lieutenant Ernesto Orlando Pelufo was a cadet at the Argentine Military Academy when he was sent to the Malvinas. The authorities graduated some of the trainee officers early so that they could go to the Islands.

Some of my relatives come from Britain, and knowing the British character I was not surprised that they decided to send a Task Force to the South Atlantic. My feeling was that if you tread on the lion's tail it sometimes turns round and bites you.

I hope one day there will be a diplomatic solution. I was not really sure that it would come to war. Our occupation of the Islands was a way of marking sovereignty. However, later on I realised that combat was inevitable. I was a fourth-year cadet at the Military Academy and I had to get up early to wake up the other cadets. The first thing I did every morning was to turn on the radio and listen to the news. That morning I switched on and learned we had recovered the Malvinas and told my other cadets about it. So the officer on duty on the parade ground greeted us: 'On the day of the recovery of the Malvinas – 1st Company – Good Morning!' That's how it all started for me.

I was sent to Goose Green and eventually found myself on the front line. The other company had been fighting all night. There was a brief lull and I knew the British Paratroopers were coming towards us. In the middle of this lull in the battle Lieutenant Estevez wanted to start a counter-attack. I told him what the situation was. I had about forty men under my command. Our flanks were not adequately protected and we were in a difficult situation. I remained quite calm in spite of everything. My mission was to hold the position. I was not thinking that

I would die. I was waiting. It was a very confusing situation when we saw troops approaching. At first we were not sure whether it was the enemy or part of our 12th Regiment that was withdrawing towards our line. We thought they could be our troops. They knew what route to take through the minefields. In fact, they were British troops and later we found out they were being guided through the minefields by Islanders who had escaped from Goose Green.

At that moment the combat started. Mortar shells exploded all around us, we jumped into our foxholes and opened up with automatic weapons. There was shooting all over the place, intense fire raining on both sides. The mortar bombs and their wire-guided missiles exploded very close to our positions, so we had to wait for a pause in the bombardment to come out and shoot at them. We carried on like this for about three hours. Several of our soldiers and officers died. One of them was Lieutenant Estevez, who was killed while he was transmitting the enemy's position to our artillery.

I didn't have much time to think about the dead or about my own safety. I did not think about my family or what I had left behind. I had done that before the battle. My duty now was to lead and to motivate my men with battle cries, especially the war chant of the province of Corrientes, which made our blood boil. We were all ready to die. The Paras got closer and closer. They were trying to outflank us. They avoided a frontal assault because we were putting up a spirited resistance. However, their fire was very precise. I remember seeing a corporal receive a direct hit from a wire-guided missile. A soldier in my trench fell wounded and I took over his automatic rifle and opened fire, but still the enemy continued in its attempt to outflank us. A soldier making very effective use of an anti-personnel missile-launcher was also hit and the launcher destroyed.

A man next to me had his rifle hit. He said: 'Sir they are very very close.' We could hear the British troops shouting at us to surrender in English and in Spanish. There were explosions all around us. At that moment I was shot in the head and fell to the bottom of my trench. Thank God the bullet didn't go through my skull. The soldier next to me gave me first-aid. At first I thought: I'm dying, but when I fell to the bottom of the trench I realised I was still alive and I still had hopes of continuing the fight. I couldn't even stand up though. The soldier treated me and when he saw the wound he said: 'Don't worry sir, it's only a flesh wound.' I tried to stand up and pick up a rifle but I couldn't. I felt very dizzy. I told the soldier to continue firing and to order the other positions to prepare to resist the enemy assault with bayonets if necessary. They continued shouting at us to surrender but I couldn't stand the idea of being defeated, of surrendering so quickly, of giving up something that was really mine – the territory of the Malvinas.

The combat had turned into individual fights from foxhole to foxhole, every man against his own enemy, trying to survive by killing him. Now it wasn't only mortar bombs but also bullets all around us. I finally understood that it was useless to continue sacrificing lives, that all was lost and there was no point in continuing the fight. I told a soldier to tie a napkin to his rifle and wave it. He was shot at and they hit the rifle. He got back into the trench very frightened. I told him to go up and wave it again, so he came out of the position and then we saw the British coming out into the open. They were going to take us prisoner. Our own soldiers started coming out of the trenches.

I was still at the bottom of my trench. I couldn't move, because not only did I have my head wound, I also had a piece of shrapnel in my left leg. I was trying to get up and help the other wounded in the trench. A British soldier arrived and asked me in English if I was all right. At first I didn't understand him. I saw him standing there pointing a sub-machine gun at me and I thought to myself: Well, this is it. They don't want prisoners – it would just make life difficult for them. Then he asked me again: 'Are you okay?' and I realised that he was not going to shoot me after all. He told me that the war was over for me and that I would be going home. So I felt a mixture of frustration because of defeat and relief because it was all over. Afterwards, I analysed every stage of the battle and thought about things I could have done, but I realised that I had done what I could to hold my position.

I remember all the soldiers who fell in the battle. I remember their bravery and conviction. I will never forget when they took us prisoner and we saw the enemy picking up our dead in the middle of the smoke and the mist. But we were at peace with ourselves because we were convinced that our cause was just. Now we think about those who stayed behind as our sentries, with the crosses on their graves marking our sovereignty of the Islands.

EWAN SOUTHBY-TAILYOUR

Major Ewan Southby-Tailyour returned to the Falklands with the British Task Force several years after having commanded the Royal Marines detachment in the Islands. An expert in amphibious warfare, his detailed knowledge of the Falklands was crucial in drawing up the invasion plans.

From 1978 to 1979 I commanded the Royal Marine detachment of forty men. A year was quite a long time to spend in the Falklands and everyone was encouraged to undertake a hobby of some sort. As a yachtsman I decided to re-examine the old charts of the coastline around the Islands. Most of the bays and anchorages a yachtsman might use were unsurveyed close inshore. Yachtsmen like to tuck their boats right in, away from the bad weather you get in the South Atlantic, so that was the task I set myself for the year. There were 15,000 miles of coastline roughly, and I surveyed about 6,000 of them. My job in the Marines is as a landing craft officer, and it was difficult to look at a beach as a yachtsman without also looking at it from the point of view of amphibious landings. We looked at a couple of beaches, just in case the Argentines might invade at some future date, but the rest were done purely for my own pleasure and for the possible help of yachtsmen who might visit the Islands.

When the invasion came none of the people in charge of planning the operation to retake the Islands had any idea of possible beaches and landing points. The afternoon 3 Commando Brigade was mobilised to go to the Falklands, I just scribbled on a map with a felt-tip pen everything I could – because everyone was in a rush to look at something. No one really had much idea what was involved. I went through the options in the Stanley, San Carlos and Port Sussex areas. Subsequently in HMS *Fearless* we used much more detailed maps and charts. People were able to look at them in simple terms because I had written down how many miles by sea, how many miles by land, for each possible landing point. I was also able to indicate where there could be no landings, and from this information Special Forces patrols of the SBS and SAS were able to go and check beaches. It was important they didn't waste their time on hundreds of beaches and landing areas which I knew were useless. This information was not known to anyone else and all I did was save them time and get them to home in on the likely options.

I would only be called in for specific discussions which usually took place in the Brigadier's cabin, a pleasant place to brainstorm after dinner in the evening. Several people would be there. Often Brigadier Julian [Thompson] would be in his dressing-gown, in his chair at the desk, pointing with his toe to the maps on the floor. I and the commander of the Royal Artillery Regiment would be on our hands and knees on the carpet for hours in the evening. Julian's big toe would suddenly point to a place and say: 'What happens there?' I probably know his big toe better than anyone else. They would have a particular option and then I was able to go away, sort through my own slides, photographs and original notes and brief them more fully.

Amphibious landing is acknowledged to be at the scholarship level of military operations. The military and naval requirements are so totally different. The military did not want to land so far away from Stanley that it meant a long yomp. On the other hand, landing close to Stanley meant very exposed naval anchorages, both to the easterly gales and to Exocet attack, aircraft and submarines. The navy liked the idea of coming into the sheltered waters of the Sound; we didn't like the idea of having to walk across the Falklands. We wanted to be able to take as many beaches as possible so you could quickly get ashore in an all-round defensive position to counter any attack from the Argentines.

We homed in on San Carlos for a number of reasons. Militarily we could contain the anchorage and look outwards and effectively meet any Argentine counter-attack. The navy could carry out the initial landings in Falkland Sound and, once we had taken the inland water of San Carlos, the ships could then move in. When we heard that it had only been visited by small parties of Argentinians we really couldn't believe our luck. Knowing the area I was very surprised that the Argentinians had not used Ajax Bay as a barracks. Of course, the Argentinians are influenced by the Americans and believed that we were also. The Argentinians therefore thought that if they were doing it they would land in Stanley, and assumed we would do the same because we had American influence. We don't do it that way. Apart from anything else it would have caused terrible and totally unforgivable casualties to civilians and it is just not the British way of doing things. We prefer a rather more subtle approach to these matters.

(Two weeks after the British landings at San Carlos the Welsh Guards were moved by ship. Their destination: Bluff Cove.)

There were serious time and tactical problems. We had troops far forward on the south flank which needed to be reinforced as quickly as possible. The Guards had to be moved quickly and there were no helicopters. Walking – yomping – would have taken an unacceptably long time. To be honest they probably weren't up to it: they certainly were not as fit as the Marines and Parachute Regiment for obvious reasons; I don't think any blame should be laid on them for that.

During the day on 7 June we had been offloading the landing ship *Sir Tristram* in Fitzroy [next to Bluff Cove] as fast as we could because we wanted to get her back to the comparative safety of San Carlos during the night. The ship's captain invited me to dinner; a lovely haven of sophistication in the middle of this ghastly business. After dinner we sat over a glass of port in his cabin and discussed in clear terms his worry and my concern over his ship staying another day, exposed to possible enemy air attack in Fitzroy. I wrote in my diary that night when I went to bed: 'This ship is in grave danger of being attacked by tomorrow morning.' We had not quite finished offloading the ammunition and I knew then she was going to have to stay there for the following day. My last comments in my diary that night made it absolutely clear to me that I did not want to be on board that ship during the day. There was no doubt in my mind, or the captain's mind, that she was in grave danger. She had been there one full day. She wasn't going to get away with it for a second day.

The following morning the captain came into my cabin in a rush and said: 'I don't think you're going to believe this Ewan, but there is another logistics ship in the anchorage and I think she has got a lot of men on board.' We both ran up to his bridge, and there facing us, inshore and probably only about 200 yards from the shore, was *Sir Galahad*. Through the binoculars we could clearly see dozens of men on the sterngate waiting for transport ashore. It was quite clear, particularly in view of our discussion the night before, that not only were the ships in great danger, but anybody, particularly masses of men on board, would be in danger. If there were men in bulk on board ships like that, even on exercise, you get them ashore first. You get the men out of the way. Even forgetting the Argentine air attacks, we wanted the men off that ship to the beach 200 yards away.

Uppermost in my mind, and the minds of many other people, was the Argentinian air threat. We had Wickham Heights to the north of us, where we were convinced they had observation posts. They had allowed one ship to sit there for the whole of one day, and now there were two ships. The 350 men on this ship had to be got off. The beach was twenty minutes away in the landing craft. It was much better that I got them off.

I put it to the most senior officer that I could find on the stern of *Galahad* that my considered and professional opinion as a landing craft officer, and somebody involved in amphibious warfare for almost all of my career, was that they should get off first and then wait. He was adamant that Bluff Cove was his destination and not Fitzroy. I was equally adamant that I was not going to take him to Bluff Cove in anything in daylight. I was proved correct only a few hours later when one of my landing craft was sunk. Unfortunately they were not prepared to go ashore and wait. To be fair they had been messed around quite a lot back in San Carlos, marching and then coming back, and then setting off and coming back. But they were in grave danger from enemy action and indeed ordinary accidents on board; there was no doubt in my mind about that.

The landing craft and the powered raft which I had to offload *Sir Tristram* had a load of ammunition on board. It was pointed out to me that men and ammunition do not travel in the same vehicles. The officer said he wouldn't put his men in a mixed load of ammunition. I explained to him that this was war and we don't operate the peacetime restrictions during war and that his men were in grave danger. I think that was probably the most serious and most often made point that I put across. It happens like that in war. You throw aside those minor peacetime restrictions. I could have got those men off in twenty minutes, no question whatsoever. Unfortunately the conversation then became rather less military and all sorts of things were levied between us. I accused him of not taking the advice of somebody who had been doing this all this life and who had witnessed Argentinian air attacks a week earlier in San Carlos.

For reasons best known to themselves, the officers decided not to take the word of a Royal Marine major and would only take an order from somebody senior. The conversation reverted to this ridiculous one of the comparative ranks between a Royal Marine major and an army major. I don't think it made or should have made any difference at all. I was the man on the spot acting for the Commodore [Mike Clapp], trying to offload these ships. Anybody with any professional sense would have taken the advice of the on-the-spot expert, regardless of rank. Unfortunately I was not wearing the rank of a lieutenant-colonel, who as far as I can make out was the only man he was prepared to listen to. There weren't that many Royal Marine lieutenant-colonels [around] on that day. And so we continued the argument.

For all these reasons the men were not allowed ashore. If I had put them ashore they could have waited until night-time, when I was very happy to take them round to Bluff Cove by a route that we had already proved, or they could have walked during daylight hours towards their objective of Bluff Cove.

I was getting more and more angry and upset that somebody who knew nothing of amphibious warfare or of being at war would not take the advice of, dare I say it, an expert. So in an extreme rage, which is the only time I felt this emotion throughout the whole war, I went ashore in the landing craft. I didn't want to stay on board that ship any longer than I wanted his men to stay on board. I personally did not want to suffer another Argentinian air attack on a most likely target. I told him he was behaving extremely irresponsibly and that I would not be held responsible for what happened to his men. Of course, tragically, three or four hours later I was proved absolutely correct.

That's where my part in this tragic saga ended, in a fit of rage and disgust that people would not listen to me. I went up the hill and took coffee with some Islanders, and a few hours later I witnessed the bombing of these two ships.

I didn't see anything to begin with. One heard the unmistakable noise of fast jets and those of us in the kitchen of the house up on the hill jumped to the window. It was quite clear they were not our jets and we saw the aircraft attacking *Tristram* and *Galahad*. Instantly there was smoke – from *Tristram* first. There was thick black smoke. I didn't see any visible signs of any drama on board *Galahad* at that moment, but I think there must have been a second attack that came in. I didn't see that because I went back to the kitchen. The girls in the kitchen burst into tears. It was the first they had seen of the war, the real war, and they were watching through the window. I knew that my fears, my very worst fears, had come about.

I ran down to the beach – it was about half a mile away. Already men were coming ashore in the most ghastly state and there was nothing I could do. In one of those strange human arrangements I stripped off my coat and jersey and picked up a stretcher, and carried stretchers for the next two hours, feeling I suppose subconsciously that having been involved in allowing this to happen, I must atone for my inability to prevent those men being bombed. Those two hours as a stretcher-bearer were certainly the most emotionally sapping thing I have ever been involved in.

I think in my career that was the most angry I have ever been. It was certainly the only time that I have felt almost shame at being involved in something which had gone wrong. Though I blame myself partly for not insisting with even more vigour that the men were brought ashore, I feel that I am not actually to blame for the deaths of those men. And it gets through to me even now.

CHRIS WHITE

Chris White served in the Royal Marines with the 1st Raiding Squadron. He was aboard the Royal Fleet Auxiliary vessel *Sir Galahad* when it was bombed by enemy aircraft and forty-eight soldiers and crew were killed, including thirty-eight Welsh Guardsmen.

The training on the way south was intense. We learned all kinds of military skills in excess of our normal training. There were even lessons in Spanish. There were intelligence briefings, actual maps were presented to every section of the areas where we would be expected to go in. As a bit of a ham artist I was asked to draw some of these maps together in detail so that at different briefings the men could see what they'd actually be looking at when they got down there.

Morale was good because we were in the tropics. We were conscious of the fact that the world was watching us, especially the Russians. They kept on sailing in and out of the Task Force. We all became qualified in light and morse and were sending messages to each other on our little hand torches, much to the annoyance of the Admiral. He once flashed a message ordering it to be stopped and there were a few rude answers sent back.

The night before the landings we got absolutely screaming drunk. It wasn't planned. The non-drinkers on board put their beer to one side. The rest started drinking and singing and having a good time. At about four o'clock in the morning the captain was sending down messages to ask us to tone it down a bit, to keep the noise down. We were actually within land sight of the Falklands at the time.

We partied until about 4.30 a.m. and slept where we fell. Reveille was at 7 a.m. and people were getting up and scratching their heads and wiping their eyes and thought to themselves: Something is happening today – Oh yes, we're going to war. We were in high spirits, and although we were well prepared it didn't seem possible that it was actually going to happen.

I started taking it personally after the first air raid. We were in San Carlos at first light, getting ready to unload. Our fibreglass raiding craft were made ready for a shore landing. About nine or ten o'clock it was very quiet, a flat calm motion. Then it started: 'Aircraft, sixty miles from the west, closing. Aircraft twenty miles from the west, closing.' 'Jesus Christ.' 'Open fire!!' And off went the guns. We were quite amazed to see the aircraft coming in. We were watching them as if it was Farnborough Air Display; 'Oh look, there's one.' It started to sink in that they were dropping bombs. We suddenly realised: 'Yes this is it, we're here and it's happening.' No amount of training can prepare you for it.

After a day of ferrying equipment the squadron was sent to the forward operating base. We went ashore in formation, down through San Carlos, passing HMS *Antelope*, which had been attacked and subsequently evacuated because there were unexploded bombs on board. We saw the hole in the side of the ship where a bomb had entered. The bomb disposal teams were on board trying to defuse it.

Later two of our raiding craft were required to go forward to Teal Inlet. We were to liaise with the Special Forces and were moved round on *Sir Galahad*. We sailed from San Carlos on a flat calm and first had to call into Bluff Cove/Fitzroy to let the Welsh Guards disembark. There was some problem with the ship – something about the hydraulics failing on the rear end. Instead of being in and out at first light we were still there at mid-afternoon, still not disembarking. A corporal and I were walking around the ship checking the craft, watching television, doing what we wanted to do and resting.

In the afternoon we were watching a movie in the recreation space. Then it came over the tannoy system: 'Air Raid Warning Red', followed by 'Action Stations!! Action Stations!!' The men at the back of the room started running forward. They were in their anti-flash gear, running for the Bofors guns on the bows of the ship. We started to stand up when the ship was hit by a bomb which went straight down into the hold, on top of a pallet of mortar bombs being pushed by some of the Welsh Guards ready for lifting out. It immediately exploded.

Two rockets sliced through the side of the ship across the room where we were sitting and blew up in the adjacent galley. It was all very sudden. One minute we were getting up from the settees and the next everything was going over to the left-hand side. The lights went out and everything became very muffled. There were shouts and screams in the room, then it went completely quiet. I was lying on the floor and started to give myself a personal check. I was bleeding from the head, but there was nothing desperately wrong with me and I knew where the door was. I started thinking about getting myself out and I tried to get up on to my knees but the thickness of the smoke stopped me breathing straight away. So I had to go back down to the floor. Unfortunately I was in someone else's remains at that time. I felt it but I couldn't see it. I started making my way to the exit. A chap from the back of the room, very very muffled because of the smoke and the darkness, started screaming that he had lost his leg.

That was the biggest deciding point in my life, whether or not I was going to go and help him or just get out. Nobody would have ever known, because it was just him and me left alive in the room. I decided I wanted to be a hero. So I went back for him and we were calling to each other through the darkness. I was desperately trying to talk myself into turning round and making my way to the exit.

I found Kevin Woodford by accident. I must have trodden on the stump of his leg because the next thing I knew, a fist came out of the darkness and clobbered me one. Kevin was obviously hysterical. I couldn't find my morphine or his morphine. We carry it round our necks, it's called 'Omnipon'. Everything was confused. He was a big man and the only thing I could do was to put my arms underneath his arms and start dragging him along the floor in the direction of where I knew the exit was. All the armchairs and settees had turned into barricades. I couldn't breathe because of the smoke. I very quickly lost all my strength. I was losing control completely.

I got him about three-quarters of the way down the room when I whispered to him that I had to leave him and I was going to go and get help. And he lay down quietly. He was out of the immediate flames anyway, and I started to feel my way along the wall, the bulkhead, in the direction of where I knew the door was. I came across another wall

162

going in the other direction, it just didn't communicate at all. I knew there should be a door there. What I couldn't see was where one of the rockets had gone through and blasted in the galley. The actual wall of the ship had peeled back and formed a small wall as well. I got a bit upset because there was a final broadcast on board the ship: 'Hands to lifeboat stations.' Being in the dark with the dead, the flames and the smoke and not knowing your way out, knowing that there should be a door there and there isn't – I started running round like a headless chicken.

Somehow I found myself out on the upper deck and there were men outside with breathing apparatus. After I finished throwing up, my one saving factor is that I told them there was a man in there with his leg off. I told them basically where he was. And that was it. I was evacuated from the ship. I managed to get to the bows and past the hold which was blowing up. There was a lot of mess coming out of there. Everybody was sitting by the bows, burned people, people with their arms and legs off, they were sitting very quietly completely dosed up with morphine. We just waited our turn calmly and were lifted off by helicopter.

I don't remember a lot after that, apart from the ride in the helicopter, which I think was more frightening than the *Sir Galahad*. They had taken all the windows out in case it crashed so it made a heck of a racket. All the wounded were taken to a ship. I was very emotionally distressed because as far as I was concerned I'd killed a man. No matter what reasoning I was going to give myself, I'd laid him down and I'd left him in a burning compartment with his leg off. It started doing strange things to me. I was being counselled by the medical staff in the sick bay. I was talking about death constantly.

During the night some time I must have wandered into the galley, where there was a pile of Argentine weapons which had obviously been taken from the prisoners of war at San Carlos. They were using this place as storage. So I helped myself to a 9 mm pistol with the intention of stopping this crushing guilt. Somebody had seen me and the gun was taken from me almost immediately by the medical staff. I was sitting back in the sick bay, taking it out from underneath my jumper. It was in the belt of my trousers. The surgeon who was there as I was taking it out put his hand on my arm and took the gun off me.

I had the sole intention of doing myself in. There was no rational explanation that I could give myself for leaving Kevin in that burning compartment, apart from fear. I knew I'd failed in the chance to actually do something, not be a hero, but actually do something for somebody, for somebody in need. He really needed my help and I blew it. That was the way I was feeling and I didn't really want to know. I had no interest in myself at all.

We were evacuated later to the field hospital at Ajax Bay and from there by helicopter to the hospital ship SS *Uganda*. I had a ticket put round my neck and I was taken away with about five other men to a white, quiet room, far away from everybody else. That's where I stayed. I noticed that they hadn't taken my morphine ampoule off me, which was fixed to my dog-tags round my neck, so I administered the morphine to myself, to my chest, aiming for the heart.

The morphine is like a little tiny tube of toothpaste with a needle in the end. I just moved my shirt over to one side and punched it in. Obviously the needle wasn't deep enough and I was spaced out for a while. The surgeon was called and he told the medical staff to check the medicine cabinets and everything else. I remember him spending a long time talking to me by my first name, which was quite unusual: 'Christopher, what have you taken?' and I finally told him that I'd taken my morphine. He said: 'Yes, right, well that's two grades down from neat heroin, so you'll have a hangover.'

A little while after that the padre came down. He'd heard about this particular person who kept on trying to do these silly things, and he had also been talking to a young man in intensive care who had had his leg taken off by the action on the *Galahad*. He put two and two together and he came down and took me to Kevin Woodford. I couldn't recognise Kevin because when I first met him it was in the dark. We took one look at each other and burst into tears, and that was it. It was the most incredible feeling. And that basically stopped me doing silly things. It didn't take away the guilt of what I'd done, that was still a very crushing thing. Although he was safe, because of my actions, I was still convinced in my own mind that I had left a man when I could perhaps have got him out. The rescue team found him where I told them he would be and brought him out. He was in a bit of a state as you can probably imagine, but he knew me immediately.

Once again the guilt was on me and I was racking my brains to see how I could deal with it. I was in the psychiatric part of the ship. I wasn't being treated in any special way, it was just everybody being quiet. There was a padre on the ship when I was transferred to the *Hydra*, which was the taxi service between the Falklands and Montevideo, in Uruguay. This chaplain counselled me and I asked for what the Catholics call 'absolution'.

He gave me absolution and he asked me afterwards: 'Do you feel any better?'

I said 'Not at all.'

So he said: 'I'm pleased you said that because it's something you've got to live with and it's something you've got to work out yourself.'

I was flown back with the others from Montevideo to Ascension Island and then back to RAF Wroughton [a military hospital] in England. I was once again segregated from everybody else and put in the psychiatric department. I was left on my own to be quiet. I sneaked out of the room, got to a telephone and phoned Gill [his wife]. She was most surprised to find out I was back in the country. I managed to have enough sense to be able to tell her where I was. My father and my wife left Weston-super-Mare immediately to come and see me.

I don't remember much about it because I was just very happy and very stupid. They were talking about all kinds of things, everything but the Falklands. I thought: This is strange, why aren't they talking about the Falklands? I didn't bother talking about it either. My father left us on our own for a few minutes and he went and saw the other lads who'd lost their arms and legs and were badly burned. He came back a few minutes later and they left.

Then I was transferred rather quickly from Wroughton to Plymouth ... to the psychiatric ward [of the naval hospital]. I had been there about a week and they gave me all the treatment, trying to make me sleep. I had gone about fourteen days without sleep and I was completely psyched up, completely alert. They were trying to induce sleep by injections, by drugs, and I was resisting everything.

I got very upset when I saw the news report about the sinking of the *Galahad* on television. I was shaking. The sister was holding me down in the chair. She was gripping my shoulders very tightly, and I was just sitting there watching it. To actually see the ship blowing up in front of me, knowing that I was inside it, Kevin with his leg off, it was just completely incredible. It made me feel very very strange. I didn't know what was wrong with me. I knew I was tired but I knew I had too much going through my mind to sleep. I was just too excited emotionally, and for some reason these people were trying to make me sleep. And when they weren't I was being put into therapy sessions. They were asking me to relate and to talk to them and I couldn't quite see what I was doing.

Sometimes I got quite angry with them and I said: 'Look, I don't know what's wrong with you, but I know that my situation is completely different. If I'm here for a psychiatric reason, then I can't possibly relate to washing up cups and whose turn it is to do the drying.' This is what the other members of this therapy group were talking about and it was making me very frustrated.

I wasn't diagnosed as a psychiatric patient; in fact, I was suffering from a thing called ABR – Acute Battle Reaction – which is another term for shell-shock. I was finally allowed to go home on a short leave where I slept for the first time, in the security of my own home.

Just before I left the hospital I was worried about my future. I still had about eight months to go in the service. I asked the doctor whether the fact that I had been there would affect me for my future employment. He said: 'I'm giving you a complete one-hundred-per-cent-clear bill of health.'

Later I went to South Armagh for six months. I volunteered for that straight after coming off sick leave with the sole intention of proving to any future would-be employer, mainly the police force, that there was no problem with me physically and mentally.

(Chris White worked for an insurance company for a short spell but became unemployed three months after leaving the Royal Marines. His wife had to give up her job on medical advice. Although he passed the exams and a medical, his application to join the police was rejected after some delay. A senior police officer told him it was because of his medical record. Even though a navy doctor declared him fully fit, the police would not change their decision.)

My relationship with Gill started to spiral downwards after that. I became very unreasonable as a father and as a husband. I am very ashamed to admit it. I was treating my family almost with contempt. My temper was something not to be witnessed, especially if I was driving a car. And I was on the dole. I went on the beer, the whisky and the gin until I reached the alcoholic state where I was drinking and not getting drunk, waking up in the middle of the night looking for the bottle. Gill asked me for a trial separation, and that frightened me, it really shocked me. I knew I didn't want to give up my family and I knew that I'd been a bit of a pig, even though it wasn't my fault. It was time for me to start putting things right. In three weeks I had a job as a bus driver, and seven months later I attained another position with a company at a very satisfactory salary and we're very happy.

DAVID GRIMSHAW

David Grimshaw was on the _Sir Galahad_ when it was bombed. He served in the 1st Battalion of the Welsh Guards during Operation Corporate. The Welsh Guards were part of 5 Infantry Brigade, which arrived in the Falklands nine days after 3 Commando Brigade, the main landing force, went ashore at San Carlos.

We do two things in the Welsh Guards. We carry out ceremonial duties but we are also infantrymen. We were a bit apprehensive I think because what we thought we were supposed to be doing was going [to the Falklands] as a garrison, to take over after the fighting was all finished. That's what we all thought. When we actually got there it was a bit of a shock. But being a soldier you knew we would have to do it some day.

From San Carlos they decided to move us round to Bluff Cove on the _Intrepid_. We had been living in trenches. Going on ship would give us the chance to wash up. We were really looking forward to getting a bit of the dirt off and cleaning our equipment. Then they decided to take _Intrepid_ back into San Carlos and transferred us to the _Sir Galahad_ to take us in by day. We didn't know what was going to happen to us . . . we were just glad to get on the ship and actually get somewhere and start doing something.

When we were at Fitzroy I was down on the tank-deck. That's where all the stores were, plus the Land-Rovers and ammunition. They opened the top deck and were going to drop a winch down to take our bergen rucksacks off. Then we were supposed to start filing out of the side of the ship. We couldn't get off the ramp because the hydraulics had gone and the landing craft couldn't get in to us. That's when we were hit by the bomb.

The crew of the *Sir Galahad* were mainly Chinese. As they slid open the top deck there were these two little Chinese men with these orange suits on. We were looking up at them at the time . . . they started shouting and screaming as they fell to the floor. As we turned round our company sergeant-major shouted: 'Hit the deck!' So I turned over, face first, and hit the deck. Then there was a pause – five or six seconds – and then a big bang. I was unconscious for a couple of seconds. There was fire and smoke everywhere. I tried to stand up then and I realised my leg had gone, so obviously I fell back down on the floor. When I came round I was lying on the floor. All I could feel was a burning sensation in the lower part of my left leg. I didn't think anything of it. I remember looking at my left hand, because that was what I was more worried about. It had melted. Then it hit me to get off the ship. Because I was a gunner I had the GPMG [general purpose machine gun] 7.62 mm ammunition – a couple of thousand rounds probably – on me at the time.

The first thing I did was take my webbing off. I had ammunition actually inside my combat jacket. I took that off as well and then I started to crawl out. There were two Land-Rovers on the ship. When I was crawling out of the tank-deck the Land-Rovers exploded. There was a lot of screaming. I can remember looking back and there was somebody running towards me fully ablaze. I never saw that person again, I don't know who it was. I remember a lot of screaming going on, people saying: 'Help me.' There was a lot of smoke and dust. I just made sure I got out. I got to a hatch on the side of the ship and shouted. Someone called to me: 'Come on, get out.' I said: 'Well, somebody's going to have to come and get me because my leg's gone. I can't get out.'

I remembered Jill, her family, my family; that must have spurred me on to get out of the ship. I crawled through the hatchway and somebody came down and carried me up the stairs.

On the deck there was a lot of running around and shouting. Someone from the field surgical team who was on the ship with us put a tourniquet on my leg and injected me with morphine. He was very good. I think if he hadn't been there I would have been a lot worse off. He acted so quickly, stopped the flow of blood and kept me calm.

I was taken by helicopter to the beach. When it landed I was in the stretcher and I was supporting my left leg in the air. There were a lot of bits hanging off it, so I suppose it looked very horrific. I looked around and there was a film crew there. They seemed to jump at me. I was a bit annoyed at that. I don't know whether I swore at them . . . or told them to go away. They were filming me because they saw the state of my leg.

At the field hospital at Ajax Bay there was a lot of confusion at first. We were in a big room. There were stretchers everywhere. People were in pain, there was a lot of moaning and groaning, people running in and out, people being taken to operating theatres. It was general confusion. But all we wanted to know was where certain people were. My best friend was in a stretcher on the other side of the room. We were shouting: 'Have you seen so and so?' and he said: 'Yes, here I am!' So there was a bit of relief then.

We didn't know who had got off the ship. It wasn't until later, when we were on the *Uganda*, that we knew exactly what had happened, who had been killed and what injuries people had. I was glad to be alive, that was the main thing, even though I had lost my leg and been burned. But I was still worried about my friends who had been with me in the army for a while. It was a relief to know that certain people were still here.

On *Uganda* we were in a hospital ward. It was run exactly the same as a hospital. The worst thing was that the ward I was in had the helicopter landing-pad directly above us. So every time a helicopter landed or took off, the vibrations were going right through the ship. That really affected me with my leg. I was in a lot of pain and I used to dread a helicopter landing or taking off.

They brought the Argentinians who had been wounded on to the ship.* They were very scruffy and soaking wet. They were suffering from petty things like trench foot and from cold; there didn't seem to be any physical injuries. What upset me and a lot of others was that they were taking up bed space which could have been used by our own troops who had very severe injuries. Just before they brought the Argentinians on board a young paratrooper came in with his left leg and his left arm blown off. There wasn't enough food – a

---

* Argentine helicopters with medical teams on board then transferred their wounded to the hospital ship *Bahia Paraiso*.

soldier always wants more food - but the nurses were all right. We were well looked after.

We left the *Uganda* on a small hospital ship and were taken to Montevideo and then transferred by ambulance to a VC10 hospital plane to be taken to Britain, to Brize Norton. When we were taxi-ing up the runway, one of the engines blew up. There was a lot of panic. I was strapped in a stretcher, and things started coming into my mind: Is it all going to happen again now? What's going to happen to me? The crew were running up and down the plane calming us down. They explained to us that a bird had been sucked into the engine and it had blown up.

The plane stopped. If it had been a couple of seconds later the aircraft would have had to have taken off, circled and used the fuel up before it would have come down. So they slammed the brakes on and the plane managed to stop. They took us back on to the ship and we were there until the following day, when we were transferred on to another VC10 which was going to take us to Brize Norton. Going on the plane the second time I just closed my eyes and lay there, praying that it would actually get off the ground. They say things happen in threes don't they? It had happened twice, I didn't want it to happen again.

I was a bit nervous at first of coming home. Things were going through my mind. We had only just got married before we left and I was into running, shooting and things like that. My life had taken a total change - I wouldn't be able to run. I was in a lot of pain. What would Jill think? When I saw Jill it didn't seem to bother her. She was so glad to see me there and that I was alive. It didn't seem to change anything. We were still the same, and with Jill being pregnant as well we had something to look forward to, so we had to carry on. There was no point in sitting back and moaning about what had happened to me, or Jill pitying me.

The employment situation seems to be zero. I was promised so much and given very little. When I was in Woolwich Hospital there was an officer who was willing to send me on all these courses. But at the time I didn't go on the courses because in the area I live there is so little to do. You can start a business up round here and nothing comes of it; but there are some big companies and good jobs. I've got a good military record. At the time of the Falklands people were looking at you, shaking your hand: 'This man's a hero.' But today people forget so quickly. I'm stuck like this now for the rest of my life. My leg's not going to grow back.

WAYNE TRIGG

Wayne Trigg was aged nineteen and in the 1st Battalion of the Welsh Guards when he was sent to the Falkland Islands on the cruise liner _QE2_. He was on board _Sir Galahad_ at Fitzroy on 8 June 1982 when it was bombed by Argentine aircraft.

We were all looking forward to getting down there. The weather remained fine right the way down past Ascension Island. We had trained with mock battles and field exercises. I had been in the Guards for four years. At the time we had been on ceremonial duties – Buckingham Palace, St James's, Windsor Castle and the Tower of London. We had been overseas. I had been to Berlin with the Grenadier Guards while all the Welsh Guards were out in Ireland. I was seventeen at the time – too young to go. We had been to Kenya for six weeks' jungle training. When we went to the Falklands I was nineteen years old.

We landed in the Falklands outside San Carlos where we dug in. We stayed two or three days and were then told to move on to catch up with the rest of the army. The truck we had couldn't get through the ground, the marsh was clogging the tyres up, so we came back to San Carlos for another night. Then we were transferred on a ship to go around to Bluff Cove. [Eventually] they transferred us from _Fearless_ on to _Sir Galahad_.

On the morning of 8 June we had got as far as Fitzroy and were moving ammunition. The spirit was high; we all wanted to catch up with the rest of the Welsh Guards. It would have been the first action we had actually seen, other than the odd air raid while we were in San Carlos. We were moving the ammunition into the centre of the ship and were told to move our rucksacks into the nets to be hoisted up and flown on to the shore by helicopters. We finished this task, got up and put our webbing on; picked up our rifles and put warm clothing on. The hatch on the top of *Sir Galahad* started to open. As it was opening we heard the screech. We saw a bloke on top, near the hatch, hit the deck. We heard there was an air raid. The planes flew over the top. We couldn't actually see them and we were not too sure whether bombs were coming towards us. Then it was one big bang. There were bodies, screaming, shouting. The ship was one big fireball.

I covered my face first as the blast came from the centre of the ship to the back end. Because the back and the front end of the ship were both closed, there was no way for the flames to escape. They rebounded and came back and caught most of my back, my legs. I actually caught fire. As I was trying to get out I fell over, and that's how I done my hands. The deck was red hot, as if the metal had been in the forge in a blacksmith's. As my hands hit the deck the skin just came off, it was as if I was seeing double: there was a hand and the ripples. The skin on my hands had actually come off. It was like a glove on top. It was flapping about on both hands.

After I had fallen over I picked myself back up. I heard screaming and shouting. I looked back but you couldn't see much as the ship was in flames. There was black smoke everywhere. I screamed to myself that I was alive. 'I'm alive. For God's sake let's get out of here.' I just ran for what I knew was the nearest door.

There were a couple of us trying to get out, pushing and shoving each other. I was helped out on to the deck. My webbing and the weapon I had were thrown overboard. The flames on my back were put out. People who weren't injured were helping those that were. They were waiting for the helicopters to come and take us out.

People were shouting at me to keep my eyes open. Most of my face had been singed and they were helping it with water, to keep it cool and stop my eyes from closing. They were calling us back. Most of us who were burned were running round to try and keep the burns cool. People were shouting. As I was looking round I could see other people who were injured, my mates. But you couldn't recognise them because of the blackness of their faces. Their hair had burned off. The medical team were rushing about with people on stretchers. I saw two or three blokes laid out on the stretchers; one of them apparently was a friend – he told me afterwards – but I couldn't recognise him.

He was shouting out names, and no one could recognise either of us. The skin on their faces had all gone black and it started bubbling and scabbing up. It smelled awful. The ammunition down below deck was still flying about, you could hear it. There was a queue for the liferafts. Three or four of us ran to the side of the ship. Knowing I couldn't use my hands I decided to climb off the side using my elbows so I could get on to the liferaft.

I got down into the bottom but I couldn't sit down because my backside was burned. I was walking about in the liferaft. Three or four others who were injured got in. The ones who were helping tried to put us in sheets, trying to get us to sit down, trying to calm us down. But I kept screaming, it was that painful. They finally helped by dipping a jacket into the salt-water to ease the pain. But I was still jumping about, I couldn't sit down for more than thirty seconds. Finally they got me to sit down and we started paddling away from the ship. Fifty to sixty yards away the oars snapped. The liferaft was getting drawn back towards *Sir Galahad*. Some people started using their hands to try and paddle ashore. A helicopter hovered above us and it took the injured from the liferaft up. The blokes inside helped put the winch around me. I was lifted up and just before the top the winchman shouted out to me not to look up just in case I banged my head on the underneath of the helicopter. They got me in and he told me to sit down at the back end of the helicopter, but I was shouting and screaming at him. I was running up and down the helicopter trying to forget about my pain. He winched two other blokes from the raft and took us ashore. It took two or three minutes.

Three of us were put in a Land-Rover. There was a slope before we actually got to the field first-aid post. The Land-Rover got so far and then couldn't get any further because the wheels were spinning in the mud. It was rolling back. This happened three or four times. The three of us who were injured decided to jump out and run to the first-aid post. My trousers kept falling down and one of the blokes helped by holding them for me. As we waited at the field first-aid post helicopters came over to land. Most of the people who were injured were burned. We ran towards the helicopters. The burns were so hot that we wanted to get cooled down by the wind off the rotor blades.

As we waited there we heard the whistles – the sign that there was another air raid. We all took cover in the nearest place – a house. We stood

behind the door. I saw my reflection in the window which was blacked
out with a black sheet. That's when I first realised that my face had
actually been burned and the scabs had built up on me. I didn't feel
anything. I just thought I was ugly. I didn't recognise myself because
the hair had gone. It was a shock. I hadn't thought it was that bad, or
even that I was badly burned around the face. It was blackened with
scabs all over it.

In my section of the mortar platoon there were ten men who went
to the Falklands. Three came back injured. Seven were killed on the
Sir Galahad.

(The injured were flown to the hospital ship Uganda.*)*

We were all in one big room on the *Uganda*. We could hear this bloke
screaming all the time. I looked over to him and the only way I could
recognise him as the company clerk was by the tattoos he had on his
arms. He was my friend but I couldn't recognise him any other way.
My eyes had closed up. The skin on my face had tightened up. That's
why they put the cream on our faces and our hands into bags. Twice
a day, in the morning and afternoon, the nurses would dip cotton wool
into water. They used to put it on to our eyes so it could soak up the
scabs. Then they would come and pick them off. It was funny at first
being able to see again. That's when I noticed there were more injured
on the ship. A lot of them had similar injuries to me and they were getting
the same treatment. Five of them I could recognise from the various
marks they had. They were friends, but none of us could actually talk
to each other because we were bed-bound.

I had been aware how many Welsh Guardsmen had been killed on
Sir Galahad but we didn't know any of the names. I discovered them
when I was back in Britain, in the RAF hospital at Wroughton. One of
the officers brought up *Soldier* magazine. They had a list of all the Welsh
Guardsmen who died, and that's when I realised most of them were
my friends. One chap I had been to school with in Holyhead when I
was eleven or twelve years old. We were in the same form. I still see his
parents now and go with the family on June 8th to lay a wreath on his
memorial. I phone them up to find out what time they are going to go

176

up to the memorial. I wait for them and then we go back to the house and have a talk and go through the old photos. I've been upset once or twice when I've been to the memorial with his family but I've gradually got over it.

I would let a son of mine go into the Welsh Guards because it is a good life. I would have loved to have stayed in. I had signed for nine years and I was hoping to finish the nine years and sign on and stay in for a couple more. But because of the injuries they decided to give me a medical discharge.

When you join up in the army you've got to remember what they do in Ireland. You don't know who they're fighting out in Ireland and whether you are going to get shot. But once you sign on the dotted line, you've got to think: 'We're going to Ireland.' You've got to think of going to war . . . that's why I signed on the dotted line . . . it happens some time.

At the time I did think it was worth going to the Falklands. All the Welsh Guardsmen were raring to go into action for the first time. But over the last couple of years, it hasn't really been worth it . . . thinking back.

KEVIN MORAN

Corporal Kevin Moran is a medical specialist with the Parachute Regiment. He served with the regiment's 2nd Battalion when it was sent to the Falklands War. On 8 June 1982 he watched from a hill above Fitzroy as Argentine jets bombed *Sir Galahad* in the bay below.

On the way down to the Falklands the unit's medical officer, Captain Steve Hughes, began something called the 'combat medic', which we ran within 2 Para. He got as many people as he could together on board *Norland* to give advanced first-aid knowledge so they could treat people when they got ashore and into battle.

Basically what he did was take the first-aid training we already had and then taught us some basic resuscitation procedures: how to deal with specific types of wounds and injuries that we might come across when we got to the Falklands. He set up a regime to treat each and every casualty as soon as we saw them. We had to try and learn it. Burns was one of the subjects on the course.

(After the battle of Goose Green 2 Para was moved forward on the way towards the final attack on Port Stanley. Corporal Moran was attached to 'C' Company near Fitzroy on the morning of 8 June 1982.)

We had been moved up on to a hill overlooking the small bay at Fitzroy to test-fire our weapons. You do that at every opportunity to ensure the sights are firing on target. We saw three or four Argentine aircraft coming in very low. We were going to leave it to the Rapier anti-aircraft missiles up on the hill to deal with the aircraft. We all watched as they came in . . . and absolutely nothing happened. The Rapier missiles never engaged the targets at all. The aircraft came in completely unhampered and dropped their bombs. We watched them as they flew over and dropped their load. One of them hit *Galahad*. There was a big bang. When a bomb falls from an aircraft it falls away slowly from the wings. They don't shoot forward, they just fall away and glide. That's what we saw. The aircraft came round again for a second pass. The first time we just sat and watched them but now we had our weapons and were all ammo'd up. The guys who had the machine guns put them on the shoulders of other lads and opened up on the aircraft on the second pass to harass them. The aircraft cleared off.

On the beach, people on the nearest boat were starting to bring survivors ashore. People were running about on the deck trying to get themselves up to the forrard end of the boat because the back end was burning. Red emergency liferafts were being launched, people were scrambling down the sides from the forrard end. There was wind blowing and there was thick smoke, the back end of the boat was completely obscured. People were being pulled off by choppers which were working in pairs. One tried to get to the survivors, the other was trying to fan the smoke away so that the other helicopter could come underneath to lift anyone who was there. Without them fanning the smoke away it would have been dangerous for the other pilot. He wouldn't have been able to see where he was flying.

The guys in the red emergency liferafts were using their hands and planks of wood to paddle along in the sea. The choppers got down behind them to create a draught to blow them towards the shore. The wind caused by the down-draught from the rotor blades blew the rafts along the water. It was a clear day and the sea was calm, so there was no danger of the waves hitting the chopper, but they were going very close to the water.

Other choppers came over the deck of the ship and hovered. A winchman came down and either hooked a stretcher or a bloke and lifted him up. They didn't just take one casualty and disappear – they waited until they had a full load of guys on board, and then off they went. Some casualties were taken to 2 Para's regimental aid post in the community centre at Fitzroy settlement. The more serious ones were taken direct to the field hospital at Ajax Bay.

Once the rafts started coming ashore we went down to help the people who were injured to get out. My immediate reaction was: 'We're going to be busy here.' Those like me who had done the advanced medical course were assisting the regimental medics. They came direct to the beach to give emergency first-aid. I helped to get the casualties to a regimental medic. We did the fastest job we could on them, enough to get back to a doctor as quickly as possible.

Some of the survivors were in severe shock from the traumatic experience of being on the boat when a bomb hit. Others were quite severely injured, they had lost limbs or had severe shrapnel wounds and were bleeding a lot. We dressed those wounds and tried to make sure that we could keep them alive long enough to get them back to a doctor. There were a lot of people who were suffering in one way or another. There was a look on their faces of complete amazement, as though they didn't know what was happening. Within themselves they were a separate community: they were mates and they were looking after each other. If there was somebody injured, someone else would be shouting for a medic. It was chaotic. You wanted to try and help everybody but you had to pick on someone and say: 'Right, I'll help him.' Then you got stuck in and dealt with that guy.

One of the paramedics called Hank was trying to get a drip into somebody's arm. When you've got someone in shock it becomes extremely difficult because the veins close down. Someone in shock and bleeding is losing body fluid, so we carried replacement fluids. You try and kid the heart really; by putting a bit more fluid in the heart thinks it's not such a bad problem.

The scene down there on the beach was quite shocking. Your training takes over, that's the way you get through it. You know what you've been taught, you know how to deal with certain things and you do your best. You can deal with a patient in different ways. I try to look at them as a lump of meat. You do all the: 'There there, kid,' and 'You're going to be all right, no problem.' Then you forget about it. Hopefully you've got someone else there who can maybe keep talking to the patient while you deal with the injury.

One guy had lost the upper part of his forearm. I looked on this as an injury I had to deal with. There is a set regime. You know if you don't do anything this guy is going to bleed to death. I had someone else with me, talking to the patient while I got a bit of shirt and tied a tourniquet quite tightly round his arm to stop the bleeding.

The worst moment of the whole business was just standing on that hill watching the aircraft come over in a perfect formation and drop the bombs without us doing anything. That was the worst thing for me – feeling we had just stood there and done nothing until they made the second pass. I sometimes think about the incident. Why did it happen? What were the circumstances? Why did those boats have to be there in that particular place? Why wasn't there something else that we could have done? I'm not haunted by it, but every now and then I do think about it.

MARCOS IRRAZABAL

Private Marcos Irrazabal comes from a working-class neighbourhood outside Buenos Aires. He was a nineteen-year-old conscripted soldier when he was sent to the Malvinas on 11 April 1982. He was with a unit guarding a mortar battery, part of the 3rd Infantry Regiment of the 10th Army Brigade, near Sapper Hill. He works as a clerk in the office of a cement manufacturing firm.

The British navy shelled our positions every night. The planes would bomb us during the day. Every day. All I wanted to do was get it over with, I couldn't bear the waiting. Once we heard that the British troops had landed we knew it was only a matter of time. I was desperate for them to reach our positions so that we could get on with the battle, get it over with, no matter what happened. Once they landed I knew that we were defeated. As the British got closer to us it got worse because we had to be constantly on guard.

I had nothing against the British troops. They thought their cause was just and so did we. I am especially thankful to them because of the way they treated friends of mine who were in hospital. It's the Yanks I cannot stand, not only because they betrayed us by giving weapons to the British and generally siding with them, but also because I have never been able to stand them. I just take one look at their flag and I feel sick. It's a personal thing.

I was on Sapper Hill with the mortar battery when I was wounded. It was 12 June – two months after we arrived.

That day I was in charge of going to get the food from Puerto Argentino [Port Stanley]. I was walking through some fields and two English planes came over us. I don't know what happened but I fell

182

wounded. I think I was hit by fire from our own side. I heard a great blow and I fell. The soldier who was with me applied a tourniquet on my arm, but I asked him where my wound was because I couldn't feel any pain.

He said: 'It's in your arm.'

He started to drag me away. At that moment stretcher-bearers arrived and put me in an ambulance and took me to hospital.

Later I was taken to Argentina on the hospital ship and then to a hospital in Buenos Aires. I used to ask the people who visited me: 'Why did it have to be me? Why should I lose an arm?' And they told me that I should look back and I would always see something worse and that my problems were not as bad as someone else's. It is true because I used to visit the boys in the psychiatric ward very often, boys who had lost their minds. The people who visited me said it was not the same losing an arm in a train accident or a car crash as losing it fighting for your country, losing it for Argentina, for something that we felt was ours.

I didn't use to agree with that then, but now I see what they meant. I don't consider myself a hero. None of those who came back is a hero. The heroes are the soldiers who stayed there, who died fighting for the Fatherland, so I will never consider myself a hero, although I fought for the Fatherland too.

The thing I love most in life is playing football. When I got gangrene in my arm, the first thing I asked the doctor is whether I could ever play football again. That was just before they amputated my arm. He told me that I would be able to play football and that I would be a normal guy. At first, when I started playing again, the other lads would treat me like a child. I told them that I wanted them to tackle me as hard as they used to before I lost my arm. They finally understood and now I'm just another player.

HORACIO BENITEZ

**Horacio Benitez from Buenos Aires was aged nineteen, and about to
complete his year-long spell of military conscription, when he was sent
to the Malvinas. He served with 'A' Company, 5th Infantry Regiment,
10th Army Brigade, at Port Stanley and was involved in the final battle
at Wireless Ridge. He manages a co-operative food and produce market
run by Malvinas veterans and is studying law part-time.**

I had eight days left with the army before I was due to return to
civilian life. I remember that we got up that morning and I found a
newspaper announcing the invasion. There was a picture of soldiers
climbing into a Hercules transport plane. We were not invaders, we were
going to recover what was ours. We knew that we had to go, although we
did not know whether our unit would be sent. They began calling up
the rest. I think we wanted to go because we felt it was now our turn
to defend the Fatherland. Also, because we were so young, we were
very naive. We didn't quite realise what it all meant. All your friends
were going so you had to go too. It was a sort of party atmosphere:
only our mothers were really worried and they were crying.

We flew out on 11 April 1982. The first thing that struck me
when we arrived at Puerto Argentino was how English it all looked.
There was nothing Argentine there. I even remember picking up a
box of nails which had 'Made in England' on them. So then you start
thinking where am I? What's this? They didn't even speak Spanish. They
were afraid of us. They didn't like us. But it turned out that the people
who we were supposedly there to defend, namely the Islanders, weren't
really our people at all, so you didn't know really who the invaders were.
At the end of it we were all invaders, they were invaders and so were we.

The man I wanted to talk to I couldn't talk to because he was English. Maybe he knew some Spanish but he wasn't saying, so I had to speak to him in English. In my own country I had to speak English? So I said to myself: I'm mad, this can't be, so where am I? From our very first day at school we had been told about the Malvinas. We had always been told that it was Argentine. It was on our continental shelf. The Islands belonged to Argentina. We all knew this was true.

At a given moment they would feed us but they would only give us soup, once in the morning and once in the afternoon. So, as in a war there is always a lack of food, or at least you cannot eat as much as you'd like to, we had to go out shopping. To buy something we had to find a journalist or anybody else in civilian clothes because we would not be allowed in the store. So that's how we bought English food – the food that had been imported from England. I especially remember the butter, it was a wonderful butter and the little biscuits were unbeliev-able. And the other thing that I had never tried in Argentina was the Aero mint chocolate, which I loved. I once bought twenty bars. So I realised that I was trying a type of food that wasn't mine, but it wasn't easy, although it helped us to get by.

I remember that I once managed to establish some communication with one of the locals in my broken English. We communicated like red-skins in the Westerns. 'How you?'; 'You buy'; 'Is good.' And he more or less understood me. He used to buy food for us and he would even give me the change in shillings and pennies. I would pay him in Argentine money. But there were others who wouldn't talk to us at all, who would close their doors on us, who were afraid. We listened to the radio – the Uruguayan Radio – to find out what the English were doing, how they were coming towards us, how they were mobilising the troops, where they were going to land, how many of them, and so on.

In the middle of all this we had absolutely no information. We knew what was happening in our zone, but we had no idea about the rest. In our calculations the [enemy] numbers kept growing. First there were 3,000 and then it was 6,000 then it was 10,000, and so on. Later on, when the British battleships would come closer to the shore to shell us, we would find out the names of the ships on the radio. By that time we knew most of what we had to know.

After May 1st we took our positions on top of a hill because intelligence had warned us that the area we were covering in the plain was about to be shelled. Up to that moment we hadn't been under heavy bombing while we were closer to the beach, but after that they started. I remember that their ships used to line up. About eight o'clock in the evening you could already see them there and they would start shelling us at about 11 p.m. It was very strange because initially you could hear four cannon firing and then they would wait. I thought that was what a bombing was like: four shells and a pause. But no, in this case it was a continuous barrage and it lasted four hours. I remember being inside my foxhole listening to the explosions and the shells whistling over us. When you can hear the sound of the shell it means it's going over you. When you stop hearing the whistle it means it is coming right on top of you.

So after the first shellings we realised that this was it, that we weren't going to hang around for much longer, wondering whether they would come or not, because they were there already. Once, when we were being shelled, there were three of us in a trench. One was praying and crying, not because he was afraid but because he knew something was going to happen to him and it did. He lost a leg. While he was praying I ate and the other man smoked. We got a bit tired of sitting there in the wet peat and we finally decided to get out and watch the show, because it *was* a real show to see the missiles and the shells flying by, and hear all the explosions. The earth seemed to be boiling and at times the whole island seemed to be moving. This was the first time that I realised that the joke was over and that we were in a serious war.

They would bomb us every night. They would start at the front of our sector and gradually work their way down with a pin-point precision as though they were placing the shells by hand. They would start working their way down, and when they reached the end of our sector they would go back to the front and start all over again. The whole world seemed to be coming on top of you. There was a feeling of impotence, as if you were just waiting for death. Then you started thinking about what you had done in your life, but since we were nineteen years old there was not much really that we could have done. Then we would start thinking about what we would do if we managed to get back.

We grew up very quickly. We asked ourselves why we were there, if we were there for a good reason, whether we were there to win or to die, or were we just being used. Mostly we were prepared to win or die, although other people wanted to go back home to their mothers. That was quite normal, but it wasn't what the majority of us thought. Most of us were prepared to die there because we thought that the whole of Argentina was behind us, that they were proud of us, and that is why we were proud of what we were doing.

We called the British Harriers the Black Death, because by the end of the war they would come down on us on Two Sisters Mountain and you could see the shadows coming towards us. They started shooting at us with their machine guns and there was nowhere to hide, so that the shadow would come at you under the Harrier and when that shadow came over you, you were a dead man. We had lost control over ourselves by that time. We were like savages, eager to kill, completely degraded. All my values had changed because my life had changed. I was no longer interested in the life I had previously led. I had become an instrument of death and my mind was concentrated on surviving to go on killing, which is the only thing which interested me and my group of comrades. We were afraid. The fear you feel when you look at yourself and you say: I am going to die. Then you ask yourself: Why am I going to die? Is my life really so worthless? That's when your values change. In the last days we would be out sunbathing or listening to music while we were being shelled. That's how we lived at that moment – a very strange life. I felt as though I had always lived that way, as though I had been born there.

[Towards the end of the war] I was on a mountain-top, cooking a stew in my helmet. There were mortar shell explosions and artillery fire all around me. You could see tracer bullets all over the place. The whole island was an inferno, but at the same time it looked like a Christmas party at home with all the fireworks. And there was I just cooking and taking in the show. One of my mates was having a siesta, another one was listening to music. Then the order arrived for us to go down into the valley. We knew then that we would be going into direct combat. Everybody was very agitated and we all talked at the same time. One talked about his sister, another about his college. Someone else talked about football, anything to evade the issue. Soon we found ourselves walking in a straight line, and all around you could hear explosions and shouts. The valley was about three kilometres long and I started feeling afraid of getting killed.

We attacked the British at the foot of the mountain. It was complete chaos. It was dark and star-shells started going off, lighting up the sky. Suddenly it was daylight. We looked at each other as if to say: What do we do now? We came under machine-gun fire and we just stood there. We stood still like tin soldiers and then the British [started] throwing anti-personnel missiles at us. They looked like balls of fire which chased you all over the place. We had never seen anything like it. It was as if they were trying to find a particular soldier. People ran away and a couple of my friends were killed. I froze. I didn't shoot, I didn't know what to do. I was desperate. Then I started to run, but I was running up, up the mountain, along with some others, in a very disorganised way. As we climbed there were helmets, weapons, bodies, strewn all around. It was a disaster. There was smoke everywhere.

We reached the top, about twenty of us, and just ahead were the British advance patrols – red berets, the Paras. The battle started. It was completely crazy, shouting everywhere. This was interspersed by periods of total silence when you could hear music or people talking and even laughing. Sometimes you would see groups coming at you and you didn't know who they were, which side they were on.

It started snowing: very thin snow, that drenched us. I was behind a rock. They were shooting at me. Under the light of the star-shell I saw this guy and I shot at him. He must have been hit because I poured a whole magazine into him and he fell. But others were coming at me. I kept on shooting but they kept coming. Some who fell got up again and kept charging on, shooting at us. By this time they were all around me. They must have thought that there were thousands of us there but we cannot have been more than twenty because the rest of the company was at the foot of the mountain. A sergeant was wounded. He shouted that he had been hit in the stomach. Another soldier was crying out for help but you couldn't help him. A grenade fell near him and it lifted him up in the air and he fell down again.

He stood up and shouted: 'I'm hit, I'm hit,' and he was swearing but he was still walking. He went round several soldiers and to one he said: 'I'm leaving you my rifle' and to another: 'I'm leaving you my magazine,' and then he started shouting: 'I'm leaving, I'm leaving, I'm leaving' as if it was all over. As he was walking away he was hit by a phosphorus grenade; his clothes caught fire and he started screaming. But he was also lighting up our positions because he was like a human torch and we were waving him away so that he wouldn't show up our position in the dark. At that moment we were not really interested in whether he died or not.

I had eight magazines with me but I had just run out of ammunition and had used all my grenades. I wasn't thinking straight any longer. The only thought in my head was to grab more ammunition and continue fighting. Something was forcing me to do it. Perhaps deep down I was even enjoying it because that's a primal instinct. I found more ammunition but as I was loading I saw an English soldier in front of me. As I lifted my rifle I was shot in the head. I seemed to fall in slow motion. I was left there.

The shot had been deflected by the helmet and had hit me in the neck. I couldn't move my head but I could still think. I can remember wondering whether I still had my arms. I tried to move my legs and I realised I had all my limbs. I thought: I'm alive. I tried to crawl back. I couldn't stand. The battle was still going on, my head was swirling.

Eventually some friends found me and dragged me down the mountain. I thought I was bleeding to death. I asked my friends for a last cigarette. We talked to each other, we wondered whether we were going to die or not. Someone else said they were killing off the wounded. Finally I passed out because I lost so much blood. I couldn't move but I could still think. When we reached the command post they told the captain: 'Here's Benitez – he's dead.'

They wrapped me up in a blanket and put me on top of a pile of corpses. A sergeant came along, he was writing down the names of the dead. He was crying. I must have blinked or moved or something because he realised I was still alive. He pulled me out, they gave me some morphine and took me to hospital.

A hospital ship took me home to Argentina, and I was at the Campo de Mayo military hospital outside Buenos Aires for two weeks. When I returned home my first weekend I went out with my two brothers. I was still fairly traumatised by the whole thing. We went to a bar. I expected everyone to be miserable because of what had happened, but everyone was having a lot of fun in the bar as if we had just won the World Cup. There was no trace of worry or sorrow on people's faces. In Buenos Aires it was as though nothing had happened. There had been a war down there and it went wrong and it was all over now, but no one was really interested in what had actually happened, in how many had died. People seemed even happier because the war was over. It was a party atmosphere. I had just seen what human beings can do to each other and all the sacrifices that our troops had made, but in Buenos Aires all that was worthless. No one was interested.

We, the veterans, soon realised we were different to those who stayed behind. I am not resentful, I wouldn't want anyone to go through what I went through, but as an Argentine it hurts to know that no one cares about what we did. If anybody cares it is usually from a political or military point of view, but not from a human point of view. Nobody cares about us. Life goes on. We don't want a reward but at least we want to know why we did it. To kill someone you must either have a cause or be mad. I don't think we were mad so we must have had a cause, but when we returned the cause seemed to have disappeared. You ask yourself: How many fathers did I kill? Why did I kill them? Was it worth it? I did it for the Fatherland. What is the Fatherland? Is it you or those who are smiling and dancing while the others suffer?

The most painful thing after the war was when we were flown home and taken to hospital and as we came out of the airport we were surrounded by a group of mothers, shouting and crying, asking: 'Where's Alberto, Where's Mario?' and they tried to reach us through the open windows of the ambulance. They were running alongside us. They wanted to know what happened to their sons. It was awful not being able to tell them.

PATRICIO PEREZ

Private Patricio Perez had just finished his high school education when he was called to do military service. He became a civilian again after a year with the army. He was aged nineteen when he was recalled to go to the Malvinas. He fought with 'A' Company, 3rd Infantry Regiment, on Wireless Ridge. After the war he trained as a book-keeper. He is treasurer of the Malvinas veterans' market co-operative in Buenos Aires.

Before the war I had just finished my secondary education. I wasn't working. I did a lot of sports and played music. I lived really like a student with my family. We rejoiced when the Islands were reoccupied but there was also concern. A week went by before I was called up. A letter arrived from my regiment telling me where to go, but at the barracks it turned out that I hadn't been included in the combat list. Some of us protested and said we should replace the soldiers who had just started military conscription because we were fully trained. For us it was very important because all our mates were going and we felt that we had to defend the Fatherland also. None of our superiors expected a war – we were just going to fortify the Islands. At the same time we knew there was a possibility of war; but because our friends were there, we thought that if we died we would all die together. Ever since we were kids we learned the Malvinas were part of our territory, part of Argentina, and therefore we had to defend them.

When we got there the first thing we did was change into winter clothes, but they were not warm enough to survive the weather in the trenches. We lived in foxholes and water kept filtering through the peat, so you would find yourself living in the water and ice with no dry clothing. You had to keep as dry as possible and try and eat as much as possible. At first we ate reasonably well, but when the British declared the Exclusion Zone very little food was brought over and our food was rationed. Sometimes we became desperate with hunger and obsessed with food. We had to find food but we had to be careful. Once a friend of mine went out looking for sheep or cows. There were mines everywhere. He stepped on a mine and lost a leg and three others with him were wounded.

Combat is an extraordinary experience. We had seen war films, but it is different being in the real thing – the noise, the excitement, the unreality, the fear. I'll never forget seeing so many explosions, so many tracer bullets flying around, seeing night turn into day with star-shells. The British anti-personnel missiles were amazing – seeing them coming at you, heading straight for you, like an undulating fire ball. I threw myself on the ground and one of the missiles passed over me. I was amazed at the explosion it made.

The battle for Wireless Ridge came right at the end of the war. As we climbed up the ridge we came under heavy fire. The worst thing was the cries of the wounded, shouting for help. You felt a lot of pain but you also wanted to avenge them. I remember thinking how important it was to cover my legs. I always thought that if I was hit in the arm or chest or stomach I could always walk out. The main thing was to keep the legs covered.

I didn't want to lose my legs. At one point I took cover behind a rock. I was carrying two rifles and I noticed that there was a sniper who was pinning me down. I wanted to come out of my rock and kill him but I couldn't because the firing was so intense. At that moment I heard somebody shout that he had seen the sniper. I came out, saw that he was leaning over the rock and shot at him and his gun fell silent. I saw him fall but I don't know whether he was wounded or dead. That kind of combat among the rocks is like a Western, but it all happens so fast that you don't quite realise what is going on.

What I felt at that moment was mostly hatred. I wanted revenge. I had forgotten fear by then, what sort of risk I was taking; the only thing I wanted to do, my obsession, was to avenge my fallen comrades. Whenever I saw one of my friends hit it was worse, it just made me want to continue fighting, it didn't matter for how long or at what cost. I didn't care about death at that time, the main thing was revenge. Looking back I now think it was all quite mad, very strange.

I once heard a Vietnam veteran talk about the 'drunkenness of war'. He was quite right, it is like being drunk and I enjoyed it at that moment. As children we all play at war because we have seen it on television or films, so as a child you play up to this role with a wooden gun, only this time I had a real gun in my hands and perhaps I forgot that I could actually kill and be killed.

Some of us went looking for the wounded. We thought they could make it back. I heard they had killed my friend Private Horacio Benitez, and the feeling for revenge came over me again.

We sent the wounded down and returned to the battle and fought on for four hours. Luckily after the surrender I found out that Horacio had survived. People greeted the surrender with relief. They were all crying. That wasn't how I reacted. I had been fighting for many hours and I was not prepared to give up my rifle until forced to do so. It's different for those who had been in actual combat. I couldn't give my rifle back until they took it away from me, and when I did give it back I made sure it was completely unusable. I felt a tremendous pain, I felt defeated. What shocked me most was when they took us to the airport and I saw the Union Jack flying on a ship. It was a tremendous blow. I was so furious I started crying. I had been so hungry, I had been so cold and so lonely. I had been through so much and had seen so many of my friends killed, and there was the British flag flying. It had been a terrible defeat. The British helicopters made a fly-past showing the battle flags. I suppose it was part of psychological warfare. They were driving the point home. I looked around me at the airport and saw 5,000 faces looking as though their mothers had just died; 5,000 faces of defeat.

On the return home on *Canberra* I became friendly with one of the guards. Little by little we realised we had a lot in common and I tried to communicate with him in my broken English. We both loved music. I played the guitar and he played the piano. He was Welsh, his name was Baker, and we also realised that we both loved rugby. He played for a Welsh club and I played in Buenos Aires. We used to sing along together in our cabin to the music from the BBC. We both realised the war was over and now we could be friends, but it was hard to think that I could have killed him.

*

When we returned to Buenos Aires they took us to the Campo de Mayo military base. It was Father's Day and we all wanted to go home. We went to bed very late that night. Next morning we saw outside the base a huge number of relatives trying to get in to see if their sons or brothers were alive. Finally they were allowed in. They rushed forward looking desperately for their sons, their friends, asking every soldier whether he had been in a certain place or with a certain unit. Sometimes we knew that that soldier was dead, but we could not tell them. In fact we didn't know whether we had to tell them or the army had to tell them.

A mother, brother and sister of a dead soldier hit in the back by a missile grabbed me and asked me: 'Are you from "A" Company?'

'Yes,' I said.

'So you must know Folt?'

When they asked me that I froze because I knew he was dead but didn't know how to tell them. So I said that I thought he was wounded but that he might be in hospital. I just walked away.

HORACIO LOSITO

Captain Horacio Losito served with a commando unit in the Malvinas War. His men patrolled behind British lines and took part in the battle for Top Malo House on 31 May. He is now studying at the Army War College in Buenos Aires.

We managed to do what every soldier aspires to, which is to prove himself in combat. In the first instance, in the occupation of the Islands, that combat was successful for the Argentine forces. I was not there in those first days but I shared the pride of the men who had recovered this part of our national heritage.

Thirteen of us in our commando unit had taken refuge in Top Malo House on our way to Fitzroy. We were ready to continue our march when we heard helicopters approaching. Initially we thought that they were our own helicopters who were coming to pick us up. But we soon realised they were not. Espinosa and Brun, who were guarding the top floor of the house, raised the alarm and at the same time opened fire on the approaching British troops. There was an explosion which shook the whole house. It was a very small wooden house and it caught fire. Several explosions followed. Hundreds of bullets were coming through the walls. It all happened very quickly. Espinosa was with Brun and three NCOs on the top floor. They could see the approaching British troops. He was told to leave the window and get out of the house as we were all trying to do at that moment, but Espinosa replied: 'You leave, I'll cover you.'

That allowed us all to get out of the house, because Espinosa

195

drew all the British fire and he was shooting back. At that moment a hand-grenade exploded on his chest and killed him instantly. Brun was wounded by that same grenade and then jumped from the first floor window. When he fell he was hit again in his leg and in the back. He managed to continue fighting with his pistol and when he ran out of ammunition he tried to throw a grenade, but he didn't even have the strength to pull out the pin.

The six of us who were downstairs had tried to leave through the door, the only door of the house. The commanding officer went up first, followed by the radio operator and myself. A grenade exploded near the door and wounded me in the head and nearly knocked me out, but I managed to continue firing. Most of us tried to head towards the Mullows stream about 200 metres away, to reach the heights beyond the stream, without realising there were more British troops there. During that withdrawal, Sergeant Esbert saw Sergeant Medina pinned down by enemy fire. He shouted to Medina: 'Run Fatso and I'll cover you.' Medina managed to get away but Esbert was killed by a hand-grenade. When he saw that Esbert had been hit he ran back to help him and was wounded himself, but he continued fighting until the end of the battle.

I was wounded again in the leg as I was trying to cover myself and I fell back into a sort of trench. I was alone. I thought they were all dead. I thought I was going to die anyway so I decided to continue fighting. At that moment I saw the radio operator, who was transmitting the CO's decision to surrender because we had run out of ammunition, and two-thirds of the unit had been knocked out. I didn't react at that moment. I had only seen a surrender in films and I never thought I myself would ever be involved in that situation. Before we surrendered I saw two British soldiers coming towards me, shooting at my position. I managed to shoot at one of them, a tall blond character I have seen in a BBC documentary. I hit him in the stomach. I tried to shoot at the other British soldier, a short man with a moustache, but I couldn't. I had lost all my strength because of all the blood I had lost. I fell into the bottom of the trench and I remember seeing the British soldier pointing his rifle at me and at that moment I commended my soul to God. I thought it was the last minute of my life. But all he said in English was: 'Hands up.' I couldn't even raise my hands. The British soldier dragged me out and said: 'The war is over for you.' He applied a tourniquet on my leg and gave me his jacket to keep me warm.

He injected morphine and painted an 'M' on my face and I was taken together with the wounded in my section to a place near the house, which was still burning. I knew that inside the house we had left Lieutenant Espinosa, but it was too late to rescue him. I didn't know him that well but we had been on patrol four days together. He was a jovial character and a devout Catholic. He was a brilliant soldier and he saved our lives. I was very confused at that moment seeing our dead and wounded all around me. On the one hand I was happy and relieved to be alive but on the other I had the anguish of defeat and the sadness of seeing our dead men. Our CO asked Captain Rod Boswell, the British commander, for permission to rescue our men inside the house, but obviously Boswell realised it was too late.

After the battle of Top Malo House I was able to appreciate the human side of the British troops. Of the thirteen men in our patrol two were killed and six were wounded quite badly. We were very well treated by Captain Boswell and his people: he was obviously a good officer. He helped the wounded as much as he could and sent us to hospital as quickly as possible. I would like to take this opportunity to thank him for the way he treated us on the battlefield. I would also like to thank Dr McGregor, the surgeon at the San Carlos hospital, and everybody on *Canberra* where we were treated so well. We were very grateful for all this. I would like to get together with Captain Boswell to discuss the battle and our common memories but obviously circumstances are not quite right yet.

When we were taken prisoner we would get together every night to pray for our dead, for our families, for the Malvinas, and we asked God to give us another chance because we felt that we had let the others down. I am a deeply religious man and that moment when we all prayed together was a great moment of peace for me. We knew that God was putting us in touch with our people. It was like being at home again. We never forgot that we were PoWs and therefore our duty was to try and escape. Obviously we were not in an ideal position to do this because we were wounded, we were on a ship and we were heavily guarded. Nevertheless we tried to recover from our wounds as quickly as possible and we waited for an occasion when we could attempt to escape.*

I am a professional soldier and I follow orders. The fact that our dead soldiers are buried in the Malvinas is just a circumstance. Whether they are buried there or not, the Islands are Argentine and they are part of our territory, and as an Argentine I will fight for our Fatherland. Our dead in the Malvinas are telling me: 'Get ready.'

* British army intelligence officers foiled one such planned escape aboard a ship as it took Argentine prisoners back home. The officers among the PoWs had been passing morse code messages to each other by tapping on the water pipes between cabins.

ALASTAIR MITCHELL

Lieutenant (now Captain) Alastair Mitchell served as a platoon commander with the 2nd Battalion Scots Guards. He was injured during the battle for Mount Tumbledown – one of the last hurdles for the British army before victory at Port Stanley on 14 June 1982.

I heard I was going to the Falklands while I was at Sandhurst on a course. We were in a lecture one day, when suddenly it stopped and all the lights went up. A chap at the back said: 'Is there a Lieutenant Mitchell here?' Everyone cheered and said: 'Well you're off to the Falklands now,' but nobody believed it. I walked to the back of the room, picked up the telephone, and said who I was. A voice at the other end said: 'This is the academy adjutant. Get your winter woollies, you're going to the Falklands.' There was a stunned pause and a few questions like 'Who is this?' from me. It turned out this *was* the academy adjutant. It was a bit of a shock really. From that moment I had something like two weeks before we actually sailed.

I'm a fairly pessimistic sort of person, and gloomy at the best of times. I've got far too much imagination to be brave or gung-ho or anything like that. I was always counting up numbers of Argentine combat aircraft – of which they had 158 and we had twenty-two Harriers. These sorts of figures and statistics didn't make very optimistic reading. I knew we were going to fight and I was quite prepared to do so. I wasn't very sanguine about what the outcome might be but I wasn't actually afraid. I just knew from the word go that it wasn't going to be very pleasant. I'm not saying that other people didn't, but they seemed to have a much more short-sighted view. My company commander, John Kiszely, was in many ways of the same opinion as me. I remember once talking to him. We had just had a photograph taken of the whole of the Left Flank company. We looked at it afterwards and he said to me: 'Well, it's rather sad but some of those faces won't be there if we take a photograph on the way back.' He realised the reality of it and so had I; perhaps one or two others hadn't quite. I wrote to my family and to the girl at home who I was going to get married to as soon as I got back. I didn't say anything quite like that because I thought it might depress them.

We did a lot of first-aid training. The look of concentration on the faces of young soldiers as they learned how to patch someone up showed that they thought that they might well be doing this for real. It gave an added impetus to the whole thing.

Training covered a variety of subjects – we learned an awful lot about the Argentine army as fast as we could, their weapons, capabilities and organisation. We were pretty *au fait* with the organisation of the enemy troops on the island. We knew which regiment was which. We had to learn Spanish. Virtually the only stuff we did learn were things like: '*Manos arriba!*' and '*Rindanse*', which means 'Hands up' and 'Surrender'. We didn't think there was much point in learning 'I surrender', or anything like that. We learned how to take care of prisoners of war, we ran through the Geneva Convention many times. All our normal stuff had to be changed because it's not really slanted towards the Argentinians. With my platoon commander's *aide-mémoire* I had to take out all the photographs of Soviet aircraft and started putting in pictures of Argentinian aircraft.

There weren't too many people in the British army who knew an awful lot about the Argentinians. We had a great deal of help from our navy, who had more contacts with them. By the time you're thirteen years old you've grown out of thinking of the Germans as the eternal enemy. As far as we were concerned the British army has fought all around the world and an enemy is an enemy.

We did a lot of fitness training as well on the way down on *QE2*. We ran round the decks, and started off with a few lighter tasks to work ourselves into it. John Kiszely was a fitness fanatic who didn't suffer fools at all, or people who were unfit. We put our bergens, weighing forty to fifty pounds, on our backs and started running round the deck. If people's knees gave way, or if people sprained their ankles, then as far as the company commander was concerned that was tough. They were just pushed to one side and the rest of us carried on. It seems rather brutal but we only had a short time, we thought we were going to fight and basically you can't suffer wasters. If they weren't fit by then they never would be. It paid off because the soldiers in our company were extremely fit. In some ways that meant they were given the hardest tasks, or so it seemed. In other ways it built up great pride within the company, so it was all to the good in the end.

Our journey in the landing craft from HMS *Intrepid* to the shore was miserable – the most miserable ten or twelve hours of my entire existence. We were the first company to be loaded and then we had to wait two hours for the rest of the battalion. We were already beginning to wonder what we had let ourselves in for. We were absolutely crushed into the landing craft, you simply could not move. You sat on your bergen and we were all wrapped up in waterproofs because we knew it was going to be a fairly hairy journey. Before we left the ship we were freezing cold – the temperature was a raw one or two degrees above freezing. There was a gentle drizzle.

When the landing craft was released, off we went. It was appalling from the word go. We were running in a heavy swell, and these things with their flat bottoms and a bevel edge at the front just smack into the waves. The spray came over and everyone was drenched within ten minutes from setting off. We had to endure nine hours of this – it just seemed to go on for ever. After an hour people were entirely numb. The bottom half of our bodies went to sleep because we were cramped so tight. We were absolutely freezing cold. People had been joking to start with but they shut up after half an hour. There was a complete silence, just the crackling of radios and the awful drumming of the waves on this craft.

At one stage we thought we were coming near to the landing – a star-shell went up which illuminated the area. We thought it was friendly forces but we were on radio silence to be safe. Dawn was fast approaching and we turned round and stood offshore until we were absolutely certain that there were no enemy about. We were terrified of getting caught in those wretched things at sea. Eventually we managed to land at Bluff Cove, but getting people off was incredible. We had to pick people up, straighten their legs, put their bergens on their backs and throw them off the front end. We hadn't had anything to eat, you couldn't do anything. So we staggered on to this beach and tried to get people sorted out. There were a few dazed specimens coming ashore.

I remember seeing one particular character who stormed on to the beach and then stood absolutely stock-still, facing the landing craft. So I thought: I'd better get him moving.

I can't recall whether I actually grabbed hold of him or not but I said: 'Who are you?' He just stared at me.

I said: 'Come on, man, who are you?'

By this time I was running out of patience with these people. I was just about to pick him up and throw him into line with the rest of them when I realised it was John Kiszely, my company commander! He was giving me a fairly icy glare and wondering what the hell I was up to. Eventually we all moved on to the shore and had a very quick kip for about half an hour in the pouring rain. It felt so good to be out on land that most people fell asleep instantly. Then we set off for Bluff Cove farmhouse.

We had heard that we might get our feet wet in the sea trying to get ashore. To an infantryman his feet are vitally important. We had no idea of how long the campaign was going to last, or for how long we were going to be required to march. We were very concerned to look after people's feet. Before we landed we got plastic bin-liners and people wrapped them round their feet. There is no point in getting wet feet if you don't have to, and if you get salt water into your clothes and boots coming ashore it can lead to problems. The salt crystals left behind are hygroscopic and will absorb water. Leather boots are ruined.

(The battle for Mount Tumbledown took place on the night of 13–14 June 1982.)

It started when we moved through one of our companies who were meant to take out an enemy position. The enemy wasn't there, so that company stopped where they were and we moved through their lines and on to our objective. Nothing happened. The tension was electric. We moved in extended line and still nothing happened. We were just waiting. After a while you felt almost a sense of relief. People were beginning to think: They've bugged out, they're not here any more. Suddenly the horizon lit up in a complete sea of white flashes.

Automatic weapons fired at night are extremely bright against this backcloth of grey sky and gloomy granite rocks. The flashes were fairly blinding at first. Everybody got down because the initial fire-fight was incredible, it was like being at the wrong end of a machine-gun range. Bullets at close range cracked like a whip over your head. The air was full of bits of lead and chunks of rock which were being broken off and were flying around all over the place. For a minute or two we were fairly stunned. You had the feeling that if you raised your hand slightly in the air it would be shot off. It was incredible. We recovered rapidly and the Argentinians never again put down quite that weight of fire. Even so, our first introduction was slightly shocking. It showed just how much firepower they had.

In that situation commanding a platoon is probably rather easier than being an ordinary soldier. I can honestly say that from the moment the firing started until much later on I wasn't scared at all. I had a job to do and I had twenty-nine people who were looking to me to do it. You don't have time to think, I barely fired my rifle. People were talking to me on the radio, asking for this and that. Section commanders were saying: 'What do we do now?' and so on. It must have been more frightening for the ordinary soldier stuck behind a rock returning fire, wondering what on earth is going to happen to him next. He probably has time to think. I didn't. I went through the normal, logical process of trying to get as much fire down on the enemy as possible, while I worked out how on earth we were going to take them out. We certainly weren't going straight in from the front. That was out from the word go. We weren't going to die like that.

The soldiers were good. You would say: 'Deal with that section out there . . .' and they would go and do it. In a strange and chaotic situation like that, which is frightening because all hell is breaking loose, soldiers like to be told what to do. Even the most bolshie individual – the typical barrack-room lawyer who would always be questioning this, that or the other on a peacetime exercise – suddenly says: 'What do you want me to do now sir?' In peacetime you go through mock battles; you practise this sort of thing but you always know that it would be worse if the enemy was actually firing back at you.

When I gave my orders for Tumbledown, twenty-four hours before we did the attack, I said to my three section commanders and platoon sergeant: 'In the end this is going to disintegrate into utter chaos. It is going to be a case of little groups of guardsmen having the courage to keep going forward.' And that is what happened – it disintegrated into a section commander's war. It was pretty much as I had imagined it.

After I gave the orders we talked and they wanted to know what we could expect in the way of casualties. I made it clear to them that there were basically three people in a platoon who were liable to get killed. One is the platoon commander, for obvious reasons: he's up there at the front and you can't always look after yourself when you're looking after other people. The other one is the chap carrying the anti-tank weapon, because it's incredibly heavy, and it limits him. And the other is the platoon commander's radio operator, because he's carrying a heavy radio. I pointed out that I had no intention of dying. They seemed quite pleased to hear that, because if I wasn't going to die it meant they probably weren't either. Funnily enough, soldiers are more likely to follow someone who makes that plain than they are with someone who wants to be a hero. Heroes are all right when they only kill themselves, but people back off a bit when they are liable to involve other people's lives.

Actually fighting the battle brought a great relief in tension. There was no going back, this was it, and I was glad to be getting it over and done with. I thought we could win. I thought we would be all right and that our casualties would be fairly light. But it got worse when I realised that the Argentines we were fighting against were the 5th Marine Infantry Battalion. We had been warned they were a hard bunch. We had spoken to people who had fought against the conscript regiments and it wasn't that bad. But it began to dawn on me that these people just weren't going to budge. They were shouting various obscene phrases at us in English, threatening what they were going to do to us. It was one thing when they started firing at us, but when they shouted at us – that was another. It's all very well shooting a target, but when the target is speaking and you realise it's a human being, things are actually rather different.

They opened up at about 300 metres. From then on we went right in close. There were many occasions where we would be sitting behind a rock and forty metres away, just out of grenade range, an Argentine would be sitting behind a rock. One of us would poke a head round the rock and take a potshot at him and he would take a shot at us, and so it went on. They didn't sit in their holes and wait to be shot at, they came out and tried to have a go at us from the flanks. They had a great weight of firepower because their FAL rifles can fire on automatic. It began to dawn on us after a few hours, when we simply couldn't move, that things were getting tough. We did get extremely close to them and we were pinned down.

We always knew we could do it in the end, I did anyway. My company commander managed to get the artillery properly adjusted. We brought the artillery in extremely close. I would say we had our own 105 mm shells landing seventy-five to eighty metres away.

We did a rather strange manoeuvre, like something out of the First World War, except there was a shorter distance of no-man's-land. The company commander ordered me to just go straight in after the third salvo of shells. The situation was deadlock and had been for many hours. We were trying to get the artillery adjusted in close to the Argentinians but we were just taking casualties. Inevitably, once every half-hour someone would be hit. We didn't seem to be getting anywhere. In the end John Kiszely gripped the situation and got hold of my platoon. He told me: 'Right, you are going to have to go straight in there. We'll give you three salvos of artillery and then in you go.'

By this stage the situation had changed slightly. The platoon on my left had managed to get up into the rocks and were able to fire down into the Argentine trenches from above. We were then able to move round to the flank. Thirteen or fourteen of us lined out and we were ready to go straight into the middle of the Argentinian position when the third salvo landed. I was worried that we were going to run into our own shells. I also thought: This is possibly the end of me and the remains of my platoon. But frankly, after four or five hours of being shot at and shooting people, I couldn't give a damn any more. I wanted to go in there and get it sorted out. So I thought I'd probably die. I know it sounds remarkable but I really had just had enough. I didn't care. I was getting quite angry and I despaired of doing anything else. I thought: Well fair enough, we'll go in there and we'll do it. I remember telling the sergeant who was going to be with me on this particular manoeuvre what was going to happen. He looked at me ... I just shrugged my shoulders. I'm sure every one of us thought we are going to get three yards and get cut down, or we are going to end up running the other way in a few moments.

We lined out, and sure enough the three salvos came in and on the last one there was almost a deathly hush in the battle. There was a plaintive cry from me of: 'Is that really the last one?' to John Kiszely and his radio operators because I was very worried of running into the incoming shells. They said: 'Yes.' Then we just got up and went in. We ran straight into the middle of the Argentinian position which was only sixty to seventy yards away. Once in there we started skirmishing through. We charged straight in and caught them as they came out of their holes. People were dropping grenades, shooting them at close range – in some cases a couple of yards. Some enemy were bayoneted. When you clear a trench it has to be done properly, because we took one or two casualties from Argentines who popped up behind us. They were in extremely deep holes which were well built.

Several times we took surrenders and would obviously keep ourselves in as good a position as possible with our sights on the Argentines. We shouted at them in Spanish to surrender, which for anybody is a pretty harrowing experience. If ever I had to surrender I would think twice about it. I would only do it if it was absolutely necessary. You have to make sure you've laid down your weapon. If an Argentine was coming out of a hole with a weapon I would be extremely careful about what I did. If he was suddenly to go down behind a rock I think I would probably give the order to fire. Argentines coming out with their hands up are a different matter – they're fairly harmless. But you've got to be watching around you to see who is behind them and who is off to the sides. It is difficult for both sides when a surrender is taking place. As soon as we got them up to us we then quickly searched them and bundled them straight back, out of the way.

In the middle of this enemy position we suddenly felt the resistance crash. It was a tangible thing. Suddenly the Argentines, who had been shouting to us a few minutes before, were now streaming down the hill, running away, although some were running *up* the hill. I will always remember my machine-gunner who was beside me. He said: 'What shall I do sir?' There were many Argentines running down the hill. Because they didn't have their weapons with them, I didn't give the order to fire. I have often wondered about that, because some of these people were later involved in mortaring our stretcher parties ... nevertheless, that's what I did.

You can always tell, if you're close to someone, when they've been hit, because you hear the crack of the bullet, but you also hear a horrible 'thwack' as the bullet hits solid flesh and bone. It's pretty unpleasant. It's an extraordinary noise, and even if you've never heard that sort of thing before you instinctively know exactly what's happened. You are quite used to hearing the crack of bullets. You are used to hearing the whine as they ricochet off rock. Then suddenly there is this dull 'thwack', and that is pretty grim.

Just before we did the final attack which cleared the enemy, we were waiting and getting in position. Some of the enemy started crawling towards us to attack. They were getting closer and closer and it was only a matter of time before they got in grenade range. You simply couldn't see them there. One of my soldiers who had a nightsight suddenly saw one of them and we heard the crack and the thump as it hit the Argentinian. There was a moment's silence and then there was the most terrible screaming from this Argentinian. He was screaming for his mother. There was complete silence from both sides at that point. Both of us listened to it and I am sure we, in a way, were just as horrified as the Argentinians. It really was an awful noise and it went on and on and on.

When we eventually got to the top of the mountain it was an amazing feeling. Seven of us got up to the top in that initial stage – John Kiszely, myself and five others. As we started going up the mountain the enemy were melting before us. We went faster and faster until we got to the top. We almost couldn't believe that we were at the top and there, just four kilometres away and clearly in view, was Stanley. We could see the lights, we could even see the lights of vehicles moving along the roads. For a second or two we just stood there looking at this with absolute euphoria: 'We've done it. We've got no more to do. This is it.'

Of course that was fatal because at that moment, from 200 metres away, an Argentine automatic weapon and several other weapons opened up on us. In that initial burst, which was almost an ambush really, three of us were hit. I saw the person in front of me just spin round, pirouette round. He had been hit in the hand and the force had literally knocked him spinning like a top. There was a crack behind me and someone had been hit. It all seemed to be in slow motion; in fact, it was my brain thinking rather faster. As I turned to run for the nearest cover myself, I suddenly felt something like enormous hammer blows to my legs. The tracer from the rounds was like scarlet rods all round me. My rifle had been hit and disappeared. I found myself crawling into the nearest dip in the ground. Rounds were cracking all around us.

I wasn't quite sure whether I'd been hit by bits of mud thrown up by the machine-gun burst or whether I had actually been hit by the rounds themselves. I noticed that my legs, and especially my right leg, were very stiff already. There was a brief burning sensation through the muscle on my right arm. I put my right hand down to touch my leg and two of my fingers went in up to the knuckles. It was at that point I realised I had actually been hit by pieces of metal. John Kiszely returned fire and was crawling around under the fire, trying to patch up various people. I somewhat apologetically let him know that I'd been hit as well. He was blaming himself for the incident. God knows why, it certainly wasn't his fault, and he did a good job of patching us up. Unfortunately, in my case he patched up the leg which didn't have too many holes in it. Neither of us realised that the other leg was completely riddled.

At first I felt almost a sense of relief. I was out of it. That sounds extraordinary but I was out of it and I knew the platoon behind me was safe. There was nothing else to do and I *knew* I was going home. It didn't take many minutes for me to start taking a slightly longer-sighted view. There were Argentinians still only 200 metres away desperately trying to kill me. I didn't know how badly I was injured and it was starting to hurt.

It was a hairy business getting the stretchers to those of us who had been wounded. They had to carry on the battle, take out the remaining Argentines, and the stretcher-bearers found it very difficult to get to us. They were very brave carrying us down. One of them was wounded in the arm as he brought the stretcher in and he plodded on regardless, carrying it with his good arm. He refused to let anyone else carry it. We set off in a convoy of three stretchers.

We were up there for several hours before we got any kind of medical attention because the fight was still going on. And there were the poor boys from my platoon carrying me over very difficult ground. We carried on down the hill and suddenly a mortar round landed 200 or 300 metres away. By now it was daylight and I can see no excuse for this whatsoever. It must have been quite obvious to the Argentinian mortar-fire controllers, who were probably on Mount William, that we were stretcher parties. Within a short time they 'walked' the mortars, adjusting them on to us. Two or three bombs went off near us. Next thing I was lying a short distance from my stretcher. There was complete silence. I had never heard the blast. I turned around. The stretcher-bearers were in pieces.

One of them was completely blown to pieces. It was really wretched. I couldn't believe it. One of those killed in this unfortunate incident was the soldier who very bravely ran to pick up the stretcher even when he had been wounded.

Guardsman Findlay, one of the others, was relatively uninjured. He had a chunk taken out of the middle of his hand. We looked at each other, we'd just about had enough. There was nothing we could do for the others, most of them were badly wounded. We started making our way down the hill. I marked on my map the position where this had taken place. As soon as I met someone else down the hill I intended getting a helicopter in. We met a corporal and told him where the casualties were. He gave them first-aid. Guardsman Findlay and I got ourselves back about a kilometre with me using his rifle as a crutch and him supporting me. At times we had to slide down because my legs were seizing up. We made our way back to the regimental aid post.

(Lieutenant Mitchell was transferred to the field hospital at Ajax Bay.)

When they carried me in to label and tag me and decide what they were going to do with me initially, the first thing I noticed was how incredibly warm it was. For six weeks I had been living in a hole in the ground. I had got used to being cold and it didn't bother me too much after a while. This warmth was so incredible that after about ten seconds of lying there on the stretcher I passed out. They took that opportunity to take off most of my clothes – it's quite a painful business. I gather that it was a fairly normal reaction for people to flake out when they were carried in to the field hospital. The next thing I noticed was that it was quite palatial for an old refrigeration hut. When you're not used to seeing a roof, a building like that can seem luxurious after a while. There was also the odd table here and there. It seemed almost civilised.

There was a queue of casualties to be operated on and they put me in a tent for a while. I went to sleep but I have no idea for how long. I remember being wheeled in for the first of several operations. I shall be eternally grateful to the surgeons for patching me up so well.

When I was waiting to go in for my operation I was on a stretcher, lying next to an Argentinian. There were quite a few of them lying around in this place and also one or two Argentinian doctors. I noticed a naval surgeon commander come over and speak to me. He mentioned that there was a ceasefire and he translated that for the Argentinian lying next to me as well. I don't know which of us looked the more relieved, him or me. This naval officer spoke a bit of Spanish and sort of squatted down and started interpreting between me and the Argentinian lying beside me. He was just a boy, an Indian who came from somewhere north of Buenos Aires and had a wife, and so on. He appeared to me not to know really what was going on. All he knew was that he had been shot through the legs as well and that it hurt a great deal. He was grateful to the British for looking after him. The next day he was shifted out by helicopter to *Uganda*. I don't know if he had been in a helicopter before but he was terrified as they lifted him up into this amazing vibrating machine. He probably thought they were going to dump him in the sea. I remember the crewman in the helicopter not quite holding his hand, but giving him a sort of pat on the head to calm him down because this chap looked absolutely terrified.

I pitied him. The Argentines who fought against the Scots Guards on Tumbledown were a tough lot, but on the whole you got the impression they were just conscripts. We were professional soldiers and much better than them. We felt rather sorry for them, they weren't volunteers.

When I was wheeled in people were being operated on all round me. I was incredibly relieved, I was almost looking forward to it. I thought: Great, they will sort me out. They explained roughly that they were going to do. They didn't know what was wrong with me. They started poking around and then shot me full of something called Omnipom [morphine], which just put me out.

They flew us home to Brize Norton. My parents and little sister were waiting to see me and the girl I was going to get married to. The workers from the local NAAFI had been hauled out to wave the flag. It was great to be back but I was slightly more worried about what they might think about me. Many of the people had much worse injuries than me. They had lost legs and were worried about how their little children would cope with this sort of thing. It wasn't too bad for me because I managed to walk off the plane, which was quite an effort but worth it because I think my parents expected me to be hauled off on a stretcher with drips and things. It seemed a bit dreamlike to be back after being in that battle on the mountain.

People in the army who weren't in the Falklands say to me: 'It must have been a great experience.' I'm not convinced. I had a platoon of twenty-nine in which there were twelve casualties, including two who were killed. If I was asked to go and do it again, obviously I would because I am a soldier. It was interesting because you lived life at a much higher level and saw human emotions at the highest and the lowest. It's not the sort of thing I'd like to go and do every morning before breakfast, frankly. And I didn't enjoy it in any sense of the word at all.

CARLOS HUGO ROBACIO

Captain Carlos Hugo Robacio, who commanded the 5th Marine Infantry Battalion, is a career Argentine soldier. He is based at the Marine Infantry's main headquarters just outside Puerto Belgrano. In the Malvinas campaign he was involved in the fighting against the Scots Guards in one of the decisive battles of the war, on Mount Tumbledown.

I'm proud of being a Marine, especially after the Malvinas war, which was a marvellous experience for a professional soldier, although it was not really a Marines operation, with the exception of the original occupation of the Islands. Despite the fact that we had to surrender I am proud of what we did. We inflicted far greater damage on the enemy than has been admitted. When it was over I not only had to bury our dead but also the British dead, and there were quite a few of them.

I was sent to the Islands after the initial occupation. When I first heard that Argentina had landed on the Islands I was proud of what the government had done, but I was even more proud when we went into actual combat. We knew that we were up against an enemy who knew his job and had adequate resources. I would not call what happened a war, it was a battle, a good battle. Lady luck may have frowned on us but I am convinced that in the long run we shall triumph.

Nobody was really surprised by what happened there. We all knew it would be a long hard battle, and we also knew that we were at a disadvantage. We went with what we had and we did what we could. It doesn't matter what the result was – we tried. I think that a nation which asks to recover part of its territory must be prepared to fight for it. Recovering the Islands was a fundamental milestone in our history.

The battle on Tumbledown was terribly hard, and I think it went

212

beyond what both sides thought modern warfare would be like. We were all surprised to see how fast and hard modern combat is. It was so quick and violent that on one occasion my subordinate asked me to order artillery fire on their positions when they were being overrun. All I could do was to warn them thirty seconds ahead so that at least they could take cover.

Nobody gave up, and we have acts of courage and valour that go beyond the call of duty. I remember two specific cases. They were not decorated because they didn't follow orders. In one case they managed to push back and attack. One of our men jumped out of his trench and actually pursued the enemy; he died five metres ahead of our positions, fighting as what he was – a brave man.

In the other case a soldier refused to withdraw when ordered to do so and finally, even after he had run out of ammunition, the only way they could get him out was by blowing him to pieces. I myself had to put those pieces in a plastic bag.

You have to be proud of these men, even though many of them weren't professional soldiers. They refused to give up and only did when circumstances forced us to do so because we ran out of ammunition. I found it especially hard to order a surrender.

All the conscripts who were wounded and taken prisoner by the British were treated very well and I am very grateful for that. When I returned to the mainland and talked to them they told me how well they had been looked after by the British doctors. This shows how humane both sides were during the war.

On the last day of the war – 14 June – at about 6.30 a.m., I thought that we were still winning. My unit hadn't suffered any real losses. We hadn't given up any of our positions. All we had lost was a very, very small part of Mount Tumbledown. I knew that we were running out of ammunition, so I asked my headquarters for more. We were concentrating our efforts on Mount Tumbledown because that was the battle which would seal the fate of Puerto Argentino. Unfortunately we never received the ammunition we needed. At about seven o'clock I received the order to withdraw prior to a surrender. Our military code states that for an Argentine military unit to surrender it must have spent all its ammunition or lost at least two-thirds of its men. It was awful to have to ask the units which were still fighting to withdraw. It was a very bitter moment. We really felt defeated. You could see the battle coming to an end. The unit withdrew in orderly fashion, under intense enemy fire and with the help of God, because God exists on the battlefield.

Then my men prepared to resist on Sapper Hill to the last man, but we were told that our commanding officers had already surrendered and I had to give my units the order to withdraw yet again. But we felt proud because we had spent all our ammunition. Obviously I think the worst thing that can happen to a soldier, the most humiliating thing in his life, must be to give up and surrender, but I hope that it is we who next time will be taking the prisoners.

We fought against very professional soldiers and I learned a lot from my enemy, and I hope to be able to apply it one day so that I can use what they showed me to reoccupy our land.

MARIO BENJAMIN MENENDEZ

General Mario Benjamin Menendez comes from one of Argentina's most distinguished military families. He was serving at the office of the Joint Chiefs of Staff in early 1982 when he was appointed military governor of the Malvinas.

I had a meeting with General Galtieri on 2 March 1982. It started out as a routine meeting. He was both army Commander-in-Chief and President of the Republic. I reported on my area of responsibility in the office of the Chiefs of Staff, and at the end of the meeting he said that he had important news for me. It was then that he told me that the junta were preparing the military occupation of the Malvinas, depending on how the negotiations with Britain evolved. This was completely unexpected – a great surprise – and I was deeply moved because of all that the Malvinas means to me as an Argentine and as a soldier. General Galtieri told me that if the military occupation took place I had been chosen to be military governor of the Islands, not the military commander, because the government did not foresee the possibility of any major military operation. As military governor I would have the great responsibility of integrating the Islands into the Argentine nation and of trying to win over the local population.

My arrival on the islands at Puerto Argentino was a dream come true for the Argentines. [The knowledge of our rights over the Malvinas] is a very profound feeling; an ambition and, at the same time, a frustration. All this was running through my mind as the plane was about to land on the Islands and, as we touched down, we all shouted: 'Long live the Fatherland!' I was very moved by this, but also worried, because by the time I arrived in the Islands there had already been the vote in the UN and the British Task Force had already sailed. So there were a few doubts and this made me feel the weight of my responsibility even more. Above all, there was a pride of knowing that I was the first Argentine governor of the Malvinas in 150 years.

I had very clear political instructions as to the way I had to carry out my job. There were three main elements. The first was to respect the habits and traditions and property of the Islanders. The second, to try and maintain their living standards and, as soon as possible, to try and improve them. There was no doubt they could have been improved. The third was to try and establish close links with the Islanders so that we could in the long run integrate them into the Argentine way of life. One measure that we had not foreseen but had to take was the change in the direction of traffic. When General Garcia first arrived he noticed many military vehicles were moving around with drivers not experienced at driving on the left. He believed it was dangerous and would cause accidents and decided to change the rule to driving on the right.

Our relations with the Islanders were not easy. We knew the local population would resent our presence, that they would be wary of us, and this is exactly what happened. Some of the inhabitants of Puerto Argentino had gone to stay with relatives in the countryside and were afraid of returning. However, little by little, we established a relationship with the locals, especially through Commodore Bloomer-Reeve, who had actually lived in the Malvinas for two years [as representative of the Argentine state airline LADE]. He knew the people well and talked to them and brought some of them over to talk to me.

We had interesting conversations about the hopes and ambitions of the Islanders: how, for example, they saw the role of the Falkland Islands Company, which employed the majority of the population and owned the Islands' main store. They wanted to have greater freedom, especially in the interior of the Island. Many things could be done. You could industrialise seaweed, increase fisheries, drill for oil – there are all sorts of possibilities. The Islanders wanted to know what role they could play in this. There were also basic improvements that could be carried out. The colonial government had been promising for ages to build a road network. All they had built in 150 years of occupation was fifteen kilometres of road. We knew that this could be improved upon and that communications with the Islands were in need of a drastic overhaul. We

216

could have done it, had we had the time.

So there were many projects that would have fulfilled the hopes and ambitions of the Islanders, but gradually, with the approach of the Task Force, we had to concentrate on other priorities. As our military presence in Puerto Argentino grew, the 600 or 700 inhabitants became a little island in a sea of 10,000 Argentine soldiers sent from the mainland. It is a great source of pride to me that during two and a half months of occupation there was not one serious incident: not one single rape or attempted rape, no assaults. There were some thefts and burglaries but it was mostly food that was taken. There was intense patrolling by our military police and a very strict discipline to ensure that soldiers could not move individually around Puerto Argentino. There were courts martial that sentenced officers and soldiers who had violated these norms. Compensation was paid for anything lost or stolen. I remember that we even paid compensation for a cat which was run over by a military truck.

The houses, jeeps and tractors that we used were not requisitioned, they were rented. We always paid for everything we used and we still have the receipts. One of the most serious problems was supplies for the local population, because the FIC ship could no longer make the journey from Britain. We solved this with our own supplies, but we also banned our troops from buying food or basic supplies from the West Store so that the Islanders would not go without. The best indication of the respect with which we treated the local populace was the visit of the International Red Cross at the beginning of June. They were allowed to interview any Islanders they wanted without any Argentines present. After that they came to see me and told me they were surprised at the absence of any serious accusations from the Islanders.

We also had to guarantee the Islanders' safety, especially in the last days of the war. We organised shelters and fire-fighting groups. On 15 June, when we had already been defeated, Commodore Bloomer-Reeve was walking towards a helicopter that was going to take him to the PoW camp, and two local women came up to him and said how grateful they were for the way they had been treated by the Argentines in the hour of victory and in the hour of defeat. This shows the attitude of the more objective Islanders.

There was no structured plan for the defence of the Island because the original plan for the occupation of the Malvinas did not contemplate the possibility of a British military reaction. Naturally this caused serious problems later on because we had to improvise a defence plan, and when other military units started arriving in the Malvinas sometimes they didn't have the proper logistical support – all the problems you encounter when you have not properly planned ahead. Then things were made even more difficult by the problems caused by the Exclusion Zone and the British blockade. We tried to organise a defence as best we could.

The British landing at San Carlos was not completely unexpected. It was one of the many places in which they could have landed. I know the British considered other sites such as Fitzroy and Barclay Sound, so we couldn't possibly cover all of them. The main target clearly was Puerto Argentino, and it was there that we had to concentrate our forces because we could not move them around. We sent out small units to San Carlos so that we would receive an early alert, but that unit could not obviously offer any resistance. It was almost impossible to prevent the landing by sending troops to the beachhead. Our helicopters could not fly because the British dominated the air. We could only send forward patrols who clashed with the British soldiers on many occasions. Their main mission was to observe and report on the deployment of the British forces, so that we could call in air strikes against the beachhead as a way of limiting the landings.

It was impossible to mount a full-scale counter-attack against the British at that stage. Initially we thought that the landing at San Carlos could have been a diversion, and that is why I ordered our planes to recce the area so we would have an idea of the magnitude of the operation. The first news of the landing came from a Lieutenant Esteban, but we lost contact shortly after he reported, and we didn't have many details. After Lieutenant Crippa flew over San Carlos and counted the number of British ships there was no longer any doubt that this was the main British landing.

The Battle of Goose Green was the first major confrontation between the two sides. The 12th Regiment fought very well and with great vigour, offering fierce resistance. We were able to send some reinforcements by helicopter because the weather conditions were so bad the British planes couldn't fly. Unfortunately the air strikes from the mainland were unable to reach their targets, again through bad weather. We made every effort, and that night when we discussed the possible courses of action with the commanding officer at Goose Green, he was authorised to surrender whenever he thought it necessary. There was not really much point in continuing the resistance against an enemy who was far stronger and had him completely surrounded.

The defence of Puerto Argentino was organised in three stages. Firstly we set up a perimeter of 360°, because initially we had thought that this would be the first British target in their attack on the Islands. After the San Carlos landing this all changed, because we could determine which way the British troops were going to advance. We then reinforced the western sector with other units and set up new minefields, but all this was done with very limited resources. It was very difficult to move our artillery around because we didn't have enough helicopters. In spite of all this our defences were reasonably strong. There was no doubt that the fight for Puerto Argentino was going to be the final battle of the war. We had prepared for this and had put up several ideas to the high command on the mainland, which sadly were not accepted. We were able to follow the British advance through the reports from our patrols. We had a good idea of where they were more than likely to attack and the possible placement of their artillery and reserve units. But we could not exploit this knowledge because of our limited transport capacity. The truth is that our commandos operated well and brought in a lot of intelligence, capturing enemy equipment and codes, which also helped. We could not prevent the British attack but we had enough information to prepare ourselves.

The British had established complete air superiority and they dominated the sea. We were completely surrounded. When the final battle started the great British strength in firepower became more evident. They also had greater skills in night-fighting. When you take all this into account it stops being a matter of courage or will to resist. We fought hard and managed to resist the enemy on the heights as long as possible. Our troops had been under intense bombardment, and on the ground for a long time in harsh weather conditions. They were extremely tired. There was a very hard fight for Mount Tumbledown involving our marines. The same for Longdon with the 7th Infantry Regiment. By the morning of 14 June, Tumbledown was on the verge of being lost and we realised that we had no cards left to play. Our artillery was reduced to ten or twelve pieces. We had no direct air support and the enemy ships were offshore reinforcing their land artillery. We had lost equipment and we had many losses through combat fatigue. Everything was very disorganised. The only high ground still in our hands was Sapper Hill and the only thing at that point which could have avoided a military defeat was a military solution. Continuing our resistance would only have meant losing lives in vain. This was the conclusion I reached, and after some contacts with my superior officers [on the mainland] I decided to accept the ceasefire offered by the British and start negotiations.

Signing the surrender was the culmination of a process of anguish and great sadness. I could not conceive of our troops being defeated because I knew they had done everything possible to defend the Islands and Puerto Argentino within their possibilities and within their limitations. Perhaps more could have been done in other circumstances. So there was a feeling of sadness and great tension but there was no shame. When I talked to Colonel Rose [CO of 22 SAS Regiment, who negotiated the surrender] my main worry was to make sure that the bravery and courage with which the Argentinians had fought be recognised by the British. He accepted this. We are not talking about efficiency here, we are talking about courage. On this basis we were to be allowed certain conditions in our defeat: to be allowed to return home with our battle flags; to allow officers to keep their personal weapons while we were on the Islands; and to retain command over our units. All these mean much to a soldier, even in defeat.

For me it was tremendously painful, but I had reached my conclusion and was conscious that we had done everything possible and that my troops, officers and soldiers, had shown great spirit of sacrifice, and of courage – as high as anything shown by Argentine troops throughout our history. When General Moore presented me with the surrender document I pointed out to him that the surrender was not unconditional and he agreed to strike that word out.

JULIAN THOMPSON

Brigadier Julian Thompson commanded 3 Commando Brigade in the Falklands campaign and planned the British landings at San Carlos. He has now retired from the Royal Marines and is a senior research fellow in the War Studies Department at King's College, London.

Planning the retaking of the Falklands started on 2 April 1982, the day the Argentines invaded. I was at Plymouth without my staff because most of them were on an exercise recce in Denmark. This was alarming because without my experts I felt somewhat naked. It became very apparent as the planning started unrolling that the superior head-quarters at Northwood [in London] didn't realise the enormous amount of shipping we would need to take all the men and stores down south. In the early hours there were heated exchanges on the telephone with Northwood, explaining why we needed a certain number of ships. This all got very much better when they started requisitioning liners like the *Canberra* and the civilian ships.

What was enormously helpful was when Major Ewan Southby-Tailyour walked in and said: 'Here, I've got all these maps and documents.' He had some years earlier commanded the Royal Marines detachment on the Falklands and had spent a lot of time studying the Islands and the coastal waters. I said: 'You'd better come with us then,' and he replied: 'There is no way I am not coming.'

The other person who was extremely important in the planning process was Commodore Mike Clapp, who was my opposite number in the Royal Navy. In this planning for an amphibious operation the troops cannot simply land where they like. It might not suit the navy to take you there because of rocks and shoals, it may not be good for

221

protection from submarines and the like. So planning this operation was a joint effort which became the theme for the whole seven weeks it took us to get down there. We had to consult the navy all the time, and inevitably when you're having consultations with people, there'll be disagreements. There were very few with Mike Clapp. We used to have our breakfast together every day for seven weeks – and if you can have breakfast with someone for seven weeks I reckon it means you're getting on with them all right.

One of the major difficulties we had was that over the years Britain's amphibious warfare capability has been cut down to such a degree that there is a large body of people in the services who have no experience of it whatsoever. This was a landing for which there would be no second chance. There was going to be no Dieppe followed by Normandy. If it didn't work the first time it would be a disaster, so we had to get it right. But we found a lack of understanding at various levels above us of the problems of making an amphibious landing. So when we said: 'We'll need this, we'll need air cover, we'll need air superiority,' we were greeted sometimes with disbelief, and were told we were exaggerating the problems.

The main worry was that we didn't have air superiority. We ran the risk that we would either have an enormous loss of life by a lot of ships being sunk on the way in, or while we were carrying out the actual invasion. It seemed to me that one way round this problem was to go for the mainland air bases in Argentina, to destroy or certainly seriously hamper their air force. I didn't actually say to Northwood: 'Why don't we do this?' but it was certainly in my mind, when I said: 'Don't you think we should do something about their air force?' Politically it plainly wasn't on, which is why it wasn't done. We made these points known – we didn't really get a very satisfactory answer. I sent a letter to Northwood in which I said: 'We will, of course, carry out the landing because that's what we have been told to do, but you should know that if we are attacked by the air, and the enemy is successful in their attack, we will take very very heavy casualties indeed.' The implication of that would have been that we might have lost all.

We had been told to land in the Falkland Islands, decide where you are going to land and how you are going to do it. All the time I was conscious of the fact that I was responsible for the lives of a large number of men and responsible also for the success of this operation.

On my shoulders rested the hopes and aspirations of rather a lot of people. I felt this pressure bearing down on me, and this coloured one's view of life as I led it.

We all had mixed feelings on the way down, when we had time to think and reflect. One emotion was the elation that we were going to do something very big, in many cases for the first time. Linked to that was the feeling of: What are we doing? Why are we here? Most of us were pretty clear we were there for a point of principle. Equally we were clear that we were there to sort out a problem that had been caused by political misjudgement. There is nothing new in that for soldiers. On the one hand this was part of the contract – you have to go and carry out an operation because this is what the taxpayer pays you to do. On the other hand you might die, and you then ask yourself: What are we dying for? In all our minds we were quite clear that there was a right cause for which we were laying down our lives. But at the same time, although you don't mind, if you like, dying for your Queen and your country, you certainly don't contemplate dying for politicians.

On board HMS *Fearless* I had a cabin where I used to meet with my planning staff. Usually we spread a map out on the floor because there wasn't room to put them anywhere else. We gathered round working out the various options. From time to time one would have a conversation on the telephone with Northwood. They would ask: 'What's your plan now?' and I would give the plan and then be grilled about it and asked why I wanted to do it in that particular way. Often the ship would be in rough seas, so one was clinging on to something to avoid being thrown about while talking over a rather bad and crackly line which would often go out and come in again. Frequently, in order to have a five- or ten-minute conversation, I would be in this little shack – where the telephone was – for half an hour, scribbling frantically with my notebook balanced on my knee, trying to remember what had been said to me over this extremely bad telephone line.

There was for me, all the time, a sense of frustration that both at Northwood and on the Admiral's staff there was not quite the fullest understanding as I saw it of the amphibious problem. I put over the points I wanted covered only to be grilled about why this or that had to be done. I assumed the reasons were pretty obvious. Plainly they didn't understand how an amphibious operation should be carried out. It was quite a low point. We were running a risk of losing a lot of people and I felt we were bashing our heads against a brick wall trying to explain this to the people back in England and they weren't hoisting it in.

To plan this landing, intelligence was absolutely vital, and there were two key things we needed to know: what were the beaches like, and what was behind them? We wanted to know things like whether the gradient was right for a landing, was there room behind the beach or was it a bog? We also needed to know where the enemy were and in what strength, because we wanted to land where the enemy wasn't. We did not want to have a head-on bloody landing with heavy casualties straight into their main force.

There are two ways you get this intelligence: you are told by your superiors from above because they and we were listening to the enemy radio transmissions; another way was by aerial photography, but we didn't have aeroplanes capable of doing that with us.

The only answer was to send men to go and look at the problem. They then had either to send a signal back, giving the information we wanted, or come back and tell us where the enemy was, what the beaches were like, what the terrain is like. This was done by our Special Forces: the Special Boat Squadron of the Royal Marines [SBS], and the SAS, the army's Special Air Service Regiment. Together these are probably the finest Special Forces troops anywhere in the world. That is their role in war: long-range intelligence gathering. In this instance they started on 1 May when the carrier battle group began inserting them covertly at night on to the Islands.

We were able to insert these patrols at night by using helicopters whose pilots were equipped with night-vision goggles. There were only four of these, so the lift capability was pretty small. They were launched from away out to sea – about seventy to eighty miles – and they landed the patrols a long way from their eventual destination because the noise of the helicopters landing near enemy troops would have given away something was going on. It was highly dangerous work. Although we picked insertion points where we thought there would be no one around, there could well have been an enemy patrol recently moved into that position.

Our patrols would then march for four or five nights to their final destination. They would only move at night, lying up by day. Towards morning they had to find somewhere to shelter. When they arrived at the final position from which they would observe the enemy, they would build a hide. This was done by placing chicken wire, which they would carry with them, over a hollow between rocks, or over a hole which they dug. This wire would be covered with peat turves and they would live in the shelter which usually filled up with water rapidly, because they were in a peat bog. By day they would lie up and observe what was going on. By night they would carry out other tasks – searching beaches, trying to get very close to enemy positions. Occasionally they got so close they could lie and hear the enemy troops talking, and see them lighting fires. They would move back before daylight, so they could hide before dawn broke. Of course it was extremely uncomfortable for them in their hides. You couldn't go out in daylight even to answer the call of nature. Once an Argentine helicopter actually landed right on one of these hides. The down-draught started blowing away the peat off the top of the chicken wire, but they were not discovered I'm glad to say.

From their hides they had to get the information they had gathered back to us. Usually in these sort of operations this would be sent back by radio. Because we didn't have short-burst transmission facility radios,* the Special Forces Patrols would have had to have spent an hour and a half, using a morse key, sending back the message. The danger of this is that it would have enabled the Argentines to have located them using direction-finding equipment. It was vitally important that they were never discovered near a site where we might land because that would immediately give away the spot we were interested in. Often I would give orders that they were to come back for debriefing personally, face to face. Of course this increased the risk, because every time you infiltrate or exfiltrate a patrol you double the risk of them being found. Not having those short-burst transmission radios was definitely a disadvantage. The patrols would have to march back overnight for several nights before they reached a predetermined rendezvous point where the helicopter would pick them up.

---

* On covert operations SAS and SBS troops normally encode a message on a special radio. It is compressed, and then transmitted at high speed – i.e. in a short-burst radio transmission – to prevent an enemy listening in and locating the source.

*

On the evening of the invasion we landed about midnight outside San Carlos Water in Falkland Sound. Standing on the bridge of *Fearless* I could see the flashes from the naval gunfire on to Fanning Head and the ribbons of tracer where SBS patrols were having a gun battle with some enemy. It got very tense. Because of various problems it became quite clear that the landing was getting later and later and we could be running into daylight if we weren't careful. Someone said to me: 'Why don't we speed things up?' I said: 'No. We won't do that.' I could imagine the chaos it would cause in the night. We were trying to maintain radio silence so as not to give away the fact that we were there. A lot of chatter on a radio to a chap standing on a landing craft in the dark, trying to take down orders, would have resulted in worse chaos than there was already.

The landing rolled ahead about an hour late, and then the sun came up as the second wave was going in. We steamed into San Carlos Water and it looked exactly like the Outer Hebrides on a sunny day. It was eerie; this rather familiar scene implanted in our minds by all the air photographs we had seen in the planning phase.

The air attacks started much earlier than we thought they would. Previously the navy's experience had been that it took about half a day for the Argentine air force to get their act together and work out where we were and what they were going to do. These aircraft came in just over an hour after dawn! I realised how vulnerable we were – sitting in something rather like a Scottish loch – to these air attacks. As they built up during the day I felt an increasing sense of frustration in the operations room of HMS *Fearless*, which is like a tin box. A lot of the radios weren't working very well. There usually is 'finger' trouble with radios at the beginning of an operation like this. Outside this small box, *Fearless* was letting off her chaff dispenser, which fires stuff like Bacofoil to fool attacking aircraft. * The noise was like having people battering on the sides of the box. And I couldn't get off the ship because every time my helicopter came to collect me the captain of the ship said: 'If the helicopter comes back again my people will shoot it down.'†

---

* 'Chaff' was a Second World War invention used to fool enemy radar. Dispensers fire containers which scatter thousands of strips of metal foil. It can confuse missiles homing in on a vessel.
    †Fear of inadvertently shooting down friendly aircraft was a constant factor. One British troop-carrying helicopter was, in fact, downed by a RN missile.

As the landings progressed the messages came in. I could hear them on the radio. Ships were being damaged and sunk. It didn't surprise me. The ships were having to stand there and trade punches with the Argentine air force, which they did remarkably gallantly. They, not us, were the people who paid the price for [our] not having air superiority. At the same time I had lost a couple of helicopters and was preoccupied with what my own troops were doing on the ground. Though I was extremely sad about these ships being sunk, at the time it didn't bear down too heavily on me.

There was continual pressure on us to get moving out of San Carlos, for reasons which I can perfectly well understand. I was summoned often to the radio telephone to speak with the superior headquarters in Northwood [over the portable satellite link]. This necessitated a trip by boat or helicopter about a mile and a half to where the radio telephone was situated. On one occasion, after a particularly irritating telephone conversation, I remember walking out of the tent and saying to myself in somewhat of a temper: I shall win the war for these buggers and then I shall go.

The seeds of the battle of Goose Green started on the second day after the landings when I decided we would do a raid in order to cause maximum damage and harassment to the enemy. We weren't actually going to stay there, in accordance with my direction to hit any enemy close to the beachhead prior to the move out. It became apparent as we had bad weather night after night that we hadn't got enough helicopter lift capacity to do the move forward on to Mount Kent and Goose Green. My main aim was to get on to Mount Kent, which overlooked Stanley.

Eventually I was told from London that Goose Green was to be captured. I didn't want to do it but that's not new. Soldiers often have to do things they don't want to do. At the time it was clear to me that back in England there was a political need for victory, so that we could be seen to be doing something, seen to be winning. War is an extension of politics, and it is something I can live with.

The turning point in the campaign for me was the end of the first full brigade night-attack when we broke through on to their main positions in the mountains – Longdon, Harriet and Two Sisters. We had by then had some experience of how they would fight, but here we were breaking into their main positions with a brigade attack against equal, if not greater, numbers than ourselves. To a degree we were taking a risk, breaking the rules which say thou shalt not attack an enemy with less than three times his power. Here we were doing it with something equal or less than equal.

The night we fought I was in my headquarters, which were a collection of vehicles around a little tent which was lit up. I sat in there listening to the radios and talking to the commanding officers who were walking forward in the darkness, fighting their own battles. I was very conscious of the fact that the Argentines could actually overhear my conversations, which were in clear, and therefore that they would be able to pick up what I was saying.

I hoped by the time they had worked out what I was trying to do it was too late. For me it was a matter of listening to reports coming back, encouraging commanders, doing a bit of chasing up from time to time. In the middle of it, just to add to the excitement, we had two reports – one from the Cymbeline mortar-locating radars, that a large force of Argentine helicopters was on its way towards us. We all thought that this was a counter-attack, though we couldn't really believe it. We had to be prepared for it and there was nothing we could do except wait for it to arrive. In fact, the radar was seeing things. We were given warnings also that we were about to be attacked by high-level Canberra bombers. They had done this a number of times, and I remember going outside the headquarters in the middle of all this, looking up at the starlit night, listening to the sound of gunfire all around, watching the flashes from artillery, looking up to see if I could see these helicopters or Canberra bombers. Then I would dive back into the smoke-filled, slightly foetid atmosphere of a busy command post as the night wore on.

I knew this was going to be a very testing night. Our boys performed well, and they did it with far fewer casualties than I expected. Next morning there was a snowstorm falling and I could hear the enemy 155 mm shells coming down all around where my brigade headquarters was positioned. I remember thinking: We can't stay here too long because if we do we're going to have a lot of casualties. We must push on.

I also remember thinking: This is it. We are going to beat these people, not necessarily tomorrow or the day after, but very soon. I didn't know how many casualties we would take in the winning, but I knew we would win. I had thought that we were going to have to fight our way through and round Stanley, but in the event, once we had broken into that outer crust of positions, we didn't have to. I felt they would not give up until they were quite clearly defeated in their own minds. I didn't know when that moment was going to come – when they would realise they had had enough and were morally defeated. So at that time I was absolutely certain we were going to have a battle in and around Stanley. There would be more bloody fighting. I viewed that prospect with apprehension, but we were set up to do it.

As we walked into Stanley I was treading on the heels of 2 Para who led the way in. The whole place was chaotic, with guns and ammunition lying about, the odd dead body. Every other building seemed to have a red cross on it. There was the smell of death, which is unmistakable, and this curious peat smoke smell which hangs over the place. The Argentine soldiers had been lighting peat fires to keep warm. As the sun went down and the evening wore on it got colder and colder. I met an Argentine military policeman who spoke excellent English and pointed out where the surrender negotiations were taking place. I turned away and tried to find myself and my headquarters somewhere to spend the night. Eventually we went to the top floor of a little house which we requisitioned and shared with one of the companies of 2 Para. During the night we turned on one of our radios to the BBC World Service. We heard from 8,000 miles away about the surrender which was being conducted in a building 800 yards from where I was sitting. We all felt the most enormous sense of relief. My main feeling was that no more young men were going to have to die. It was just an enormous sense of relief that it was all over. We could all go home.

From the very beginning I was never in any doubt that the Argentines would fight. After all, they were only 350 miles from their own home, they had been there five or six weeks, they had plenty of opportunity to get together the right amount of troops and support. Had they got their act together I am quite clear they could have won. Their biggest problem was that at the higher level their three services didn't get together. There didn't seem to be an overall plan for how they were going to win the war. Each service seemed to go its own way. Their army didn't get air support when they wanted it, the navy more or less opted out of the war and didn't engage our surface fleet and give them problems. At the lower level the conscripts were not well trained and they lacked this feeling that we had – that we were all fighting for each other. They seemed to have this idea they were fighting for their flag, for their country, which is a very fragile foundation on which to base morale, because in the stress of battle it evaporates. Whereas, if you're fighting for yourself, your comrades, for each other, that sustains you in the moments when you think you might be losing.

The main lesson for me that comes out of this war was that there was a failure of deterrence and that we must be absolutely clear next time, in future times, that we never get ourselves into that sort of situation. You do that by making signals, in the truest sense of the word, to any would-be aggressor, that are absolutely clear. It is very important to realise that you cannot run away from war, you have to face it if it has to be. You don't stop wars by running away from them, you stop them by making it plain to the person on the other side that you are not going to be pushed any further and that the results are going to be pretty awful if he starts pushing you.

The homecoming was a marvellous experience in that it showed the appreciation of the country to the young men for what they had done, and I am glad it happened from that point of view. It was a fairly subdued personal experience for many of us. There was a feeling that we didn't want to leave the familiar surroundings of our friends, comrades and men we knew, to go back to what was going to be unfamiliar. We were going among people who did not totally understand what we had done; into a world full of people who didn't know what we had gone through, who were perhaps putting the wrong connotation on what had happened, revelling in the fact of victory for the wrong reasons, as if it had been a football match, which it was certainly not. There is no fun in killing people and no fun in the actual effects of war, which are death and mutilation and terrible bereavement. I actually in some ways felt reluctant to walk off that ship among it all.

Once ashore I chose a route back to Plymouth which would avoid every town I could find on the map, because I didn't want to get involved in the homecoming razzamatazz in any way. I did not feel I wanted adulation or any of the things that went with it. I didn't feel that it was like a victory, I felt just great thankfulness that it was over and that we had brought more people back than I thought we were going to bring back.

LOU ARMOUR

Sergeant Lou Armour of the Royal Marines was serving as a corporal in the Falklands when the Islands were invaded on 2 April 1982. He was captured, sent back to Britain and, with the rest of his comrades, returned to the South Atlantic to join up with the Task Force. He has now left the services and is studying for a degree.

We had been on the Islands for four days when the Argentines invaded. We had just moved into our accommodation [at Moody Brook] and were finding out where we were going to sleep, meeting the lads who were already there whom we were going to replace. We were 'sussing' out what we were going to do for a year, which didn't seem like very much. I hadn't had a chance to see all the Island but my first impression was that it was pretty barren. I went out there with positive thoughts, mainly because I am a weapon instructor and I was told that there was a big opportunity for a lot of field-firing. That was the sort of thing I was interested in. We were looking forward to what was going to be a fairly quiet year. Wrong.

Before they invaded there were hints of it all the time during the day. Then we had a briefing from our boss. We knew something was going to go on but we really believed it was going to be a show of strength. We thought the Argentines would land and then say: 'We can land here if we want.' We didn't really believe there was going to be a full-scale invasion. I was sat in the bar talking with the lads and we were called together and given our orders. We didn't know where they were going to come from and we didn't have the equipment to defend the Island. The armoury was opened about six hours before the invasion and we had the pick of the equipment. We took what we wanted.

I was sent to a place called The Isthmus – a strip of land near the airfield – about five miles from Stanley. If any Argentine troops approached us we were to open fire, and when they went to ground we were to double back to the section behind us and then keep pepper-potting them like that. The other section behind us were half a mile away and it was flat ground, so it was going to have to be a running half-mile. We had seen Moody Brook being mortared about an hour after we got our last message over the radio. It said: 'Good luck. Good luck.' Actually I laughed at that message because it was ironic. 'Good luck. Good luck.' Wow! Thanks! We dug our shell scrapes a bit faster. I told the lads in my section not to do anything stupid and to play it off the cuff. It might have been a bit easier for me because I had them to worry about. It was worse for the lads because they were just thinking about themselves.

When they mortared Moody Brook we could see the flashes and hear the guns. We heard a lot of chat over the radio. We stayed where we were, because we were told not to move until we were either called or actually engaged with somebody. Eventually we were told to move to Government House. We had a lot of ammunition with us which was quite heavy. We packed up the kit and started running back to Stanley. A Land-Rover pulled up. I couldn't believe it. Moody Brook had been bombed, over the radio we could hear: 'Stanley is under fire,' and some Marine casually pulls over in a Land-Rover and says: 'Get in.' On the way back to Stanley another corporal, Dave Carr, waved me down. I was half-in and half-hanging out of the Land-Rover and he told me Government House was being attacked by the Argentines. A lot of tracer started flying down the road and we just scattered, we jumped out of the Rover and dived into the gardens, trying to figure out what the hell was going on. It was pitch-black, we didn't know exactly where they were around Government House – it was defining their exact position, how many there were. It was all a bit chaotic. Dave Carr began returning the fire and there was fire being exchanged down the road I had to go along. We skirmished our way along the road, firing at gun flashes. We got to the hospital wall and then we had no choice, we had to leap across the football field.

Getting into Government House was dodgy because we were frightened of getting shot at by our own guys. We were actually shot at and we ran forward shouting like crazy: 'Marines, Marines, Marines.' We didn't want to get killed by our own guys at that stage. I got into the kitchen and the first thing that struck me was that there was water everywhere from burst pipes that had been shot away. My boss, Major Norman, said: 'Well done,' and told me to put some of the lads upstairs. I was relieved to be among the crowd, there was some sniper fire going on. It was the first battle I had fought in. I was frightened. The scariest bit is before it all happens and you think: 'I'm going to be scared and run away.' You don't know what you are going to do. In training you're all sort of 'gung-ho', leading the way, but that's with blanks.

Inside Government House, where we could have a rest, my mouth was all dry. I've never felt so knackered in my life. I felt tired and thirsty and all I wanted to do was drink. I drank my whole water bottle more or less straight off. It took the fear away, although I was still apprehensive.

The Argies had some armoured vehicles moved up. At the time of the surrender, when Rex Hunt went out to talk with them, I was actually quite pleased we were stopping, I make no bones about it . . . I didn't fancy getting shot to bits. I was just glad it was finished. They made us lie down. Suddenly you're in their hands. There were two APCs [armoured personnel carriers] of theirs hit; they must have lost guys in them. There were three casualties lying in the garden of Government House. You think: What sort of mood are they going to be in when their oppos are shot up?

When we were actually lying down I felt a bit humiliated but I also felt apprehensive about what was going to happen next. One of the Argentine officers came along and actually struck one of the guards and told us to stand up. We stood up and he shook my hand and a few other guys' hands and said that we shouldn't lie down, that we should be proud of what we'd done. I liked him. We were put in the back of a Hercules to be taken to Argentina. I was worried about the prospect of that because I'm not daft. I'm not too bad on current affairs and I know that a favourite ploy during their own Dirty War was to toss people out of Hercules over the sea. But they treated us okay. I think they were more nervous of us, they were continually searching us for knives. They had this image of the Second World War commando, knives all over his body, so they were quite nervous of us.

They didn't interrogate us and we were sent back to Britain fairly quickly via Uruguay. It was a relief to get back to the UK.

*

When I got home I didn't really enjoy it. I couldn't sleep. I was a bit nervous for a couple of days about anything that would shock me, like somebody tapping me on the shoulder, or a noise. I didn't like people talking about it, they were all patting me on the back, my family were trying to drag me up to the pub. I was still coming down from the adrenalin high and I didn't want to be the centre of attraction. We were suddenly media stars but I didn't feel like it. If you go through something where you think you're going to die or even be badly injured, then it's hard to talk to people who have not been in that position. I think I was a bit of a shit to the people around me. I didn't know how to explain myself to them, so I wanted to get back to Poole to the guys that I'd been with, because I knew we all felt the same.

When they told us we were going back down to the Falklands you had to put on this: 'Great, let's go back and do it.' I was willing to go back down and do it and I did go back, but it wasn't for the same reasons as everybody else. It wasn't for the old patriotic fervour which had caught the country. We were getting carried along by the other Marines saying: 'Nice one lads. Well done.' In a sense it was good, it made you feel good. It was about things like pride. There's a bit of stigma about surrendering. One politician said how come during the Second World War Germans were holding off the British or the Soviets with just a few men for weeks on end? I suppose when you're at the top of a mountain and you're on dominating ground or something like that then you can hold off people for a period: it's things like that which irked us. We had done exactly what we were told to do. The Governor decided enough was enough because of civilian casualties, but there is still that stigma to the surrender bit. That might have played a factor.

When we got on the *Canberra* among our own unit we had a little bit of a celebrity status with the other Marines: 'What was it like being under fire?' . . . you were swept along with the whole thing . . . 'We're going to go down there and "dick" that lot.' As we got closer I was changing my mind slightly, the real me. As we got nearer, the old 'For Queen and Country' bit was going out the window. It was more: 'Let's get down there, do it and let's get back. And if we don't have to go down and do it, great.'

Everybody in the Task Force, the Marines, the Paras on *Canberra* – we were all keen to get ashore. There was lots of singing, ending off the evening with 'God Save the Queen': stacks of bravado. But I found myself, and my troop, tended not to sing so loudly. It doesn't mean to say we were any less loyal, it's that we had just been involved in it. We were more aware of what we were going into. The younger lads felt a bit like I did the first time, before the shooting started. This time around I was more aware of what was going to happen.

(Armour's company of marines were held in reserve after the initial landings at San Carlos. Then they were moved forward to Goose Green to reinforce a second-stage attack on the settlement by 2 Para.)

The Paras had put in the first attack and they had a hard time of it and quite a few casualties. They asked for reinforcements and our company was chosen. We moved during the night to an area where the helicopters had dropped a load of artillery rounds and mortar bombs, which the Paras really needed for the assault the next morning. It meant we had to leave our bergens behind and we went in with fighting order, which weighed about 40 lbs. To fight with this is quite difficult really. You had to carry your ammunition. We had to move some of the mortar bombs up to the mortar pits. Our boss went to see the CO, who was the second-in-command of 2 Para. We were told there would probably be an assault in the morning which we would take part in. The Argentines might get the chance to surrender first.

It was pitch-black, there was a lot of smoke, the gorse was smouldering. I said a few words to a couple of the Paras. We knew this was going to be a cruncher just from looking at the Paras and seeing how shagged out they were. The next morning was going to be pretty horrendous. We were told to dig shell scrapes and wait to see what transpired. There would either be an Argentine surrender or another assault by the Paras with our company in support. We were told about the air threat from Pucaras – propeller-driven aircraft which carry a lot of armament. They are quite formidable and would scare the ground troops more than anything else.

We wanted to dig in but couldn't because the ground was so hard. I remember hitting the ground with a pickaxe and nothing happened. In the end we had to lie down where we were and stayed awake all night.

You couldn't go to sleep because it was freezing. The temperature was below zero; it snowed. I've been to Norway and I know what cold is. I was wearing an Arctic windproof jacket which doesn't have a lining because it is a windproof and if it gets wet the wind dries it out pretty quickly. It was about ten below zero and I was lying in a scrape that was full of snow. I was cuddling up to another marine who was my number two. We stayed there for a couple of nights until they brought our bergens and we got our sleeping bags. After that we took them everywhere with us, we took them out of our packs and tied them on to our fighting orders. When you're that cold you're no use to anyone.

By this stage a couple of guys were having problems with their feet. The correct name is immersion foot, but grandads know it as trench foot. There was also the danger of frost-bite and you have to be careful in these situations. Some of the Marines had had frost-bite in Norway, and it is very dodgy going back into a cold environment if you've had it. One guy in my section, a chap called Johnny Oldham, was practically in tears with every step he took when we were doing yomp. People don't realise what it is like to be in a combat situation when you are fighting not just the enemy but also the environment. It's not a case of 'K' Company move here, 'J' Company move there, 2 Para move here. It is a Marine carrying a GPMG [general purpose machine gun], which weighs 24 lbs, and all the ammunition, practically crying with every step he's taking rather than not stay with his section. He was in absolute agony with his feet. But what could you do – you could only casevac [casualty evacuate] him anyway, and you couldn't do that because the 'cabs' [helicopters] were being used for ferrying supplies. Apart from that he wouldn't have gone, he wouldn't let us casevac him even if we wanted to. He wanted to stay, that's why he carried on walking, and I felt pretty bad about seeing the state he was in. He had done all the right things, changed his socks, powdered his feet. But when you're wet in the freezing cold, eventually all your socks become wet. My troop officer had a parcel sent out to him and he had four pairs in it. He kept one for himself and gave three away. Socks were the big thing. We took Argentine boots whenever we could find them, and socks. They had polythene bags full of socks.

The average Marine or Para at that stage had to drink peat water. Streams were negligible, fresh water you couldn't get. You had to take what you could out of the ground by stamping on to the peat or digging holes until you got a puddle, because it was all sodden ground. You had to scoop the water into a mug and put a sterilising tablet in it. The water was absolutely black but you drank it. Our rations were Arctic rations, but it wasn't as snowy as the planners thought it might be and those rations need water. They were good rations, 5,000 calories, but no matter how many steri tabs [sterilising tablets] you used, it ended up taking it out on you. I never had any underpants on by the time we got to Stanley, and there were quite a few guys like that because of having the shits. That would put pressure on you: if a guy has already got bad feet and has to live with the shits. You only carry so many pairs of pants in your pack. In the end you might be yomping and suddenly you go. It's not very nice when you've got rampant diarrhoea and you've still got to keep walking. You can't stop, obviously. One of the lads in our troop just undone his zip, cut through his underpants and just tossed them away and carried on walking. The doc said the only thing you can do, because you're losing body fluid, is just to drink lots of water, and of course we were drinking that crap again. You don't read about that in the paper.

One night 42 Commando assaulted Mount Harriet, 45 Commando did Two Sisters and 3 Para did Mount Longdon. 'K' and 'L' Company were moving up and 'J' Company (us) were placed down by the mortar pits to go wherever the CO wanted us. We had spent a lot of time in the previous few days taking mortars to the pits. It was a pain in the arse. They weigh 80 lbs. We had to carry them two kilometres and we had done that for two days. I remember saying that I hoped they were going to use them all when the assaults went in.

That night we were told to move up to support 'K' and 'L' Companies. We had to go along the Darwin Road, some of which had been cleared but the rest of it was no-man's-land. We were not sure how heavily mined it was, but we did know it was mined. It was pitch-black but it was good to get on the move again because it had been pissing down with rain and we were getting stiff with cold. We started getting shelled, but we couldn't take cover because there were mines either side of us. We just kept our heads down and kept on running. That's all we could do. All I remember was seeing the flashes and hearing fzzzzzzzzing sounds. It just didn't seem to be real, it was weird. It was nothing like I thought it would be.

We went up Mount Harriet in an extended line and advanced up the mountain. By this time 'K' and 'L' Companies had swung round on their axis. As we were near the top daylight started to appear. It was weird. It was misty, snow was on the mountain and it was a bit frightening. At the top we started to consolidate, move in to some of the old Argentine positions and rebuild sangars [fortified firing positions, using rocks or peat] for ourselves. Military rule dictates that if you lose a position you immediately start shelling it, and that's what happened for the rest of the day. That really scared me. There is nothing you can do about it, you just listen to them coming in. In the end you knew which ones were going to miss you and which were going to land in amongst you. We got really blasé about the ones going over the top. We'd tell jokes and laugh – it's where the military humour comes out. It's much better to crack a joke than stand there shaking. You would try and make yourself as small as possible. Two lads in my company were hit by artillery and were injured. We got a 'cab' in to lift them out. Luckily they were okay.

The next day we had to deal with the Argentine dead. My section was detailed to bury them. You had to take off their dog-tags or anything that could identify them, and put a rifle in the ground with the helmet on top and the dog-tags wrapped around the rifle. Later on a padre was supposed to come along and do a quick prayer over them. I took two Marines, the eldest guy and the youngest guy. We had to go and look for them. I've been at odds with myself over this. Suddenly they weren't the enemy any more. The first guy I came across, he had all of the side of his face totally missing and he had upper chest wounds. I took his dog-tags off and while I was doing it I was talking all the time: 'Okay, right, I'm just going to undo his dog-tags, and yes, right, here they come . . .' not because I was trying to tell the lads what I was doing. I was just trying to stop myself from thinking about this guy. You'd find a wallet on them and there'd be a picture in there of them with their wife and kids. And I was looking around and I thought: 'Well, fucking hell, that could have been me lying there.' He was just another bloke. At the time I didn't feel too bad because I had these other two lads with me and I was the section commander . . . 'Joe Cool'. We started to bury them but the ground was too hard to dig holes, so we dragged them over to a depression and I'll never forget the way they looked.

Every body we came across was all twisted. You could see the agony that these guys had been in when they died.

We dragged them over to these depressions and we started making jokes then about the fact they were dead. We just covered them with boulders. We were knackered and cold as well. We put their rifles on them. Then we found an Argentine officer who'd been injured. He had a belly wound. I can't remember who found him. They called me over and said: 'Come on over here Lou and have a look at this guy here.' I went over and he started speaking to me in English. He was telling me he didn't know why we were fighting either. We tried to get him casevaced, but we couldn't because we were still being shelled, on and off, even while we were trying to bury them. Suddenly you'd have to take cover.

I was still coming on with being pretty cool, that I could hack it. It wasn't until later on, when I got home, that I realised that it had quite an effect on me. I didn't admit it at the time, it was so easy to hide because I was in charge of the section and I had other things to concentrate on. I had a bad feeling about the bodies, the state of them and how we just tossed them into a hole. They were just kids. The guy that was injured . . . I wish now that he'd never spoken English.

At the time you've got so much on your plate, but when you get home you see that he was just another ordinary guy, in exactly the same position as me. I was keyed up that day and I hid it all. It took me four years to cry about a few dead people, because obviously you can't cry then, you've got a job to do and you do it. I still feel, even now: Why am I crying? I'm afraid I just don't see him as enemy.

Coming home was great. I was feeling pretty good along with everybody else. I felt great because I had the best compliment you can get if you've been in that situation . . . your lads turning round and telling you that they thought you were bloody good down there, that you'd handled the section well. That does mean a hell of a lot to me. It was great coming home while you were still part of the group. It's the getting home and the splitting up: that was the time I started getting problems emotionally. While you're with all the lads, because you've all been in it together, you know each other's feelings. Only people who've been in that situation really understand.

That is really my only criticism of the forces. We all flowed along with the tide, the flag-waving, the coming into Southampton on the *Canberra* . . . you're still with the lads all together, you can come out and wave. But then you all split up. You're told: 'Go on leave for eight weeks, get pissed and forget about it.'

It was only a short conflict, but from the time the Argentines invaded the Falklands I had been off on this emotional charge. We didn't know it was only going to last four weeks, the land phase. We were expecting six months. All the while you are keyed up ready for the massive battle that might take place. There were battles but we were expecting a real big bang, and of course we only had a little bang, although it was a big one to me personally. It's all that pent-up apprehension, excitement, you can contain it when you are with the lads . . . but then suddenly you're on leave.

I'm not really close to anybody, I've always been a bit of a loner, and suddenly I'm away from all the guys. My only criticism is that I'd have liked it if there'd been some sort of doc who could have turned round and said: 'Look when you get home, all this emotion is going to come out . . . when you leave the blokes, leave the bonding, you're going to find it hard talking about it.' If a few docs could have been there to say: 'If you're married try and talk to your wife . . .' or if you were a loner, like me: 'Come and talk to us.' That's my only criticism.

I went on leave for eight weeks and had a good time . . . But all the back-slapping from friends, from relatives, I couldn't hack it. I didn't go home for the first few days. I didn't like all the flag-waving. I think I only stayed at home a week, then I just shot off all round the country. I hired a car. I started to get feelings I wanted to tell people about. I wanted people to know about the dead people and what it's like to be shit-scared. I just wanted to get it off my chest. Instead I kept it cooped up because strangers would come up to me and say something stupid like: 'Did you kill anybody?' Or they'd be slapping you on the back, buying you pints, and you'd go along with it a bit. But you'd never really tell them what it was like . . . you'd just tell them, well basically as much as the British public do know. At the end I had eight weeks of not telling anybody anything. I just pushed it all to the back of my mind. When I did start to feel a bit depressed over the next couple of years I'd get stroppy very quickly. I'd say to myself: 'Stop being a wanker, stacks of other guys have hacked it.'

Young Argentine conscripts faced many hardships as they waited for the British to attack, especially cold and hunger. Defeat was hard for them . . . but all were glad when the time came to go home.

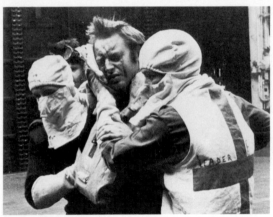

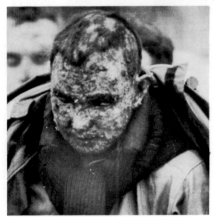

Top: *Guardsman David Grimshaw's agony brought home the reality of the conflict to millions of viewers when a BBC TV-crew captured the aftermath of the bombing of* Sir Galahad.
Above: *A wounded sailor from* HMS Sheffield *is helped on board* HMS Ark Royal.
Left: *A burned soldier from* Sir Galahad.

Chris White, a Royal Marine casualty aboard Uganda.

Casualties from the war were taken to the British hospital ship SS Uganda *where they were cared for by staff from QARNNS, the Queen Alexandra's Royal Naval Nursing Service.*

Chris White – centre, wearing camouflage trousers – with other survivors from Sir Galahad.

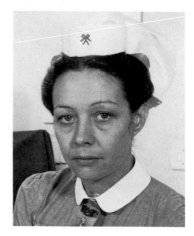

Nurse Marion Stock

Top: *Flight-Lieutenant Jeff Glover, the only British PoW in Argentine hands, shortly after he was captured when he bailed out of his Harrier jet over West Falkland.*
Middle: *A joyful wife: Mrs Dee Glover watches as her husband's plane lands in Britain.*
Bottom: *Together again.*

An emotional moment as a young soldier of the Parachute Regiment arrives back in Britain from the Falklands War. Prince Charles was at RAF Brize Norton to greet them, but there was only one person this mother wanted to see.

Homecomings:-
Top: *Dead sailors from the torpedoed* General Belgrano *receive a blessing from a priest when they arrive back on Argentine soil.*
Above: *The friends and families of the British Task Force collect on the quayside at Portsmouth to welcome them home.*

Mrs Hulda Stewart, a Falkland Islander.

Mrs Dorothy Foulkes, whose husband Frank was killed on board Atlantic Conveyor.

Mrs Gill White, the wife of Chris White, who survived the bombing of Sir Galahad *and then tried to take his own life.*

The legacy of battle:-
British troops begin the massive task of clearing up in Port Stanley after the surrender.
Among the leftovers, thousands of rounds of anti-aircraft ammunition.

Playtime, once a carefree occasion for the schoolchildren
of the Falkland Islands, took on a very sinister
meaning once the war was over.

They've always hacked it through the years. I am proud of being in the Marines.

I had a good career. I liked doing all the roughie, toughie things that the Marines do. I even like yomping with heavy packs. But I've got to be honest . . . I don't want to go to war again – which doesn't make me a pacifist, because if the country was threatened by someone else I would pick up a rifle and I would fight. I didn't want to stay in the Marines in case I end up in a fight I don't believe in. I'm not saying I disbelieved in the war against Argentina. I've got my own views on that which, out of respect for people who are bereaved or guys who are injured, I will keep to myself. I would fight again but I'd have to believe in it.

People say: 'You know, you're crazy going outside.' Security, money, all that is fine. I'm not married so I don't have a commitment to look after a wife and family. I could actually take the risk and go. I think if I'd stayed in, it would be just my luck that in three years' time I'd end up going to war again and I'd be saying: 'Stupid bastard, I told you you should have got out.'

CIVILIANS

GERALD CHEEK

Gerald Cheek was born in the Falklands and runs the Falkland Island Government Air Service (FIGAS), which operates throughout the Islands. During the Argentine occupation he was arrested at gunpoint by armed soldiers and deported to Fox Bay on West Falkland.

The atmosphere in Stanley when the Argentines arrived was very oppressive. I was out with the local Falkland Island Defence Force the night they came in. We were taken away from the area we were guarding when they arrived and sent back to our homes. It was a dreadful feeling. Everybody was shocked. We were under house arrest practically for the whole day on 2 April. It was very bad, everybody was depressed and apprehensive as to what was going to happen next – whether we were going to be shot or whether we would be taken back to Argentina. Everybody knew of the regime over there, the military government, and what they'd done to their own people. We knew they wanted the Falklands – we didn't know what our future would be. It was very alarming to say the least.

We were very restricted in Stanley by the Argentines. One of the first things they said when they arrived was that nothing would change. The next thing they said was how things had to change. We had to drive on the other side of the road, we had to have passes to go around Stanley. We weren't allowed out of Stanley, although some people did drive out to some of the farms. After two or three days the airport was a no-go area. There were lots of restricted areas. It was very trying.

I elected to stay, as quite a few of us did, to look after Stanley as best we could. People began thinking back to the Second World War and how it must have felt for the French and the Dutch and the countries in Europe occupied by the Germans. It was, I am sure, very similar. There were some very tense moments. We – the heads of the various Falklands Island Government departments – were called to a meeting at the secretariat to meet the Argentine High Command and were told what each department would have to do. In my case they insisted that the internal air service should keep functioning. I said that there was no way it could keep going with all the Argentine soldiers around – who knows what they might have done: 'That's a strange aeroplane, we'll shoot that down.' So even if told to, our pilots wouldn't have flown their aircraft, it was far too dangerous. Of course this cut the Islands off. Our air service is an essential part of the community life in the Falklands.

Three weeks later – on 27 April, I'll never forget that date – they came for me one afternoon and said I was being taken away. I didn't know where to. Four of them came in with pistols and threatened my family, saying to me: 'You've got to go, you've got ten minutes to pack.' I thought I was being taken to Argentina, I didn't have a clue where I was going. They took me and several other people – fourteen in all – down to Stanley Airport. We were taken by helicopter out to Fox Bay and were put under house arrest for the remaining seven weeks of the war. Initially I thought we were going to be taken out and shot. I thought back to what had happened to their people – the 'Disappeared Ones' in Argentina. I thought 'That's it, I'll never see my family again.' I've never felt so low or bad in my life.

I said: 'Where am I going. Do I need my passport?'

They said: 'No – internal.'

That's one word that they said, I remember that well. It was very upsetting for my two young daughters and my wife. They were crying. I'm not a big toughie, I was on the verge of tears as well. Absolutely.

I've often wondered why they chose me. I was summoned before their second-in-command a few days before this and he said that the military police were after my blood. They knew I was a member of the local defence force. I was a member of the Falkland Islands Committee. I was quite a good marksman in the local rifle range and they knew I didn't like Argentinians, which was absolutely correct. I think all these things mounted up and they swooped one day.

When we arrived at Fox Bay the Argentinians there thought that this was the day when the Task Force was going to make an all-out attack.

They wanted people like us out of the way in case we could assist the British forces. They really believed this was the day they were going to attack all their positions, an all-out attack overnight on Port Howard, Fox Bay, Goose Green, Stanley. It would be one glorious battle.

At Fox Bay the local manager, Richard Cockwell, and his wife Griselda very kindly offered to put us up – all fourteen of us, so we had a very crowded household. There were 200 Argentines based at the Fox Bay settlement and they were always around. There was no communication with the outside world but we used to listen to the BBC to see what was happening in Stanley. They searched the house on more than one occasion trying to find radios. They thought we might have had transmitters. But we managed to keep the radio receiver hidden away, thank God. That was the only way we knew what was happening in the rest of the Falklands. Our families back in Stanley did not know what was happening to us but at least we managed to keep some [listening] contact.

We had to keep the fact that we had a radio very secret, even from the children. There were six small children there. The Argentine major and captain in charge of the detachment there used to come in quite often. They spoke good English, so there was no way we could let the children know that we were getting news from outside. We could talk about the war as it happened only among the adults. We had the radio hidden in a small room at the back, under some boxes and bits and pieces – rather like a junk room. One of us would go in there and listen to the radio, checking there were no Argentinians round at the window.

After the first Harrier raid we used to hide underneath the floor-boards. The Brits were also shelling the Argentinian positions pretty close to where we were living, so we elected to go under the house at night because the stone foundations gave us some protection. We virtually lived under the house for the remainder of the war. Conditions were pretty cramped but reasonably comfortable. We also had another radio hidden under the floorboards. We took it to pieces and scattered it round, so that during the searches the Argentinians, if they did find out, would think it was an old radio which didn't work. If they discovered the first radio we always had this one as a back-up.

On one occasion about twenty soldiers surrounded the house and took us all down to the shearing shed. They searched the house thoroughly.

One of them told Richard Cockwell that we were to stay there in the shed and if we were to step outside we could well be shot. They were very agitated on this particular day. I don't know what prompted that but there were quite a few terrifying moments like that. They actually opened fire on us on one occasion. Richard had permission from the major to go down to the harbour to his yacht to get some blankets and things we needed. I went with him and on the way back in the small open motor boat one of the guards opened fire. The bullets came fairly close. We didn't know whether he was firing at us or trying to scare us. It was damned close and very terrifying.

I used to get depressed because we didn't know what was happening in Stanley where my family were. The BBC was telling us on the radio that the Brits were getting closer and closer. The shelling was on the fringe of Stanley more and more and we were always wondering whether the next shell would hit a civilian house and someone would get killed. We listened to the 'Doctor's Hour', which they run every morning from Stanley to the 'Camp' [back-country] stations, and heard that three people had died. That really was a very sad day for everybody. We thought: 'Well, hell, who will be next? Where will the next shell land?'

There was no way of communicating with our families or them with us. We knew when we came to Fox Bay that the Task Force was on its way. Most of us thought it would be a couple of weeks, that there would be a big glorious battle, the Brits would have the Falklands back and that would be the end of it. But we were held at Fox Bay for seven long weeks.

Looking back, it's very sad to think that so many people lost their lives. Perhaps in some ways it was a fruitless war. We are very happy that the Brits came back and threw the Argentinians out, but it was so unnecessary. It should never have happened. It should never have come to war and bloodshed. I think it was badly handled by the Foreign Office. The Argentinians were led on and on. We've learned now that they were told to win our hearts and minds, to woo the Islanders and one day they would have the Falklands. They got fed up with wooing. They didn't do that very well. Finally they decided they would come in and take it. I'm sure they thought they would stay.

We were angry at them being there. I personally didn't have any compassion for them. We didn't see them so much in Fox Bay as they did in Stanley, where they saw the young conscripts and they realised they were suffering, and a lot of people did have some compassion. But I didn't feel that.

Listening to the radio every day we finally heard about the surrender, or the possibility of a surrender. It finally came for us at midnight. The Argentinians came and said it was all over. They just couldn't wait to get back home again. They were fed up, they just wanted to get out of the Falklands. A Lynx helicopter off HMS *Avenger* came in the morning after the surrender. That was a great moment to see the British people on the ground and we knew then that it was all over, and we were going home.

We got back to Stanley two days later. A Sea King helicopter from HMS *Invincible* was sent in to Fox Bay to take the doctor and his wife, who was also a doctor, back to Stanley, where they were wanted at the hospital because there were a lot of injured people to attend to.

When the Sea King landed on the green in front of the house we all went, all fourteen of us, and said: 'You're not taking off until we're all on board.'

He said: 'Well I haven't got room.'

But he made room and we all got back to Stanley together, which was a pretty happy day. The town was a dreadful sight. We flew over the *Sir Galahad* first on the way past Fitzroy and it was still ablaze. In Stanley there were still a few smoking buildings and lots of wreckage. It was nice to get back home but it was a pitiful sight. It wasn't our little town any more. It had changed dramatically.

I don't think too much about it now – I think it's best forgotten. I hope never to see an Argentinian on Falkland Island soil again. I've got to be honest. They had their chance, they had lots of opportunities to win our hearts and minds and woo us. And they made a bad job of it from day one. They completely blew it on the 2nd of April 1982. And that's it. You know I think I can speak for well over ninety per cent, probably ninety-nine per cent of the Islanders. They had their chance. Tough mate. We don't want them back. Ever.

HULDA STEWART

Mrs Hulda Stewart is a Falkland Islander, married to a former British serviceman. She teaches at a school in Stanley and was living there when the Argentine soldiers invaded the Islands on 2 April 1982. Their house is on the outskirts of the town close to where the final battles took place.

I was absolutely horrified by the arrival of the Argentine soldiers. Things had been hotting up beforehand but I never actually thought they would invade. At four o'clock in the morning we heard bangs and when we looked out of the window we saw smoke coming from Moody Brook, the barracks where the Royal Marines lived. Then we realised it was happening. They had arrived. We saw their special forces – the Buzos Tacticos – with their blackened faces and their black clothes, coming down the road. We were very apprehensive because we weren't sure what would happen. We didn't know if they were going to come in and shoot us.

They came in as far as the gate, which they left open. My husband went out to close it, so that the dog wouldn't get out, and then they were a little bolshie. When it was explained, one of them who spoke English told the others and said we didn't want the dog getting out and getting killed. They seemed to accept it, and then they carried on, they left us alone.

We had a mixture of feelings. First there was absolute fury. How dare they come here and invade a peaceful colony where people just wanted to be left alone to live their lives. People here are not particularly materialistic, they just want a peaceful existence. How dare they come and commit an act of war – we had the British Royal Marines here. Then there was a feeling of frustration at not being able to go out where we wanted. But there was also a feeling of fear, not necessarily on one's own account, but for the old people especially. I'm very involved with the old folks and a lot of them had never been out of the Islands.

Within a few hours the Argentines started issuing their edicts. The first one said that they would respect people and property. Because of various things I knew about Argentina, having been there, I felt that they wouldn't stick to that for very long. Life actually changed quite a lot. We knew they weren't going to respect our property or our way of life as they promised. One of the first things was: 'You must not drive on the left-hand side of the road.' Now if I go to another country and they drive on the right, I'm prepared to accept that, but not in my own country. Then of course the curfew came into being, the fact that you were shut in your house from 4 p.m. until 8 a.m. If you wanted to go out to 'Camp' you had to get a pass. There was no way you could just go. The Argentinians came to all the houses in turn, they had a tremendous amount of information and knowledge about the Islanders.

There was a meeting held with all the teachers. Only two of us were Falkland Islanders, the others – apart from three or four – decided they did not want to stay. They left the Island, the school closed. I continued to have children in my own home. I collected them so many times a week and brought them to my home for lessons.

It felt like we were living in an armed camp. The West Store, our biggest shop in Stanley, became very much the centre of life. People went there sometimes to buy things, not because they really required them, but because it was a meeting point. It was somewhere you could receive and impart information. Outside the stores often you had rather ragged-looking young Argentinian conscripts asking you for money to buy food or for food itself. I found this very difficult as a committed Christian. We are told to give to your enemy, to love your enemy, to be good to them. I found that impossible.

We had some friends, our neighbours from next door, staying with us because the Argentinians broke into their house. We knew that the prisons in Argentina had been emptied of rapists, burglars and so on. Houses were being broken into. Our friends, two doors away, had woken up in the middle of the night to find Argentinians in their bedroom.

The 1st of May [when the British bombed Port Stanley for the first time] was very exciting. We were woken up by a banging on the door. Our friend, who is normally a very quiet, steady sort of person, was saying: 'They're here, they're here, the British are here.' We hadn't been sleeping well and said: 'Oh how marvellous,' and went off to sleep again. In the morning the impact of this really hit us. Shortly after we got up we were looking towards the airport and we saw smoke and we realised there were more bombs going off, and I was so elated. I stood in the front window and jumped up and down. And as I turned round, I realised that the Argentine machine-gun nest just a few yards away from our house was pointing the gun at me, indicating that unless I got down they were going to shoot me. So needless to say I very quickly got out of the window.

When news came through of the British landings at San Carlos the joy was incredible. It showed on people's faces. We heard it first from the BBC. Apart from the bombing of the airport on 1 May, this was the first time we felt real contact with the British. It was a tremendous feeling. One was naturally very apprehensive then because we realised that the Argentinians had well and truly entrenched themselves. They used to hide among the civil population in Stanley. They had their machine-gun nests in peat sheds between people's houses. Although we had no doubt that the British would get the Argentines out, we knew it was not going to be as easy as some people thought.

When the news came through that British boys were being killed, when the ships started sinking, people felt very very sad. One felt very conscious that it was a tremendous price really for our freedom. We fully anticipated that about fifty per cent of the population would probably die. We lived with that knowledge. Death faced us daily. When we heard of a ship being bombed, or a British aircraft coming down, we knew all the time that these people were dying for us, that people were being maimed for life, people were being blinded. It's something even now that I find very hard to live with. When relatives [of servicemen who died] come down they make me feel very humble. They have no bitterness towards us. They are so grateful for anything we can do, but yet they gave their all. We can do so little in return.

As the British troops got nearer and nearer to Stanley we realised we would be in a very vulnerable position because our home was the furthest house to the west that was actually occupied. We knew that the Argentinians were very suspicious about why we were staying in the house. We thought we might be taken as hostages when the British

252

troops came. My husband, Ian, decided the best thing was to make a hidey-hole under the sitting-room floor, through the foundations of the house. He padded it out with underlay. We took down water, food, some axes, various things like that, so that if the house caught fire we could perhaps bash our way out. It wasn't very pleasant down there. We didn't stay there all the time. We didn't know when the shelling would stop or start. We got out to make tea and coffee but it was very oppressive. Being down there you didn't really know what was going on around you. We weren't too sure if the Argentinians were perhaps trying to get in the back door.

For three weeks during which the British shelled Argentine positions we had shrapnel raining down every night. As the British troops got closer and closer we had air-burst shells landing in front of the house in the sea. Our big picture-window suddenly shattered. Four neighbours were living with us in the house by then, and we would suddenly all find ourselves lying flat down on the floor. A shell went off just beside our fence at the back of the house. The neighbours were actually down in the hidey-hole but I was in the house with my husband. We were lying on the floor in the passage with him on top of me, trying to protect me from the shrapnel and bullets that were flying around. Our greenhouse exploded and we had shrapnel, glass and bullets coming through the windows – right through from the back of the house to the front. There were Argentinians firing at Argentinians because they thought they were British troops and vice versa. We were caught in the crossfire.

We could see the British troops through binoculars on the mountains to the west of the house, on Tumbledown and Two Sisters, so we realised how close they were to us. Eventually we were told in no uncertain terms by the Argentinians that we were to leave. We did, but came back to the house when we found out there was a ceasefire and the possibility of a surrender. We talked about it and decided we wanted to be here, closer to where the British were, rather than down in town, which was where the Argentine forces were, or the no-man's-land in between. We thought we would try and get through to where the British troops were so that if the surrender didn't actually take place then we would move out with the British troops. Somehow we managed to get past an Argentinian guard, possibly because my husband told him that he worked for Cable & Wireless and had to get out of the centre of Stanley to get something from his office [near their home].

We came up to the house and were absolutely astounded to find fifty or sixty Paras living in there, in the garage, workshops, everywhere. I think that's when the full impact, that the British were actually there, hit us. All I can remember is those people with camouflage cream on their faces. I went down to our hidey-hole where I had hidden twenty-odd tins of cakes. I knew that the Paras and Marines were on field rations and probably wanted sweet food. They took some of the tins of cakes to their friends in some of the other houses – it was an incredible scene. We thanked them over and over again. Occasionally it was very sad. Someone would mention a friend. On one occasion I was trying to get a primus stove going to give them hot tea because some of them were very shocked.

Someone turned round and said: 'Oh we need so-and-so here for that.'

So I said: 'Well, will you go along and get him please.'

Then suddenly it hit this Para. He said: 'He's no longer with us. He died, he died before he could be carted back out.'

To actually speak to these people who had lost their friends, it was something I find even now very difficult to live with. We all had a good cry. It was easy to laugh, we could laugh over the smallest things that wouldn't even raise a smile now. But it was even easier to cry.

Looking back on it now it makes me extremely sad. I have tremendous feeling for those relatives who have no bitterness and who are willing to accept us as we are and who say: 'He was doing his job. He was in the services.'

The last time the relatives from the Falklands Families Association came down we put on a buffet supper party. All the relatives who didn't go out to Goose Green came up here, and I had an absolute houseful. I saw a little girl here in my house who must have been three or four months old when her father died in the Falklands. As a teacher, knowing what it's like with children, I think about one-parent families and to realise that a child would go through life not knowing her father, because of us, really ... I get depressed. Speaking with those families helped me to live with it, they have no bitterness.

During the occupation, to be perfectly honest, I had no compassion whatsoever. It was all black and white to me. If I gave food to

Argentinians then perhaps tomorrow they would kill my brother-in-law, who was serving with the Marines, or any other British troops. It was something I felt I couldn't do. Now, yes, I do have compassion after going to the Argentine cemetery and seeing all those crosses there. I feel very bitter about the Argentine government, that they caused all those deaths.

I want the British people to know how grateful we are. I realise it cost so much. I came across some people in Britain who were so sympathetic, but others told me how much we were costing the British taxpayer. I feel extremely sorry about that. There's nothing I personally can do.

I remember my fear when they took Ian. Every day I lived with fear that he would be taken out and shot. He's a former British serviceman. They knew that we would, if possible, contact British troops. Then one day my worst fears were realised. The house next door was unoccupied: the neighbours were in the UK and we had a key. There were a lot of Argentinians standing at their door and knocking. My husband said: 'Well, rather than let them break the door down I'll go out and give them a key.' He was immediately taken by the Argentinians and made to kneel at our front gate. It was a bitterly cold day, a Sunday afternoon. For over twenty minutes he was kneeling there, in his shirt-sleeves, with a sub-machine gun in his back. I never realised just what it was like when you can't sit down. I tried to sit down and couldn't, I was so tensed up, I was so worried.

All I did really was walk to the kitchen, make a cup of coffee and come back. I didn't know that in twenty minutes one could drink so many cups of coffee. I put on 'Land of Hope and Glory' [on the record player] and opened the windows. I felt, knowing my husband's sense of humour, that if he were to die, if that was the last thing he heard, at least he would die with perhaps a little smile on his face. Then they released him. My views haven't changed at all. I still want the Falklands to remain British.

JUNE McMULLEN

June McMullen is in her early thirties and married with two young children. She was born and brought up at the settlement of Goose Green on East Falkland. She was living there with her husband, then a shepherd and now manager of the settlement, when the Argentine troops invaded.

It was pretty scary the night we first heard that they were invading. We couldn't really believe it and we had to wait another two days before they came to Goose Green. We didn't know what was going to happen. When they finally arrived here it wasn't too bad at first, they left us alone. But it was frustrating. Suddenly it wasn't your home any more. You had foreigners here telling you what to do and what not to do. It made me angry but I didn't say anything because I didn't want to have any contact with them personally.

At the beginning of May the soldiers started to bring the helicopters down very early in the morning and put them in among the houses. That was the day Stanley Airport had been bombed, although we didn't know that at the time. Then we realised why they had put the helicopters in among the houses. It was so the RAF wouldn't touch the settlement – wouldn't bomb Goose Green. If they saw the helicopters in among the houses they wouldn't dare bomb them for fear of hitting us.

The Harriers still came and bombed the airstrip. It wasn't long after that the Argentine troops herded us out of our homes at gunpoint and put us into the community hall. I had my two children: Lucille, who was four, and Matthew, my young baby, who was three and a half months old. And there was Tony, my husband.

When we first went into the hall we were told it was for a meeting.

We thought they simply wanted to talk to us and then we would go back home. Nobody brought any food with them or changes of underwear or anything like that. There were no blankets. We just had what we stood up in. The first night it was pretty cold, nobody had any extra clothes or blankets. Then we were able to sort something out and go and get mattresses and blankets.

Conditions in the hall were pretty grim. There were 114 of us in there and only two toilets and two wash basins. There were no proper sleeping arrangements, everybody was just sleeping on the floor. We each had a little area where we would put mattresses or blankets down to sleep on. We were lucky, we had got hold of a mattress but some people had nothing. Being the community hall we had a billiard table, and people would play darts, cards or read during the day.

Everybody got sick with bad diarrhoea because the water supply wasn't that good. The baby was no problem because he was so small. He just would have his feed and I would put him in his pram. But it was difficult to get clothes dried. He never had a bath all the time we were in there. I used to lay him out on a towel. I had a 5 lb margarine tin which I kept for him to have his water in. I would sponge and soap him and wash him down like that.

We didn't know anything at first about what was happening in the outside world. Some of the blokes found an old radio that was in bits and pieces. Each night a couple of them would work on it in secret and eventually put it together. We used to listen to the news and that's how we heard that the *Belgrano* had been sunk. And then, when the *Sheffield* had been sunk, we realised there would be a war.

When we heard about the *Belgrano* the mood inside was that we were all quite happy. But then, when we heard about the *Sheffield*, it was a bit of a different story. We wondered what would happen next. Each time a plane flew over the settlement an air-raid siren went off. Everybody in the hall would try and take cover somewhere. As the Task Force got closer and closer we got more and more worried. We were hostages and we didn't quite know what they would do with us, or how they would use us. We knew that they had shot a lot of people in their own country, so we thought they wouldn't be too worried about shooting us to get us out of the way.

We used to have a prayer meeting each evening in the hall. Brook Hardcastle [the local Falkland Island Company manager] used to lead the prayer meeting with a few prayers and then we'd all say the Lord's Prayer. We never sang any hymns.

After the first week the Argentines let two women go out each day to the galley in the cookhouse, where all the men would normally eat together. They were allowed to cook up a big meal, with bread and cakes, and bring it down to the hall. Considering we were all cramped together in a small place everybody got on very well. People were generally good-natured. There weren't any rows. The kids seemed to enjoy it, they thought it was one big party.

On 21 May when the Task Force actually landed, we were all delighted to hear the news. But then we got worried. The Argentines kept moving more and more troops in here. We were wondering what would happen if there was a battle for Goose Green. We wondered if any of us would be killed. Whether they would bomb the place. There were times that I wondered whether we would get out alive. Some of the men cut holes, so that if the battle reached Goose Green we could go underneath the floorboards to get a little bit of safety. And when the battle finally came, this is what most of us did. It was pretty grim: dark and cold and wet in places. We all went down there, my husband and the two children. We stayed there for over six hours. We could hear the big guns going off. There was a lot of noise. The Argentines had moved the big guns close in to the hall. They were firing all the time and then there was small-gun fire. Later on the Harriers came in and there was a terrific noise.

We heard the battle was over from the BBC, on the six o'clock news in the hall. They said: 'Goose Green has been liberated.' But we hadn't. We had to wait until the next morning. The British soldiers started to come in about ten o'clock after they had taken the surrender. They came down through the fields and into the hall. We gave them tea and cigarettes and shared what we had with them. We really felt as if we'd been liberated. We were pleased. We knew they'd come eventually, but when the Paras came into the hall we were very pleased to see them. They were just as pleased to be there and to relax and have a cup of tea. One fellow, a Paratrooper, asked if he could have his photograph taken with baby Matthew. I think when they saw little Matthew that's when they thought it had all been worth while. They could see then what they had been fighting for. One Para, only a young fellow, gave Matthew his cap badge.

When we got out of the hall we found the settlement in a complete mess. Before they surrendered the Argentines looted the place. They went into all the houses and made a general mess of everything. We were very upset when we got back to our house, it was in a terrible mess. They had pulled things out of cupboards and drawers, just scattered them all over the place and walked all over them. They hadn't used the toilet – they had gone on the beds, on the floor, in the bath, everywhere. It was just a mess from top to bottom. I'd packed the things that I really treasured away when we went to get a mattress and blankets on the second day. But I was very depressed with what they had done. It was pretty sickening. But the troops helped us clear it all up.

MARIA KRAUSE

Señora Maria Krause is in her early thirties and was married to an Argentine air force Hercules pilot, Major Carlos Eduardo Krause, shot down and killed in the Malvinas War. She is bringing up three children alone.

I went to the Malvinas in 1979 for a visit, because my husband used to fly there regularly from the mainland with the Argentine state airline, LADE. For me it was a big thrill because I had always felt very strongly about the Islands. I supported the occupation of the Malvinas and I hope that one day I will be able to return.

My husband was a great man, very generous, not materialistic at all. I used to call him a professional Bohemian; he loved the simple life, and open-air life. I was his friend, his companion, his wife, and he looked after me and pampered me in our years together. He was an extrovert and always loved telling jokes. He had a funny accent because he came from the north of Argentina.

Right from the start I had the feeling that my husband was going to die, I don't know why. I lived with this anguish and asked my mother-in-law to stay with me during those days. We talked a lot. We both suffered but she gave me great support. When Carlos returned home after forty-eight or seventy-two hours on duty we would prepare his favourite dishes. We would listen to music and then all go walking together. We would go to the cinema and play with the kids. We didn't watch television or mention the war. In those brief moments we tried to live our last minutes of happiness.

The officers' wives lent to each other a lot of support. We all lived in the same neighbourhood and had known each other for a long time. We had always helped each other, for instance when we were pregnant and our husbands were away. It was like a big family. Sometimes one of us would get more depressed than the rest and we would all go over to her house and try to cheer her up. We would iron her clothes for her, or cook for her kids, because we were all in the same situation. You could not afford to lose your spirit, it would have been terrible.

My husband was unable to call me every day because he was flying most of the time, so another pilot would call his wife and maybe say that he had seen my husband and that he was okay and she would then tell me. Sometimes a pilot coming back to Buenos Aires would bring letters for all the wives and we would try and send them chocolates and sweets. I was possessed by the war. I sometimes think women have the knack of pushing their husbands to do something without them or us realising it. I knew what my husband was doing. Initially he flew food and soldiers to the Islands but later he flew the Hercules which refuelled the fighters. He died when he was on a mission looking for British warships.

On his last visit home he stayed with us for five days, which was very rare. It was near the end of the war and I thought he must have been assigned a dangerous job because he had been given such a long leave before it. Later I learned that he had volunteered for this mission. I learned of his death on 1 June at seven-thirty in the evening. Two air-force officers came to my home and told me there was still a possibility that he could have been found and rescued by the British navy after the plane was shot down.

At that moment I felt inside of me that it was all over. They asked me what I needed and I in turn asked them to talk to my father. When my husband's friend came over I asked him what he was feeling and he replied: 'Carlos is dead.' From that moment I never doubted it. Although they kept looking for him I knew he was dead. At first I thought I would go into hysterics, but I didn't. I took it very calmly and it was only the next day, when we still had not received any news, that I locked myself in my room and cried all the tears that no one had seen me cry in public.

I found out exactly how my husband died after four years. It was in a Spanish book about the Malvinas War and I read the account by the British pilot of how he had shot down the Hercules. I cried a lot then because my husband had never been a coward and he would not have acted as the English pilot did. He shot all his weapons at a defenceless plane and overflew it three times. This 'gentleman' ended his account by explaining how the plane disappeared into the sea in a big splash, a mountain of froth, implying that he had accomplished his mission and that it had been very successful. In my opinion it was like killing a pregnant woman; a real pilot would never do that. He could have given that plane the chance of staying afloat even if it had only been for a few seconds. Had they been able to try and ditch they would at least have had some chance.*

I'm proud of my husband, I think his sacrifice was worth it because that was the way he chose to live and to die. He was convinced that what he was doing was right, that is why it was worth it. You have to separate what our government did from what our men did. The whole world recognises that our men were people of great courage who did amazing things with very little. Many years will pass before we see the results of that sacrifice. Maybe I won't see it, perhaps it will be my children or my grandchildren, but I am at peace with myself because I supported him to the very last moment. I would not forgive myself now if I had objected to him going to war, because he really wanted to go. My children remember their father with great pride. They asked their school to put up a plaque to their father, which they did. For them that is a great source of pride. There are several schools in the province of Misiones which bear my husband's name, even an international airport has been named after him, and that makes us all very proud.

*Señora Krause would obviously see the exigencies of warfare in a different light to the fighter pilot executing the proper and lawful orders to which he was subject, and which probably caused him equal anguish. No criticism can be made of the pilot in such circumstances, but Senora Krause's account demonstrates the emotional reaction of a widow who will never be persuaded otherwise.

EDA MASSE DE SEVILLA

Señora Eda Masse de Sevilla is in her fifties. She is the widow of an Argentine naval officer who died a year before the Malvinas War. Her son, Lieutenant Gerardo Sevilla, was aged twenty-two and was a junior officer on board the _General Belgrano_ when it was sunk by a British submarine in the South Atlantic.

That Sunday I had gone to lunch at my mother's house, and as I was going to bed in the evening my eldest son called. He said: 'Are you listening to the news on the radio?'

I said: 'No, I am watching television.'

And he said: 'They are putting out unbelievable news on Uruguayan radio.' He didn't say anything else so I went to sleep.

At six o'clock in the morning I switched on the radio and the first thing I heard was that the _Belgrano_ had been attacked. I rushed to the telephone and talked to my son and to my sister. It turned out they had been up all night listening to the news. That was the start of my long nights. On Monday: no news. On Tuesday: no news. On Tuesday afternoon: the parish priest said a mass at the church opposite my home, St James's church. All my neighbours and relatives were there, praying for my son's safe return. On Wednesday, at about 1.30 p.m., I received a call from navy headquarters. They wouldn't tell me anything but I somehow knew he had been found. I realised that if he had been found alive the lieutenant who was calling would have said: 'He's alive.' So I called my son and said: 'Look, it must be serious because they won't tell me anything.' He went straight to navy headquarters and returned with a navy doctor. He said; 'Mum they have found him dead.' They gave me an injection and I slept all night.

263

It was awful – the anguish. He was such a healthy boy, so active. He was 1.90 metres (6ft 5in). He would not like to see me crying.

They brought him back on 10 May and gave him a funeral with full honours the next day. Then they buried him at the navy mausoleum. In his letters from the ship he would tell me about his duties and about the music he listened to, because he loved music. He would tell me not to worry, not to listen to the news and to go out and have fun with my friends and try and forget about the war. That is what he told me in his letters. He loved being a disc jockey at parties and he had a hi-fi which he loved – the sounds and the flashing lights and that sort of thing. He was a good sportsman and a good swimmer. He once won the inter-services athletic championship and competed in the Latin American military championships in Brazil.

He was very gregarious and had several girlfriends. At one point he was going out with three girls – all of them called Veronica! He was an extrovert but he also liked reading quietly. He was a normal healthy boy, I suppose. I would not say he was the best because for a mother every son is the best.

My life has changed completely now. I am alone, because my husband died a year before the war. So I lost my husband and my son in the period of six months. All the hopes I held for the future are now completely lost. I have to say that the pain I feel outweighs the pride. In spite of all the tributes to the heroes of the Malvinas I feel more the pain of the mother than the pride for the hero. For me he is not a hero, he is a son.

The sinking of the *Belgrano* was a political matter, perhaps the whole war was a political matter. When Mrs Thatcher ordered the sinking of the ship she forgot that she was a mother and that on that ship there were over 1,000 men who had mothers. The ship was not carrying out any mission at that moment, it was not fighting. It was completely unfair, it was treacherous.

A year after the Malvinas War I went on a trip to Europe. I was on a ship in the Greek Islands when I saw an English lady. I don't know what came over me. I went up to her and asked her: 'Do you like Mrs Thatcher?' She was a bit taken aback but she replied: 'Yes I do.' I said that I hated Mrs Thatcher because I blamed her for my son's death in the war. Then I walked away.

I would say that we have to recover the Malvinas but we have to do it peacefully. When you take up arms you lose the young men who are the future of the country. So we must find a way to bring the Argentines and the English together and to recover our islands. There must be a way. I would say to English mothers to struggle too, so that there will not be another war. In the last war we all lost – the English and the Argentine mothers.

JOHN WITHEROE

John Witheroe is a journalist. He sailed with the Task Force as a correspondent for *The Times* aboard HMS *Invincible*, one of the two aircraft carriers sent to the South Atlantic. He is now diplomatic correspondent of *The Sunday Times*.

I was told on the Sunday before the Task Force sailed that I was to go on *Invincible*. I drove down at 2 a.m. that morning, about eight hours before the ship left Portsmouth. The atmosphere was quite extraordinary, there were hundreds of thousands of people lining the quay, waving. The entire ship's crew of a thousand men turned out on the deck and saluted as we left Portsmouth, followed by *Hermes* and some other warships.

Within the ship there was a curious mood of ebullience and aggressiveness. A lot of crewmen were singing 'Don't cry for me Argentina'. That mood of expectation, combined with a lack of perception that this really was going to be a war, survived for some time, almost until we reached Ascension Island. Most of the crewmen were perfectly happy being there. They thought that the whole escapade would soon be settled diplomatically, and that all the training was just training and we would not actually go to war.

The only person on board ship who said he thought it would come to fighting was the captain. He identified the issue of sovereignty as the main stumbling block, and of course he was proved to be right. He showed a certain nervousness because as an experienced sailor he knew the abilities of the Argentine fleet. Many of them had trained in Britain. He knew about the Exocet missiles and the capabilities of their air force. Almost from the beginning he was

266

cautioning us against taking an over-positive line about how to report this.

There was a huge amount of activity at Ascension Island. Ships were constantly being replenished by helicopters from the island. We had expected a vast fleet to be assembled, but by the time we got there we were told several had set off south. We were expecting to be there several days when we were suddenly turned about and sent off south ourselves. The mood on the ship then changed dramatically.

There were five journalists on *Invincible*. They were forced to take us, the navy didn't want us on board at all. One of the reasons was that Prince Andrew was on board. Yet the navy, in its wisdom, decided to put two correspondents from the *Sun* and the *Daily Star* on board. This made the captain nervous, and Prince Andrew more so, at least for the first couple of weeks.

Among the officers the attitude initially was rather resentful, but that quickly changed. They began to realise that we would serve a purpose. We could report to their families much faster about what was going on, because they had very little communication with them. The captain, slightly cautious at first, began to refer to the journalists as one of his weapon systems in the war against Argentina, obviously meaning that for him we could be a tool of propaganda.

The sailors were amazed that we were still on board after Ascension Island. They thought we were going to get off and wave goodbye. They started asking how much we were being paid for being there – was it huge amounts of money? Had we volunteered or had we been press-ganged? They were amazed that we wanted to go all the way.

We had one of the Ministry of Defence Press officers with us as minder. He had to vet everything we wrote and could object, and did object sometimes, to the sort of things we wanted to put in. By and large their system of controlling us was by denying us access to information rather than trying to prevent us writing what we knew. And even when we wrote things that were fairly uncomplimentary they didn't stop us writing them. The captain would call us in and say: 'This isn't really to our advantage.' He would point out why it might affect the morale of the ship. Everything we wrote was pinned up on notice-boards the same day, so that the crew could read them. He was worried that if we were writing about changes in mood, or about some crewmen being afraid, this might spread ill-feeling throughout the ship and lower morale.

The transition from peace to war was a gradual process. As we sailed south the training became much more intensified. There was a lot of flying by the Harriers and by the Sea Kings. One of the Harrier pilots became very nervous and we tried to convince him there was going to be a diplomatic settlement, although we thought it would end in fighting. The mood among the Harrier pilots was interesting. They tended to be older than other crewmen on board and they were really in the front line. It became noticeable, south of Ascension, that they were drinking less. They kept more to themselves, they did more briefings, they smoked more. The helicopter pilots were younger men and tended to be more belligerent in their attitude and less affected by the dangers that were about to emerge.

On board ship we did far more exercises at Action Stations, where the whole ship would be brought to a state of alert. It would take anything between ten and twenty-five minutes. This heightened the sense of unease. People had to put on their anti-flash gear, they were told to go to their action stations, where they might have to spend hours waiting. All the hatches were closed, the pressure in the ship built up. It was this regular training, as we went to Ascension and beyond, that created a warlike atmosphere.

The mood of levity disappeared very suddenly. Crewmen would come up to us and talk very seriously about their families. What would happen to them if they were killed? Some spoke about what they felt about killing Argentinians. Most of them were worried about what killing meant, now that the reality had come home to them. A few days after we left Portsmouth one of the helicopter pilots told me that he wanted to drop a depth charge on a real submarine. He'd never done it and he just wanted to do it. And when I spoke to him just before the fighting began, he said it was the last thing he ever wanted to do. So it was that change of mood.

Everybody became caught up in the fear that we might get killed, especially when the war started and the raids began on Port Stanley and the *Sheffield* was hit. We were relatively close to *Sheffield* – about twenty miles. She was on the horizon and we assumed we were under missile attack that day. The crew realised at that stage that they were vulnerable to the Argentine air force. It seemed they could sink us at their will and that thought transformed the general feeling on board. Special arrangements were made. We had to make a will and on the closed-circuit television we were shown by the surgeon commander how to jab morphine into our legs in case we were injured. We constantly had to carry lifejackets and gas-masks. This made one aware all the time that we were at risk.

A ship is a very confined area. One tried to maintain one's distance but inevitably you begin to identify not only with the people on that ship, but the fate of the ship. We tried to be objective. If there was something critical to report we tended to do it. But one naturally began to report in a sense what one felt could be said about the war. There was a kind of self-censorship. Because it was such a short war, people didn't build up any great hostility towards the Argentinians, but we obviously wanted to win and we didn't want to be sunk.

After South Georgia was taken a number of Special Forces troops started arriving on the ship for insertions on to East and West Falkland. During May a number of these trips were made. The Special Forces units would be taken in by helicopter, landed and brought back, some-times within a few days. We generally got to know when they were going and when they were coming back.

They were a curious mix of men. Some of them used to come into the wardroom. We would ask them what they were doing, and they would refuse to reply. We'd ask their names and they'd give us their Christian names. We found them sometimes in the hangar, studying their equipment, polishing it. We saw one pair of Marines exchanging a pullover for a couple of hand-grenades. They became obsessed by their kit.

The SBS [Special Boat Squadron of the Royal Marines] took over one of the offices on the ship, next to the Admiral's quarters. They put up loads of maps and attended to their equipment, various rifles and night-sights and weapons. I once tried going in but was ushered out very quickly. It was always hard to tell who were officers and who were men. Some of the naval officers began to worry that they were bringing ordinary men into the wardroom, rather than officers. But none of them ever dared challenge the SBS, who had a slight air of menace about them. One of them was training on the quarter-deck for the world record at press-ups – which was 9,000 consecutive press-ups. They were obsessive about fitness.

In 18 May we were told by the captain, over the ship's tannoy, that we were going on a special operation north-west of the Falklands to insert SBS on to West Falkland. That is what we had been doing, inserting troops backwards and forwards. But this seemed slightly different in that they announced it over the tannoy. The ship then set off with one escort – HMS *Broadsword* – sailing very fast, over 25 knots, westwards. That night I went up to the bridge and found it in utter and complete blackness, which was unusual. On these operations the bridge was normally darkened, but this time there were no lights showing. It took twenty minutes to get used to the darkness, to be able to see what was happening. A few cables away, *Broadsword* was steaming alongside us, showing no lights at all. There was complete radar silence. Nothing. I asked the officer-of-the-watch what was happening, where we were going. He said he didn't know because the course was being given to him segment by segment. He only learned about the next stage as it was brought up by the captain.

I went downstairs into the ship and spoke to someone in the operations room and said this seemed extraordinary, it didn't seem like any of the other operations we had been on. He took me to one side and said he didn't think it was. He thought this was a secret operation to launch a helicopter towards the Argentine mainland. That was as much as one could know at that time.

Throughout the night we steamed at high speed. The whole ship was vibrating. We turned round at some stage, presumably the helicopters took off. We were not allowed to know about that because we were kept away. *Invincible* and *Broadsword* then returned towards the rest of the fleet who were east of the Falklands. As day broke *Broadsword* was once again alongside, still maintaining radio silence. She started signalling to the Captain of *Invincible* [with an Aldis lamp]. I was with the signaller in the Admiral's bridge. He took the message down, which he read back to us: 'Pray God we were successful.' Such a message was extremely unusual. Normally these Special Forces insertions into the Falklands would be done as a matter of routine. We could only reach the conclusion that this had referred to an extraordinary event, the insertion of Special Forces into Argentina. We were told shortly afterwards by somebody on the flight-deck that this helicopter had not returned. Normally when they put people secretly on to the Falklands the helicopter would come back to the *Invincible*. But on this occasion we were told the Sea King had not come back. We were also told it had been carrying Special Forces. Two days later we heard on the BBC World Service that a helicopter had crashed in Chile. We assumed it was the same helicopter and that it had taken SBS or SAS men to Argentina.

(John Witheroe later landed on the Falkland Islands and went forward with soldiers involved in the battle for the mountains around Port Stanley.)

We were involved with one night attack on Mount Harriet, when the Welsh Guards were coming up as a back-up. This involved marching for several hours on a very dark night, through a minefield. Sporadic shellfire slowed our progress tremendously. Eventually we made the base of Mount Harriet, which was coming under incredible fire from a frigate offshore. The whole mountain seemed to erupt in flame. It seemed impossible that anybody could survive an attack like that. This went on for well over an hour, shell after shell whistling over our heads and hitting the mountain. Eventually this was lifted and the Marines [42 Commando] went in. To our amazement there seemed to be an incredible amount of fighting going on. There was a lot of tracer fire. The whole night was being lit up by flares, which cast a dead, unrealistic, pall over the whole scene.

Near us there was a Milan anti-tank missile unit, who were trying to take out a bunker that had been putting up fierce fire on the advancing Marines. One attempt missed. They then fired a missile straight into this bunker, which exploded completely, and the firing then ceased. The battle must have gone on for hours. The air was full of the smell of cordite and shouts that we could occasionally hear. Men advancing. Cries of pain.

By the time dawn came we could see the Marines up on the mountain. Our feeling was one of curious detachment. We weren't directly in the line of fire, but we knew at any moment there could be a breakout, or that it could come down to us. It was bitterly cold. We stomped up and down trying to watch what was going on.

News came through to us on the radio-net that the Argentines were close to surrender. We were back at Mount Harriet at that stage with the Welsh Guards who were to take Sapper Hill, the final step before Stanley itself. We flew in a helicopter to the base of Sapper Hill. The Marines had just been involved in a fire-fight with retreating Argentinians and we found several wounded Marines by the roadside being tended by medical orderlies. We jumped on a Scorpion tank that was heading up towards Sapper Hill. Troops around us were all running to the hill. They were determined to get to Stanley as quickly as possible because there was intense competition between the rival units to be first into Stanley. The Welsh Guards still thought they could be first in.

We mounted Sapper Hill and got our first view of Stanley. After ten weeks of fighting we didn't know what to expect. We looked down on this curiously insubstantial little town, with smoke coming up from the surrounding houses, several of which seemed to be burning. There was no sign of any Argentinians, anywhere. The senior officers from the Guards gathered on the hill and looked down. They realised they had to stop there. They were not going to be the first in. Mixed with their jubilation was intense disappointment that they were not the first liberating troops.

The journalists' aim was to get into Stanley as quickly as possible. We took off our army camouflage gear, realising that if we marched into Stanley like that we could be shot, because we didn't know if the war had finished or not. Underneath we had blue sweaters and jeans. So we discarded the kit and walked down this long road into Stanley. On either side of the road were Argentine positions, men with guns pointing at us. We really didn't know if they were going to shoot or not, because none of them waved. We waved at them hoping they would wave back but there was no response until, on the outskirts of Stanley, three Argentines came up carrying no weapons and insisted on shaking our hands and saying: 'It's over.'

As we arrived in Stanley a helicopter was coming in. It had a big white flag draped underneath it. This was Lieutenant-Colonel Mike Rose [Commander of 22 SAS Regiment], who was going to negotiate the surrender with Menendez. We saw Rose going into the negotiations. As we wandered through Stanley it was deserted. There was no sign of any Argentine troops, and no British troops because they had been kept outside the perimeter. We came across locals who seemed blasé about finding us there.

The local priest invited us in and gave us a meal, our first wash in two weeks, and showed us some of the damage. Stanley had been quite badly hit by some of the shelling and firing that had been going on. He showed us a volume of theology which had two bullet holes going right through it, fired by nervous Argentine troops inside the town. He said: 'They got through this quicker than I did.' Elsewhere the locals were celebrating but in a low-key kind of way. They were just grateful that the whole thing was over.

GILLIAN WHITE

Mrs Gillian White is married to Chris White, who served in the Falklands campaign with the Royal Marines and was hospitalised when he returned to Britain after *Sir Galahad*, the ship he was on, was sunk by enemy bombing.

I was slightly apprehensive and annoyed when I heard that Christopher was going off to the Falklands. We had a wedding to attend that weekend and I was going to be chief bridesmaid – the first time I had ever done it. It was Christopher's sister's wedding and he was meant to be an usher. At the last moment everybody was rushing around trying to find new ushers. At the time I thought a war wasn't really going to happen, and I was upset on the evening of the wedding because I thought he was going to be there and he wasn't. Then there was a delay and the departure was stopped several times. He would ring up and say: 'I'm still here, I haven't gone yet, we're still loading up the ship, half the supplies haven't arrived.'

It was a couple of days before he left and it would have been nice if he could have come home for a few hours. They had to keep him all the way down there [in Plymouth], so the only contact we had was by telephone. When he actually said: 'I'm on my way' I thought they were bound to find a solution before he got there, that it would just be a joy ride for him.

When I first heard, over the radio, that the *Sir Galahad* had been hit I wasn't at all worried. Christopher left Britain on the *Sir Galahad*, but at Ascension Island he changed to *Sir Tristram*. I knew this because he was sending me letters all the time, full of things about what they had been doing, more jokey than anything else. He wasn't worried about what was going to happen and I didn't worry about it.

And then while I was at work I got a phone call from my father-in-law. He phoned the barracks and asked whether Christopher was on the *Galahad* when she went up. He was told 'Yes', but they couldn't give any more information, we would have to ring back later because it was very difficult to find out exactly how many people were on the ship – survivors, wounded or whatever. So I had to wait.

I rang a number we were given in Plymouth and was told that he was perfectly all right. They then phoned and told me that he was on the wounded list but they couldn't tell me what was wrong with him, so of course my imagination ran riot. I decided not to do anything about it, just wait. Then I got a call from Christopher's sergeant, who said he wasn't physically injured, but he wasn't very well and I'd just have to wait and see.

(Chris White made an unauthorised telephone call to Gill from RAF Wroughton, a military hospital – see p.165.)

I was annoyed that Christopher had had to ring me. I had a three-and-a-half hour drive [to RAF Wroughton], but I really shouldn't have done it. I should have taken a taxi. I started off in the wrong frame of mind. I was very upset. I didn't know what was going on, I didn't know why he had to ring me and why we weren't informed that he was in the country. On the way down we blew a tyre at 70 mph on the outside lane of the motorway, so we very nearly didn't get there. When we did, we went to the ward where they had the physically wounded. It was a bit horrific. There were people in there talking to the kids without any legs in wheel chairs. They were brilliant, until they walked out. Then you could see wives and families just breaking down. They had had to be so strong when they were in there with their sons, but when they walked out they were breaking down. They were very upset.

We were taken to one side by one of the psychiatric nurses and told not to expect very much; Christopher had to be kept very quiet. Basically we had to talk about anything we wanted to, but were not to upset him too much and not to push him in any direction.

We were taken down to this tiny little room. It was lovely. It was quiet and the curtains were drawn. The hospital itself was out in the countryside, so it was peaceful. But he looked an absolute wreck. That was our first thought as we walked through the door. He had bags under his eyes. They were black. He was wearing different people's clothing because his clothes had literally been blown off his back from the *Galahad*. He was grinning away, very pleased to see us of course, but it was difficult to talk to him, to contact him in any way. He was obviously on something they had given him to try and make him sleep, so even conversation was a bit difficult. We just had to play it by ear.

I think he was confused more than anything else. When you think of a psychiatric case you think of someone who's a bit doolally, bouncing all over the place. But he was very quiet. He had a stubborn look about him so I knew that obviously he'd come to a decision in his own mind about something, either that he was going to say nothing, or he wasn't going to sleep. He was quite willing to talk to us but not to anybody else, which is why the people at RAF Wroughton decided that the family was so important to his therapy, because we were the only ones that he would really talk to.

When he was in the hospital at Plymouth he started to tell us what had actually happened, little bits and pieces started to come out. They were pretty horrific, you just had to sit there and let it go all over the top of your head. It was no use showing any emotion, he didn't want any emotion showed. If I had broken down and started crying it would have made him feel really awful and he probably wouldn't have said anything to me again. He would have bottled it up inside him. So I just sat there and let him pour it out, time after time. It had to go over my head until I could accept it. When I had begun to accept what he had actually been through then I could start asking him questions, to try and draw it out of him even more.

I was shocked when I learned that he had tried to take his own life, shocked because he hadn't told me the whole story. As it unfolded I was angry at him because he'd allowed himself to think the way he had done. I think anybody listening to his story would know automatically: he had a choice and he'd chosen to go back to try and help Kevin to get out of the flames. He had done as much as he could and when he couldn't do any more he had got help as fast as he could. The fact that he decided to take all this guilt on his own shoulders annoyed me to begin with. I could understand it after a while. In fact I varied from understanding him to being annoyed. I would say to him: 'Don't be so stupid, you're not to feel any guilt. You couldn't have done any more.' I was angry then.

Initially when he came home he just slept. He hadn't slept all the time he'd been in the hospital. I had these great big bottles of pills given to me and was told: 'He won't sleep.' As soon as we got home I threw the pills away and he slept for almost twenty-four hours. He was in his own environment and that's where he wanted to be. He said to me previously that the hospital was far too big, he didn't like the space, he just wanted to be quiet. Really, he just needed a time of adjustment, or so I thought.

He was all right until he came out of the Marines. He went back and did a stint in Northern Ireland and he seemed to be far more balanced. He seemed to have started to enjoy himself again. And he was really looking forward with some optimism about what he was going to do when he came out of the Marines. That's really when the problems started. He hit this awful wall of people not wanting to know because of his medical record. I became very bitter about it because he wasn't a psychiatric case, they didn't have any facility for Acute Battle Reaction patients. It was either a medical ward or a psychiatric ward and that was it. So I became quite embittered and had a battle with the authorities in the navy that if he had to be readmitted for any other treatment it would be to a hospital nearer to home. The effect on both my health and Christopher's of the travelling and expense caused me to lose my job as well, under doctor's orders. We went from both being employed to both being unemployed, and that was a terrific financial strain, which we didn't really need at the time.

We got an interim payment – about £500 – from the South Atlantic Fund to pay my travelling costs; I was commuting every day to Plymouth, having to hijack members of my family with better cars than we had to take me down there. Later a letter said they were reviewing the case and they would inform us about any other payments being made. Eventually Chris had to ring up himself, and he was told that we really ought to be grateful for what we'd got. We were not going to have any more assistance.

I was looking after a three-year-old child, our son, and trying to do a full-time job. It meant I had very little time for relaxation. My constant worry was trying to get down to Plymouth to give Chris as much time as he needed. He wasn't talking to anyone else about what had happened to him. Once they actually showed the *Galahad* on television. I was talking to him and holding his hand. He was far more relaxed about what he had gone through and then I knew he had to come home. But it was a fight, they didn't want to let him home. I wasn't having that, I was taking him home.

He is fine now. Over the last year our relationship has improved tremendously. He's got his self-respect back. I'm working again. I went through almost a period of resentment towards him because I was working and he was going out and using my money for his drinking. I got to the stage where I looked at myself in the mirror one day and thought: I don't like what I see and I'm just going to tell him I don't like it, if not for my sake then for our son's. He's going to have to go or pull himself back together.

I know very well that if we'd had some financial back-up or we had had a commitment from the services behind us about his medical record, then all of this really needn't have happened. It wasn't necessary. He needn't have gone through all of that, he would have taken a year off, relaxed and got himself well again.

He wasn't physically injured, he had to go through a lot of trauma because of his condition. It wasn't a psychiatric condition but it was complicated, worsened, by the fact that he was unemployed for so long and he became very depressed. I think any ordinary person would become depressed when they're unemployed for any length of time. When you've fought so hard to come out of the services with a normal medical record as he had done, then to be turned down for jobs because of his medical record and still receive no assistance . . . it became very very hard. It was very difficult for us to accept. I became much more bitter than Christopher. He was quite happy to disappear into the bottle. I could see what was happening and it made me very annoyed.

I have changed my attitude towards the system. It was totally lacking in any emotion whatsoever. You were in the navy and that was how you were listed. You weren't 'White – human being' you were 'White – navy', so you had to go where the navy said you had to go. As a civilian I found it extremely annoying that they were going to take him further away from us when it was obvious he needed us more than ever. So when I was called in front of the [navy] surgeon I told him exactly what I thought of him and the system. It didn't make me popular but I was past caring by then. As far as the navy was concerned, he was navy property almost. He was going to be moved to Plymouth whether we liked it or not. My parents and I complained about it. To me Christopher wasn't part of the navy, he was my husband and he needed his family around him at that time. That was all that concerned me.

We've lost several years because of the attitude of the services. I didn't get any back-up when he did leave hospital, I was totally on my own. I didn't have any person to ring, any particular person to contact if I thought he was going back into a deep depression. I was out on a limb over 100 miles away. Well, I coped with that. I had my own doctor to go to who is very good. It was just the general lack of assistance that I find very difficult.

My attitude to the war didn't change because of what happened to us. He was there, he had a job to do. He'd been in the Marines several years by then, he'd done different jobs in the Marines and he was more at ease and relaxed in a Raiding Squadron than any other thing he'd done. That was what he'd chosen to do.

In retrospect I think if he had stayed in he might have got the back-up, but he wouldn't have got it out of his system half as quickly as he has done. It's taken long enough as it is to work its way through. He still thinks about it, but he's learned to live with it.

When you hear the old soldiers talk about the wars they've been in, they haven't forgotten anything. They can recall it all at an instant. But they learn to live with it, learn to accept it, and they get on with their lives. Chris has done this. He's got through the tunnel, he's come out of the other end and we're a family again. It almost destroyed us as a family but we did it, and that was without any help from the services. I would say to anybody going through it: 'Just hang on in there – but don't expect the services to support you. You've got to do it on your own.' It's the only way.

MARY WATSON

Mrs Mary Watson lives in Sheffield. Her only son, Tony, was a sailor on board HMS *Glamorgan*, which was on Exercise Springtrain off Gibraltar when the Falklands crisis broke. The ship was diverted to the South Atlantic instead of coming home to Britain. Throughout the war, as she waited for news, Mrs Watson's constant worry was whether she would ever see her son again.

When Tony's ship was diverted to the Falklands I felt panic, wondering what it was all about from the political point of view. I couldn't understand it, not many women did at that time. It was national pride I suppose. I agree with that but I still think, like all females, that a life is very precious. I'm anti-war, but Tony was out there fighting the war; Tony my son. He was trained to do that but I was scared for him.

I felt proud when I saw the pictures of the ships leaving Portsmouth, saying goodbye. I didn't get the chance to see Tony because they were deployed straight from Gibraltar. I suppose they had to get there quick. It made it difficult. I don't know whether it was a good thing because I'd have probably broken down if I had seen him. Maybe it was for the best.

From then on it was just one long night really. I couldn't concentrate on anything so I wrote a diary. Every morning I used to write to him. The Post Office were very good because they gave us the airmail letters for free. I wrote every day, just nonsense, home news, silly things. I used to send him parcels – pot noodles, he used to like pot noodles. They used to laugh at me at the Post Office because I was always sending him silly parcels. I don't know whether he got them all or not. It was just a case of trying to be near to him.

I felt very alone at the time, I wrote that in my diary. When I used to go out into the street the world was going on. It was a different world outside. In the home he was missing and I didn't know whether he would be missing forever. I used to sit and write and write and write. That way I'd feel closer to him. I wanted them to come to a peaceful solution. I listened for every snippet of news on the radio or television. I used to sleep on the settee, whatever sleep I could get. As soon as it was on the television news I turned it on. I'd have the radio on just for news. Until you're a mother you don't realise what it's like. When I saw Argentinians on television, I looked at it from the mother's point of view. Those boys were just boys. They had mothers worrying about them just the same. I couldn't see anything from the political point of view, I just saw mothers with sons fighting, that's all. Killing each other. I just can't see the point in it. I suppose somewhere along the line there was a reason – it was our territory. But I've known one or two boys, nice boys, that have been killed. If it had been my son as well I should have broken up.

I heard the *Glamorgan* was hit [by an Exocet missile two days before the war ended] when it came over the news. I had just come back from church. As I was walking back one of the neighbours asked me how Tony was getting on. I said: 'Oh, last letter I had from him, he was fine.' Then I got in the house. I heard that the ship had been hit. I can remember I had the flowers from the altar at that time. I just threw them on the floor and collapsed because I didn't know whether he was alive or dead then.

You pull yourself together and you start phoning until you get some news. I got the little slip of paper – the Familygram – with a few words on it, saying that he was alive. There must have been families that got bad news. They're the ones I think of.

We used to have these meetings of families from the *Glamorgan*. We met once in York, it was very nice, very pleasant. When the surrender happened I felt as if all the weight had been lifted off me. I cried, but they were tears of joy. I had been wondering whether I'd ever see Tony again. It's as simple as that. It seemed so long and drawn-out. Now that he's home we argue like mad. But he's here to argue with, that's the main thing. He is an only child and I had no other children to turn to, so therefore it was very lonely for me at the time. I used to pray very hard. I found a lot of comfort in church, I used to sit and cry there.

I just couldn't wait for the boys to get back. There were a lot of them down there and it must have been a very long journey home. The homecoming itself was brilliant. Brilliant. We went down to Portsmouth and stayed in the Home Club. It was good to hear the older generation of the navy, the old salts. They thought the lads did a brilliant job. They did too, let's face it. The older ones tend to think the younger ones can't do anything. But they showed their spirit in the Falklands. We talked to a lot of the older chaps and they were so proud of the lads. Then we went on to the quay to meet the *Glamorgan* coming back. She was so rusty because she'd been at sea a lot of days. I've never seen so many men cry in all my life. They were all crying, waiting for their sons coming home, you see. And it was a marvellous sight.

Some families had gone down in busloads to meet the ship coming in. I had an umbrella – I had painted a big hand on top of the umbrella so that he could see it. He saw me when the boys came in and were lined up along the sides of the ship, looking very smart. It was a very emotional time.

It was a bit frustrating really greeting Tony off the ship. At that time he had been writing to a girl, and I'm afraid the girl pipped me to the post. She was there waiting, a very nice girl, but I wanted to get there first and unfortunately I didn't. But nevertheless it was marvellous because there were so many families greeting their boys.

He said: 'Hello mum.'

I said: 'Hello son.' That's all. We're not flowery speakers, just ordinary people. But it was good to hold him. I think that's the first and the last time, because he's not a mother's boy.

It was a sad occasion as well. As we were crying with joy, others would be crying with sorrow, because some of the boys hadn't come back. The boys on the ship felt very sad. I feel so empty for the families that have lost their boys. Every war claims some victims, I realise that, but when it comes into your life it's very scary, very scary.

At the time I felt very guilty. I felt it was my fault that he was in the navy, but if he had been in the army or RAF I would have felt the same way. I felt as if I had encouraged him to be where he was. The diary I wrote is riddled with guilt, I realise that now. It's years since I read it. I just used to write and write, in the early hours of the morning when I couldn't sleep. I just felt guilty. When he was born in Jessops

Hospital a friend of mine had a baby boy at the same time. Now Ian is in college. He has done very well, I don't know what he's studying for, but he's gone up the ladder. I just wish now I'd encouraged that, rather than the navy side of it. But I'm very proud of him. I think he's a man's man. He's a very very good son to me, very good. I don't think there's anything wrong in that, do you?

The whole experience of the Falklands War changed my life – I'm frightened of what's round the corner. I'm more wary. I just want to see him settled and married. I want the future to happen that's all, being the only one. I need him as a continuation I suppose.

JANE KEOGHANE

Mrs Jane Keoghane is a widow from the Falklands War. She was married to Kevin Keoghane of the 1st Battalion Welsh Guards, who was killed aboard *Sir Galahad* when it was bombed on 8 June 1982. Their only child was born after the conflict ended.

The thought of Kevin going to the Falklands didn't seem too bad. It was a long way off and I think most people thought by the time the *QE2* got there it would all be over. So it didn't seem as real as Ireland. It was a fairly important period for us both because I was six months' pregnant with our first child when he left. It was very exciting: we'd been married for six years and then I'd actually become pregnant.

He sent letters while he was on the way down. He wrote about what we were going to do when he came home, and things like that. He hoped I was keeping fit and well and that the baby was okay. I was a district nurse at the time and he was concerned about me driving. From his letters he seemed very happy. It was a bit of excitement, especially being on the *QE2* – he would never have gone on a ship like that otherwise. He was very impressed. He and a colleague were sharing a luxury cabin.

The *QE2* went first to South Georgia. Then they changed to the *Canberra* and were taken to the Falkland Islands. When they got ashore they were digging in and marching forward – for five days. They then went back and got on a ship. His last letter was written in a shower cubicle on board the ship. They were crammed in together and it was easier for him to sit in the shower cubicle with the light on and write his letter. Apparently they had been messed around for five days – digging in, marching and then being brought back again. In spite of that, morale

284

was very high and everyone seemed happy. They were being taken to a place called Bluff Cove the next day.

On the night of 8 June I watched television, which is something I don't normally do. I put the TV in the bedroom. The BBC2 news said that a ship had been bombed and that Welsh Guards were on it. I didn't do anything that night because it was 11.30 p.m., but the next morning I checked with the guardroom [at Pirbright Barracks where Jane and Kevin had a married quarter]. They told me Kevin was all right because he wasn't on the list. In fact they had only got the list of people injured, which of course he wasn't. I was relieved because his name wasn't on the list. I didn't think anything other than that.

On the Friday the ex-families officer came to tell me Kevin was missing. He had obviously been brought in because of the numbers of people involved. I was getting ready to go to work. A friend who lived in the same area was driving to work and saw him coming into our cul-de-sac. She realised what was happening and came with him. He just stood in the living-room and said Kevin was missing. It was all very quick. He left then and said he would be back later. I don't think it really sank in an awful lot because of the shock. In retrospect there were ways it could have been handled better. No one likes telling somebody that someone has died, or – in this case – is missing. He seemed embarrassed. That's not the right word – he certainly wasn't comfortable with the situation he had been placed in. I don't think he had ever had to do anything like that before in his career. I'm sure he doesn't want to do anything like it again.

Later on the colonel's wife, Mrs Rickett, came in to see me. I got very cross with her because she said that it was all very final. I suppose really that she was the only one who was being realistic. She said that there wasn't much hope because it was then two days after it happened. Given the conditions out there it was pretty unlikely they'd have any survivors. I did get cross with her because she said it. But she was very kind and very nice. I suppose, looking back, she was very helpful. But at the time it didn't appear that way, on that particular day. It wasn't until the following day that I heard for certain. [It was five days after the ship was hit.] The officer's words were: 'We must presume that they're dead.' And that was it.

I know nothing of the circumstances of Kevin's death – that was of my own choosing. I'd seen the TV account of it. Lieutenant-Colonel

Rickett [CO 1 Battalion Welsh Guards] visited me on his return from the Falklands. I had letters from the colonel and from another officer who knew Kevin very well. He had been his platoon commander at one point and he felt better qualified to write to me than the existing officer. Lieutenant-Colonel Rickett visited me in hospital. I had been taken in because I had toxaemia. I didn't have any details because at that point I didn't want to hear any. I never knew where he was on the ship, or anything like that.

(Her husband's death meant that Jane had to give up her married quarter in Pirbright and move in with her family in Newport.)

Kevin's pay was stopped on 8 June, which was the day that the *Galahad* went down. This is where the confusion arose with the demand for the rent on the married quarter at Pirbright. I didn't realise Kevin's pay had been stopped. I was informed by the bank that his money hadn't gone in. My main objection wasn't the fact that I'd had a demand for rent on the house, it was the way it was demanded. My name wasn't on it. It was addressed to 'The Co-op Widow', whatever 'Co-op' stands for. I don't really know. I've never found out. But I did feel that it was totally unnecessary, that they could have written it either to myself or 'The Occupant' but the 'Co-op Widow' I thought was pretty heartless. I did ignore the first demand I had for payment because I just filed it away, it didn't seem important at the time. Then I had another letter stating that if I didn't pay, they would take legal action. Kevin's pay was stopped on 8 June but I was actually informed of his death on 13 June.

When I returned to Newport my sister arranged for my name to go on the waiting list for a council house. This was a week or two after my return. We were then told I would have to wait between three and nine years. This we challenged because it obviously wasn't very satisfactory. Apart from the hassle with the council there was also the DHSS. They said I wasn't entitled to claim my maternity benefit because of Kevin's death. I wasn't entitled to claim a widow's benefit plus maternity benefit. I couldn't understand why because the maternity benefit was my contributions. I worked for those and then I was told I couldn't have them.

A representative of the DHSS actually called at my father's house where I was staying and demanded my book from me. But he didn't really explain why I had to give it in. He just said I wasn't entitled to it, which I couldn't understand because it was my benefit. I was told that if I didn't hand it over that he would have to take me along to the local police cells. I was then seven months' pregnant.

Eventually I was rehoused by the local council under the Homeless Persons Act, which meant I could have a property, but if Philip hadn't survived the birth they could have evicted me because I wouldn't be entitled to a house. So they were just covering their own backs, I suppose.

When Kevin was serving with the Welsh Guards you always got the impression that it was a family unit and that they always looked after their own. But my feeling is that when things go wrong then they are not a family unit. I certainly found the family unit lacking when I needed help. The first six months there was very little contact. You don't want people falling over you, but it would have been nice to have been visited without them having been asked to visit.

Kevin lived and breathed the Welsh Guards. They were everything to him. He was a very loyal member of the regiment and he really loved his job. It had a lot to do with the fact that his father was a Welsh Guard. He had been brought up Welsh Guards and that's where Kevin got his love for the regiment.

I don't want my son to join the army. There is no training for them, they're just soldiers. I don't mean they're 'just soldiers', they do a very important job. But at the end of the day they've got nothing to show for it. Kevin did fifteen years. Had he come out, apart from the police force there is not an awful lot he could have done. He wasn't trained to do anything and in this day and age you need a profession.

I don't think the cause was worth Kevin's death. I've got to say 'No.' He was my husband. I think it was a necessary cause. I don't think it could be left to the Argentines just to take over and leave it at that. There are other little islands we've got nearer home. We've got Jersey and Guernsey. I mean there would be nothing stopping a tinpot dictator getting a foothold in any of those. I thought it was a necessary cause, but I just hope it was worth the lives.

I think everybody knew from the beginning [the bombing of the *Sir Galahad*] that it was one big cock-up. You only have to look at the news footage to see that. They were just sitting ducks. Whatever you say about it, nothing is going to alter the fact that it happened, and nothing is going to make him come back. People tell you that time heals, but it doesn't. You just have to cope with it.

People will tell you that you look well. What they expect you to look like I don't know. But they say: 'Well you *look* well.' I suppose that's just their way of saying something but saying nothing. There's not a lot you can say, is there? But time isn't a healer. It doesn't heal.

I still feel very bitter because it's something which shouldn't have happened. There are cock-ups in every war, but when it affects you it is totally different. It's you it's happening to. It still doesn't alter the fact that it's happened; you just have to cope with it, and get on with your life the best you can.

DOROTHY FOULKES

Mrs Dorothy Foulkes lives in Lancashire. She was widowed during the Falklands War. Her husband, Frank, was a mechanic aboard the container ship *Atlantic Conveyor*, which was hit by an Exocet missile on 25 May 1982 – Argentina's Independence Day.

Frank had been in the Royal Navy for a number of years and then went in the Merchant Navy, so he was essentially a navy man. He was also a great one for home. He loved his navy life but the minute he shipped up, he loved to get home. He was for his country and the Royal Family. He was very patriotic and wouldn't have hesitated to go to war. He never thought twice about going. He was also a happy-go-lucky type, and we had a nice relaxed life. They were away nine weeks and home for three so you never really had time to get bored with each other. It was a good life we had together.

He got a telephone call from Cunard. They said: 'Your ship's sailing tomorrow. You know where they're going – are you sailing with her?' Of course he said Yes. I never thought twice about it; they needed the ship and obviously he would go. It was the same as if he was in the Royal Navy.

He described the journey on the way down in his letters. He was thrilled because it took him back twenty years. On board they had the Royal Navy, RAF, there was a Marine and also helicopter pilots. He said the social life was fantastic. They were playing darts, cards and cribbage. There were deck games and plenty of people to chat to. He talked to some of the younger sailors about when he was in the navy. He couldn't get over the pay they were receiving, compared with what he got when he first went in.

He said in one of his letters: 'Whatever is waiting for us down there, nothing will look so bad if we've still got this happy atmosphere on board ship.' So he was really enjoying it. They were working long hours and it was hard work. When they were not working they would get together for a drink. Normally it was a quiet ship, it didn't carry a big crew. Frank usually spent his evenings in his cabin playing tapes and reading. He kept a bottle of whisky in there, and his mixers. All of a sudden there were a lot of people on board, as well as helicopters, planes, ammunition, cluster bombs and thousands of large tents. He didn't think the Falkland Islands were big enough to take all these tents. He had been up in a helicopter twice while they were going down there and was thrilled to bits.

I had heard one morning on the radio that there had been a fire on one of the merchant ships. They had put it out and everything was all right. I took the children to the dentist. The taxi driver asked me whether Frank was okay because a merchant ship was on fire. I said: 'They put it out. Everything's all right. You know what they say: "No news is good news." '

We didn't get back until about 12.30 p.m. I believe by then it had already been announced on the news. When we drove up there was a chaplain from the Merchant Seaman's Mission in Manchester sat in his car by the door. He was waiting for us. I saw this little blue badge on his lapel. I automatically thought: Something's wrong.

He said: 'Can I speak to you in the house please?'

I said: 'Yes, come on,' and we sent the children away into the kitchen. He put me in the lounge and said: 'I'm afraid I've some bad news for you.' I said: 'Just how bad?'

'I'm afraid it's the very worst.'

I sat down. The telephone rang and it was my daughter from Germany. She had heard the *Conveyor* had been hit. She said: 'Mum, have you heard anything?' So of course I had to tell her. No sooner had I put the phone down than my mother rang. I had to tell her. I was quite concerned because she is old and on her own.

I couldn't get rid of the man. I just wanted him to go. He said: 'Do you want me to tell the children?'

I said: 'Oh no. No. I'll tell the children in my own way thank

290

you.' He told them: 'Make your mother a strong cup of tea.' I can remember that.

They came in and kept saying: 'What's the matter?' When he went I told the children that the ship had been hit and their dad had been killed. It was all I knew at the time. They were very good. The youngsters were still at home. Charlotte was only ten; she couldn't quite take it all in. Later on she said: 'You mean my Dad's dead?' Victoria keeps everything to herself anyway so she just went very quiet. Elizabeth, being the eldest, tried to help shoulder the responsibility of looking after her sisters and me.

I'm a strong character and I didn't break down – not at the time. I remember seeing on the television the first report that the *Conveyor* had been hit and that there was only one casualty – a Chinese seaman. I was so mad about that I just wanted to ring up and tell them they were idiots: 'He wasn't Chinese!' I was so mad with anger. You don't take it in at first. Even now, years later, you don't believe it. Sometimes I still think: 'He's at sea.' You carry on as though he is still at sea. But now and again it comes home.

I found out that his body had been picked up and that he was buried at sea. I got a telephone call, I think it was on 27 May, saying: 'Frank Foulkes was buried at sea at 3 p.m. on Wednesday 26th May,' and they gave me the longitude and latitude. I then got it in writing from Cunard two or three days later. I did ask what happened. I'm still asking. I ask everybody I see who is connected with it for information. I asked the Seamen's Union if they could get me some information, because I couldn't. Cunard answered and sent me a duplicate map of the Falkland Islands, one of those maps that you roll out. There are sea-currents on it and there was a cross with a circle. It says on it: 'Position at sea of burial of Mr Frank Foulkes.' I didn't think it was an awful lot of information. I wanted to know why he died when there were so many rescued. There were only three bodies picked up. I presume the rest were still on the ship. Why did they die? Since then I've spoken to two of the relatives and they were given reasons. I was never given a reason.

It worries you, it gnaws at you all the time – not knowing. Frank was a strong swimmer. He had been a sailor practically all his life. It makes me wonder why he didn't survive when the others did. What went wrong? I knew Frank was fire-fighting, this young man told me. He saw the fire-fighters going down in the hold after the order to abandon ship had been given. People were climbing down the rope-ladders. Even at this stage there were explosions and the ship was on fire in different places. The fire-fighters were still going down. Maybe he was very tired. I've thought about this. That could be the answer why he didn't make it. Apparently he was swimming in the water. It could have been cold, but I think perhaps he was just very tired because he had been fire-fighting. They had quite a lot of equipment when they went down in the hold – big tanks on their backs.

I got his belongings back in a jiffy-bag. It was upsetting. Inside was a plastic bag and there was his pipe, his wristwatch, his St Christopher, his wedding ring. I was very upset about them taking his wedding ring off, because it worried me. It was very tight and he had never taken it off. I was worried how they got it off his fingers. He always used to wear a cap when he was down below because he didn't like to get oil in his hair. His cap was in this plastic bag and they were all wet still, as if they had come out of the sea. His pen and pencil were in a little velvet box. It was all wet. Funny enough the ink was still running in the pen. The biro and his wristwatch were still working. The tobacco had come out of the pouch and was spread among all his belongings. They only picked up three dead men and sent off the belongings of three men. Couldn't they have just wiped them over or dried them first? We were glad we got them because at the time I was very worried he had been trapped in the ship and he had been burned or badly injured. Getting all his belongings back in one piece reassured us that at least he had got off the ship and that he wasn't trapped. It does help to know things like that.

He was presented with a South Atlantic campaign medal that came through the post. It was in three pieces. There was a bit of ribbon, and you got a medal in another jiffy-bag. They are good with jiffy-bags, the Ministry of Defence. There was this little rose that goes with it. When I opened it there was a letter inside, which upset me a bit. I was crying at the time and I dropped it on the floor. I didn't know what I'd dropped because it had all fallen out of the envelope, and I thought there was a piece missing. I couldn't make up my mind. I thought: 'No, the medal is here and the piece of ribbon is here.' And I got them together. It was a few days later that I found this little rosette – I think it was in the fruit bowl, under the oranges. I suddenly realised it belonged to the medal.

It was a bit upsetting because we have got an army camp and HMS *Inskip* only three miles away. Every night in the local paper there would be pictures of soldiers being presented with their medals. It would have been rather nice if they had written to me and said: 'If you would like to go along to the camp, one of the officers will give it to you.' It would have been nice if we had all been assembled and had it given to us with a pin, so that I could use it. You know, put it on. But no. I got it through the post with a jiffy-bag. '

I think we had to fight because they had invaded British territory. It's really all a question of pride. I think Britain had to have that pride in herself or, as a nation, what would we have been now? They had to do it. But the price my family paid ... no one will ever know exactly what price we paid. Perhaps it was worth it, for Britain's sake.

It has changed me. I'm a lot harder. I don't believe anything anybody tells me quite as easily. I'm very bitter. I think a lot has to do with the way we were treated afterwards. I never in my life had been treated as a third-rate citizen until I got among the services and the Ministry of Defence. Suddenly, if you're not an officer's wife, you're nothing. I couldn't understand this at all. Years later it is no easier to cope.

There are times when I think: 'I used to get like this when he was away at sea. I'll be glad when he comes home on leave. When he comes through the door I'm going to say: "Right. You make all the decisions now. I'm not going to make another decision for three weeks." ' It was great just to be able to hand over all the reins and say: 'You run every-thing. Let someone else advise all the children when they say: "What do you think I should do? Should I do this?" ' He used to say: 'Right I'll cope from now on.'

I talk about him all the time to the girls. And they will say something like: 'My Dad would have liked this.' Or I say: 'Frank would have gone mad if he'd seen this.' We speak about him in the house and have his pictures in all the rooms. I don't want the children to forget their father, particularly the two younger ones. I don't think they will. He was a good father to them.

When the others came back home after the war it just upset you.

You felt very bitter towards people coming back, not as individuals, just because they had come back and Frank hadn't. There were a lot of things which hurt. There was a service for the *Atlantic Conveyor*. We knew nothing about it, we just saw it on television. Something like that really hurts you because you feel you want to go to everything connected with it. Whether they think they are protecting you by not telling you I don't know. But it's very hurtful when they do these things.

When they launched the new *Atlantic Conveyor*, my daughters didn't like it being called that. They said: 'They shouldn't have called it that, Mum, there can't be another one.' Of course they do that with ships at sea, they always do. I would have loved to have gone and seen it launched. I believe there were thousands who went to see it launched. But apparently not us. If I had been told about it I would have gone, just to see it.

LORD WHITELAW

Lord Whitelaw, now retired, was the most senior member of Mrs Thatcher's Cabinet. During the Falklands War he was Home Secretary and a member of the War Cabinet. As a young officer in the Second World War he served in the Scots Guards and won the Military Cross for gallantry.

There had been talk that the Argentines were going to invade the Falklands and there was a good deal of intelligence to point that they might. They had threatened to do so before. They had talked about sovereignty of the Malvinas, as they called the Falklands. One felt they might do it, but one never really believed they would. Then suddenly, on that Friday morning, 2 April, they invaded.

I was actually away during the day. I had gone as Home Secretary to visit the Fire Brigade in Southampton. I was immediately called back and we had a Cabinet meeting on that Friday evening. Our first thought was that it would have been totally inconceivable to have simply sent a protest or a diplomatic note. Some really firm action had to be taken. The question was: Should the Task Force be assembled? I think what was in our minds was: We have to do something, and if we don't send a Task Force, what else shall we do? Parliament was going to meet on Saturday, we were going to have a very hostile House of Commons, a hostile Press and many criticisms of what had happened. And if we hadn't reacted very sharply then we probably wouldn't have survived as a government. The decision was taken to assemble the Task Force and send it. That really was enough for one day.

There was an amazing reaction by the British nation: people getting the ships ready, assembling the Task Force in the ports; the seamen. It was a very remarkable feeling. People felt they were doing something for Britain, and were determined to do it. The speed with which everything was assembled was far quicker than most people thought it would be. It beat all the estimates of what the military and naval advisers said we could do. There was a sense of how marvellous it was, but behind it was the nagging feeling: Would it all work? When you think of the distances and the risks involved, the particular problems of the South Atlantic and of not knowing whether the Argentines were capable of fighting – nobody knew. Some thought: 'The Argies will never fight.' That wasn't the view of people who analysed the Argentine forces. Their air force was very powerful indeed. Fortunately their naval forces were not exactly keen for conflict and that helped a good deal. But nobody knew what the soldiers would do. So there was this great surge of emotion and the nagging fear of whether it would all actually work if it was put to the test.

It was important that we kept the Americans with us, not only from the point of view of world opinion – of United Nations opinion – as far as we could get it with us, but we had to have their co-operation for some of the planning. Some of the equipment they had was very important to us. There was the Haig shuttle, and we relied on the Americans for the use of the Ascension Island base. The Americans generously gave it to us. If we hadn't had the use of that base, we would not have been able to send the Task Force down to the Falklands.* The Americans could have said 'No' at any stage if they disapproved of what we were doing. So it was essential for us to be seen to be reasonable with Haig. One has a great deal of admiration for him. He conducted those negotiations extremely skilfully when one thinks of the time he spent flying between the two countries; the changes of mood and everything else.

I don't think any of us in the final event believed that he would succeed, because we thought the Argentines had probably gone too far. They had stirred up their people too much and really they couldn't retreat.

Initially the idea was that we must try and persuade Haig of the rightness of our case – which I think we did. We had to remember too

---

* Under the 1962 US/UK Agreement, the UK has the right to use Wideawake airfield on Ascension Island, subject to giving specified periods of notice. During the Falklands operation the notice requirement was effectively waived.

296

that the Americans have a very strong South American lobby of their own. There were very strong pressures in the South American wing of the State Department. Haig himself was under pressure, and some of the people who held those views came over with him. There were advisers who were pro-British and those who, if they weren't anti-British, felt that America had to keep in with South American opinion.

That kind of pressure on any American president is always very great, remains great today and must never be discounted. We always thought Haig was very fair to us, although inevitably there were moments when you had these two wings in the administration pulling in different directions, times when he would appear to be more under the influence of one rather than the other.

But he was desperate to get a settlement. We had to show him that we wanted a settlement too, but not at any price. There were moments when we felt we could not give in to the points that he was making because to do so would have sold out our position as far as the Islanders and the sovereignty of the Falkland Islands was concerned. Inevitably, the invasion by the Argentines had stirred up the British people, and for us to give way on some of those things would have been wrong. We would have been giving way under pressure. It would have been fatal for us as far as our own public opinion was concerned.

At the back of the minds of those who thought more deeply about the military side of it was the anxiety. Could you mount an invasion at that distance from any base – from ships tossing about in the South Atlantic? There was a moment when the Chiefs of Staff told us that we couldn't just sit and hope for something to turn up. They warned us that we couldn't keep ships with all the troops on them stationed for long periods of time in the South Atlantic. They would be unable to exercise sufficiently, inevitably getting stale, somewhat restive. Morale was remarkably good, but the effect on troops of sitting on ships bobbing about in the South Atlantic for a long period of time, on their fitness, and on their capacity once they landed would have been bad. We also had to think about the big ships with large numbers of troops on them: imagine if we'd lost them – that was possible.

One of the amazing features of the Prime Minister's leadership was that we might have to go to war if the Argentines didn't accept a diplomatic settlement. She was never in any doubt. There may have been those of us who at one moment or another thought: Shall we just give a little bit more? Would it finally end the problems – which we hadn't yet faced – of actually invading from ships in the South Atlantic? But she was totally resolute and she was proved right; there was a point we could not go beyond.

We had our position; we had the rights of the Falkland Islanders to think of. She felt that Britain must stand up for them, and the mood of this country was very much that we should. It would have been easy to have gone just a little bit further but she was quite determined that there was a point beyond which she was not going to go; the point where she would appear to be sacrificing British honour and the interests of the Falkland Islanders themselves.

The War Cabinet was a group of politicians and senior military advisers. We formed a very close-knit team; you do if you're working together all the time. We met mostly in the Cabinet Room at Number Ten to discuss all these matters. We learned how to deal with the problems together, and always in the most amicable way. It was a remarkable feeling. I found it strange. I had, after all, been at the receiving end of politicians both during the Second World War and, particularly, when I was a staff officer in Palestine in 1945 to 1946. I remember then cursing the politicians for the stupid decisions that they made and the maddening things we had to do. Then suddenly I found myself at the opposite end, saying to myself: Now I wonder what all these people who are mixed up with this are thinking of the decisions I am making. It was a rather humbling experience, because one realised they were saying exactly the selfsame things about me, as I said about politicians when I was a soldier myself. I used to laugh about it sometimes, it kept one's feet on the ground.

There was one thing we had to get used to – and this was very much for the Prime Minister: Politicians must never show military advisers that they are fearful of too many casualties, however much they mind about casualties once they start. If you do you will put caution on the commanders right the way down, when caution probably may not be the right answer. They're as worried about casualties as anybody. I had some experience in Northern Ireland of casualties, and used to get terribly worried myself. I always tried desperately not to show it because you have a bad effect. And that was particularly true at the time of the *Sheffield*. You must not allow yourself to appear upset. You obviously are upset, we were all frightfully upset about the loss of HMS *Sheffield*, but we were determined not to show it.

The sinking of the *Belgrano* became a great issue, yet at the time it was one of the simplest decisions that I personally found myself involved in. It was taken when some of us had gone down to Chequers at the weekend for lunch. It was heard that one of the submarines was in contact with the *Belgrano*. I remember asking Admiral Lewin [Chief of the Defence Staff]: 'Can you be in contact with *Belgrano* and just choose the time, if we are going to give permission for an attack when she may obviously be moving towards the Falklands? Can we follow her in the South Atlantic and judge the moment?' He said: 'There is no chance of you doing that. You may lose contact and may never get contact again.' One came hard up against the very simple decision. I think some of the critics have never perhaps thought of it in the way that one does at the time. What would everybody have said? What would our sailors, the families and the whole of the Task Force have said if it had become known that we had the chance to attack the *Belgrano* and wouldn't do it because we were waiting to see what would happen? And then if the *Belgrano* had got away from our submarine and steamed in and caused havoc in the Task Force? Just imagine what the feelings of those of us who were there would have been if that had been the result. It could have been, and the moment that I was told that, I had no doubt we had to take the opportunity we had.

Sometimes I was laughed at as being 'the old soldier', but I tried not to be 'an old soldier'. I did occasionally interpose a soldier's point of view as against a sailor's point of view, which was useful. When it came to deciding on the invasion by 3 Commando Brigade at San Carlos it was a matter for the politicians to approve the invasion plan. This was a very major exercise. Once something succeeds everybody says: 'Oh, how easy it was; whoever thought it wouldn't work?' It's all very well, but when you're taking a decision to invade territory held by an enemy whose forces you don't really know, whose fighting power you have not really ever been able to properly assess ... the invasion plan was crucially important. We discussed it and I remember saying: 'Why are you going to land in San Carlos Bay – quite a long way from Port Stanley, which is the main objective? Surely from the military point of view we ought to be landing as close as we can to give our soldiers less distance to go?'

I discovered that this had been the opinion of General Bramall [Chief of the General Staff] from a soldier's point of view as well, though I don't think he would mind me attributing it to him. So he was amused when I raised it. But it was clear, when we had it explained to us, that the need was to get the ships into a reasonably safe anchorage. We needed to get them somewhere where they couldn't be so effectively bombed. San Carlos was the best place. It was a balance between the naval, the air and the military judgement. It was a very interesting and important discussion. I remember asking how on earth we would get ships into such a small space. It was obviously a silly question because all of the navy staff who were assembled said: 'Of course you can get ships into an area like that.' Afterwards they said: 'Well, we weren't quite as sure but we thought we ought to assure you. None of us was certain.'

We had to think about the Argentine air force and what would happen if they got good weather and simply bombed the narrow concentration of San Carlos with those big ships in it. Think of the prestige of those liners if they had been bombed. It could have happened. On the day of the invasion, these were the things that terrified us most.

We had some very low times. The *Sheffield*'s loss was the first major blow – a very big blow. There was the problem of our supplies when the *Atlantic Conveyor* went down. That was very serious. And then, of course, Bluff Cove and the Welsh Guards. That was a terrible blow too. The numbers. One felt awful about it at the time, but I was obsessed with not allowing oneself to be too worried by the casualties, while worrying about them deeply behind the scenes, and never showing it.

I used to talk to the Prime Minister and she was absolutely marvellous about it. I thought it was amazing. When you're at the very top, at moments of great tension in public life, there is all the difference in the world in being the person with whom the buck stops, and, as I was, the person next closest. That's where the slight difference between her and people like me came. It is a slight difference but it's very real. That was why I admired her so much. It made me all the more determined that under no circumstances would I show any feelings [about casualties] even to her. It was my job to bolster her up, not to show any doubts.

I think it is fair to say that she has all the qualities that go to make a great wartime leader. She had enormous courage, and it is not always realised how much courage she had at difficult moments. She has immense determination. She will not be easily shaken from a point of view. Sometimes people find that disappointing and they would like to shake her. But when it comes to leading a country in war, determination and singlemindedness of purpose are very important; coupled with something she doesn't always show – which is a very remarkable degree of compassion. That's necessary because you need the emotion which is stirred by the events in a wartime situation. I've worked with her in many different situations and I think she showed she is absolutely at her best with that sort of challenge because all these qualities come out at their strongest.

The Paras' victory at Goose Green was a very considerable boost to our morale. I think there were many of us who were worried initially that having got a beachhead at San Carlos we were going to get stuck there and not be able to break out of it. Everybody had memories of the time it took to break out of the beachhead at Normandy. In terms of the whole of the Falklands it was not a big area, but to be stuck in a very small area and confined there would have caused all sorts of trouble in every way, not least on the diplomatic front. If we didn't get a move on all the proposals for ceasefires would become stronger and the conditions would not have been beneficial from our point of view. There were all those risks. A breakout was important and we were very keen to see one. Goose Green was very important because it made us realise that, if really pushed by first-class troops, probably the Argentines were not as strong soldiers as all that. And that gave us a great hope for the future.

I was very concerned with the battle for Mount Tumbledown because it was my old regiment, the Scots Guards, who were making the assault. It came on the famous last day of the whole campaign. That morning we assembled for our usual meeting at Number Ten and Admiral Lewin spoke, looking straight at me. He knew I had served in the Scots Guards during the war, that I was immensely proud of my old regiment and had great feelings for them.

He said: 'Well, there is really only one problem left. If the Scots Guards can succeed in taking Tumbledown – and it's a very big assignment – then we shall probably be in Port Stanley tonight, and maybe that will be the final blow in the war. It's a very major issue and really I don't know whether they will succeed.'

This was a great challenge to me in a way. So I laughingly said: 'Of course they will succeed, I know they will.' I don't think I had any right to say it, because how did I know what an enormous task it was to be? But I did have my anxieties.

At 10 a.m. I went back to my normal work at the Home Office. I could not get it out of my mind all day. I had the usual problems which one does as Home Secretary but I couldn't keep my mind on them. Probably my staff realised that most of the day I was thinking about something else and wasn't addressing my mind to the problems in hand, although I suppose it happens to all staff with all ministers from time to time.

About five o'clock in the afternoon I said to my private secretary: 'Do you think I could reasonably ask you to ring up the Chief of Staff and find out what's happened in that battle?'

He said: 'Of course, why not?' So they rang and the message came back that it was still going on but it looked as though they had won, although they had taken fairly considerable casualties. It looked as if it was going to be a success. I remember my anxieties then. About half an hour later Admiral Lewin himself came on and said: 'They've succeeded. You were right.'

My reaction was one of immense relief, very great relief, because after this success we were into Port Stanley that night. I felt my old regiment had a major effect on the outcome of the war. I felt part of it at that moment because we had the news of the Scots Guards' victory and our final victory at the same time.

You don't adjust yourself quickly to that sort of occasion, when you've been dealing with a crisis for so long. Suddenly I thought: Oh, what's going to happen tomorrow? There'll be no meeting. That is the rather absurd feeling you get in your mind. One could scarcely quite believe that after all the troubles and problems there had been, it was a success. I remember going over to the House of Commons and meeting the Prime Minister in her room. We were obviously delighted. I then went home and had a quiet dinner with my wife. It takes quite a bit of time to accustom oneself to the situation. We didn't have any particular celebrations at that moment. We just sat and I said: 'Do you think this is quite real?'

Epilogue

Six and a half years after the conflict ended, the deadly remnants of war continue to be uncovered across the vast wilderness of the Falkland Islands. Grenades, rockets, mines, booby-traps, anti-personnel bombs, shells and countless millions of rounds of small-arms ammunition are regularly discovered. The Royal Engineers' bomb-disposal squad, now housed in a newish Portakabin just behind Port Stanley's main Post Office in Ross Road, keeps a running total. They have found and disposed of 2,664,780 pieces of 'ordnance', the technical term for the refuse of death, wounding and maiming. Beaches at York Bay, Gypsy Cove and Surf Bay, where once Islanders walked with only penguins for company, are now fenced off with barbed wire. Red warning signs showing a white skull and crossbones emphasise that this particular Argentine minefield has not been cleared. For the Islanders these leftovers from the war are a permanent reminder of the events from April to June 1982, and the fact that Argentina is only 400 miles away and that within only a few hours a massive military force was able to take over the Islands.

The civilian government in Buenos Aires wants talks to resume on the future of the Falklands. In November 1988 the people responsible for the Argentine débâcle, the members of the military junta, were sent to prison for twelve years. The Islanders, however, are in no mood for a dialogue. Before the war they never trusted the politicians in London, believing they simply wanted to be rid of the Islands because they had become an awkward diplomatic problem which soured relations with Argentina. Now in Downing Street they have Mrs Thatcher, who is much more to their liking. They see her almost as a saviour. She is their talisman. Not only did she send the Task Force to recapture the Islands; where another Prime Minister might have settled for UN intervention, Mrs Thatcher continues steadfastly to insist that sovereignty of the Falklands is non-negotiable and that the Islanders' wishes are paramount.

Seven years later a lot has changed. Although the streets of Stanley are not paved with gold, Islanders can see a period of economic prosperity ahead. The Falklands are positively awash with cash – £25 million in 1988–9 from licensing fishing in the South Atlantic. The annual budget for the Island's government is £34 million compared with £2.5 million in 1984–5. The gross national product per head for the 2,000 Falklanders means that they are twice as rich as the average Briton. The money has meant a lowering of personal taxes and long-awaited development projects in the Islands – better local services, a new swimming pool and school, and a modern telephone system to replace the antiquated exchange and the hand-cranked WT wireless sets in some of the more remote homes. In 1982 this kind of windfall was only a dream.

Not long before the Argentine invasion the British government turned down pleadings for a £12 million extension to the small airport at Stanley, which would have allowed bigger passenger planes to come from the South American mainland. Now the Islands have a £500 million international airport at Mount Pleasant – a showpiece of British civil engineering skills – but few people to show it to. It is the headquarters of the British military presence. Where once the British government was set to withdraw the single patrol ship HMS *Endurance*, now the Royal Navy has a frigate permanently on station in the South Atlantic. RAF Phantoms patrol the skies; troops garrison the Islands; missile batteries and sophisticated radar sites act as silent sentries.

All this – economic prosperity, Mrs Thatcher in Number Ten, a permanent military presence – makes the Islanders feel more secure. At the same time, it is open to question whether future governments will wish to continue Mrs Thatcher's 'Fortress Falklands' policy. On the surface perhaps a lot has changed. Yet nothing of substance has changed. The Falklands are no longer the quiet and forgotten backwater they once were, but in the consciousness of the general British public the Islands have reverted to the level of importance they held before the events of 1982. Few people, apart from those directly affected by the war, spend much time thinking about the Falklands, but at least they now know they are not at the top of Scotland.

How extraordinary it is that only a few years after the Second World War the Allies settled most of their differences with West Germany and Japan. Yet seven years after the Falklands War the central issue is not resolved; indeed, it seems unsolvable. Argentina's people may have been glad to be rid of the military junta, but they still think of the Malvinas as theirs. So Argentina's claims to the Islands won't go away – and neither will the casualties from the bloody war fought in the South Atlantic.

After a war, people naturally remember those who died – both Argentina and Britain have their own particular fallen heroes – but perhaps it is also fitting that we should remember the living, those who came back. If *Speaking Out* is about anything it is about changing our perceptions, the way we think about war and the men who fight wars. What we discover is what we should have known all along: that soldiers, sailors and airmen, whichever side they are on, are human beings who experience human emotions. Their experiences are etched in their memories. Beneath the tough and rugged exterior, beyond the popular imagery of the fighting man, beyond the medals and the guns, the uniform and the training, they are merely flesh and blood, and just as vulnerable as the rest of us.

Index